Personal Being

american
university
studies

Series VII
Theology and Religion

Vol. 258

PETER LANG
New York • Washington, D.C./Baltimore • Bern
Frankfurt am Main • Berlin • Brussels • Vienna • Oxford

Andrew T. Grosso

Personal Being

Polanyi, Ontology, and Christian Theology

PETER LANG
New York • Washington, D.C./Baltimore • Bern
Frankfurt am Main • Berlin • Brussels • Vienna • Oxford

Library of Congress Cataloging-in-Publication Data

Grosso, Andrew T.
Personal being: Polanyi, ontology,
and Christian theology / Andrew T. Grosso.
p. cm. — (American university studies.
Series VII, Theology and religion; v. 258)
Includes bibliographical references.
1. Polanyi, Michael, 1891–1976. I. Title.
B945.P584G76   192—dc22   2006100648
ISBN 978-0-8204-8897-4
ISSN 0740-0446

Bibliographic information published by **Die Deutsche Bibliothek**.
Die Deutsche Bibliothek lists this publication in the "Deutsche
Nationalbibliografie"; detailed bibliographic data is available
on the Internet at http://dnb.ddb.de/.

The paper in this book meets the guidelines for permanence and durability
of the Committee on Production Guidelines for Book Longevity
of the Council of Library Resources.

Printed in Germany

Contents

Acknowledgments

This study is a revised version of the doctoral dissertation I completed at Marquette University. I should therefore first acknowledge with gratitude the contributions made to this project by the members of my dissertation committee, including my director, Ralph Del Colle, as well as the Rev. David Coffey, D. Lyle Dabney, Robert L. Masson, and the Rev. Philip J. Rossi, S.J. They each provided me with valuable insights when I was still in the early stages of researching and writing and thereby helped me clarify my intentions and organize my thoughts. The conversations I shared with my director likewise helped me focus and refine my arguments. I especially appreciated the constructive comments each member of the board offered once they had read through the completed manuscript. I also wish to thank Bradford Hinze for serving as an alternate reader and helping me complete the dissertation process in a timely manner.

I would also like to acknowledge several others whose teaching and guidance have been invaluable to me. The Rev. D. Thomas Hughson, S.J., provided me with an opportunity to pursue some of the ideas I develop in this study within the context of my doctoral qualifying examinations. While in the midst of writing chapters two and three of the original manuscript, I shared a brief but helpful conversation with Andrew Tallon that helped me clarify several ideas and also provided me with some valuable insights into the relationship between scholastic thought and personalism. Deirdre Dempsey helped me translate some of the more technical passages in Gregory of Nyssa's *Ad Ablabius*. James Dunkly did the same with several passages from the *Ambigua* of Maximus the Confessor, and also graciously provided me with space to work at the duPont Library of the University of the South while I was writing chapters four and five. Finally, I owe a more general but no less substantial debt to both Michel René Barnes and Mark Noll, both of whom instilled in me an appreciation for the historical heritage of the church as well as a respect for the practice of theological scholarship.

The formation I experienced during my graduate studies was influenced at least as much by my nascent experiences as a teacher as they were by my experiences as a student, and I appreciate both those who have provided me with opportunities to hone my skills as an instructor as well as those who have participated in the courses I have facilitated. In particular, I am indebted to Robert Deahl of the College of Professional Studies at Marquette University and to David Stosur of St. Francis Seminary for allowing me the chance to serve as an instructor at their respective institutions.

I have been encouraged and energized by conversations I have shared with others engaged in pursuing their own studies and vocations. Scott Geis, The Rev. Thomas Holtzen, Wolfgang Vondey, Skip Jenkins, the Rev. William Danaher, Jr., and the Rev. William Carroll all provided me with opportunities to talk about my efforts while also broadening my horizons by sharing their own work.

Several people were instrumental in helping me prepare the revised version of this study for publication. I am grateful to Heidi Burns and Richard Atkins at Peter Lang Publishing for guiding me through the publication process. The Very Rev. R. Steve Lipscomb, Dean of Grace Episcopal Cathedral, provided me with time away from my pastoral responsibilities to complete revisions on the manuscript. I received much-needed financial support from Tom and Cheri Gross and the Rt. Rev. Dean E. Wolfe, Bishop of the Episcopal Diocese of Kansas, without which I would not have been able to see this project through to publication.

My wife, Diana, has more than anyone else provided me with the support I needed in order to finish this project (in both its forms). Her unstinting willingness to grant me the time and space necessary to work, her providence for our well-being, and her patience and encouragement throughout this process account for only a small measure of my regard and affection for her.

This project is dedicated to my parents, Sharon M. Kruse and Thomas E. Gross, Jr., who gave me the freedom to pursue the path that I have chosen, encouraged and supported me throughout my years as a student, and helped instill in me the values that have made me who I am.

Introduction

A few years ago, the Rev. Frederic Burnham, director of the Trinity Institute at Trinity Episcopal Church in New York City, mailed a survey to a number of individuals who had participated in the work of the Institute. The purpose of Burnham's survey was to elicit the opinions of his colleagues regarding their perception of the most important and pressing theological questions and "horizon issues" of the day, those they believed should be of special interest to the Institute. Two issues consistently topped the lists Burnham received in response: first, the question of identity; and second, the question of what it means to exist as a relational being.[1]

Both of these issues are to no small degree representative of a wider concern in the contemporary theological enterprise, one that can be characterized as an abiding preoccupation with the concept of the person. The range of theological studies published in recent times that seek to address the nature of personhood is telling, and such studies invariably involve some consideration of the proper means whereby we should interpret those theological traditions of the church particularly associated with this concept.[2] That the personhood is (in general) a distinctly Christian and (in particular) theological contribution to the Western intellectual heritage has been repeatedly affirmed, but there is little consensus on either the precise meaning of the term or its currency in contemporary theology.[3]

The challenge of the question of personhood in contemporary theological studies can be seen as having two aspects. On the one hand, the question of personhood is not just a distinct matter of interest within the broader context of theological inquiry, but is close to the heart of many, if not all, issues of central theological concern. What, for example, does it mean to confess that God is "three persons in one being"? What does it mean to confess that Christ bears "two natures united in one person"? How are we to understand the distinct personhood of the Holy Spirit? What does it mean to say that human beings in some way manifest the image of God, and that do so as a result of the creative personal act of God? Relative to each of these ques-

tions, no less than the correspondence between them, the question of personhood is one of most salient issues needing to be addressed.[4]

At the same time, the question of personhood also reveals some profound
tensions. Chief among these is probably the very real distance that exists
between contemporary efforts at treating the question of personhood and
similar efforts conducted during the patristic and medieval periods, during
which time the classic theological understanding of personhood was ham-
mered out. Whereas early Christian treatments of personhood were informed
by Jewish monotheism and Greek metaphysics, the intellectual milieu within
which Christianity finds itself at present is marked by a considerably different set of expectations and assumptions, and more recent treatments of the
problem seem as often as not to characterize the indebtedness of the tradition
to earlier religious and philosophical formulations as hindrances to be overcome rather than resources to be employed.[5] As noted above, this perceived
problem is one that crosses the lines of various doctrinal loci, including
trinitarian theology, christology, pneumatology, and anthropology.[6] Not
surprisingly, we should also expect that any shifts in perspective in these
core areas of theological inquiry will have ramifications for other issues not
immediately related to the problem of personhood, such as ethics, hamartol-
ogy, soteriology, and ecclesiology.

We also find that the question of personhood has made in-roads into the
consideration of the relationship between formal reflection and the actual
exercise or practice of faith. There have been, for example, a number of
studies dedicated to exploring how the question of personhood informs the
life of faith and one's experience of worship, prayer, and spiritual discipline.[7]
Additionally, the question of personhood has served as an organizing theme
in certain ecumenical efforts, such as those dedicated to exploring rapprochement through the clarification of trinitarian formulations.[8] Similarly,
the question of personhood has served to foster dialogue between members
of different religious traditions that subscribe to a personal view of the divine.[9] Finally, we have already mentioned the need to balance fidelity to the
theological tradition with a commitment to working out problems in terms
approachable and understandable to contemporary thought.[10] Alongside these
developments, some have also made determined efforts to undermine the
theological viability of the concept of the person (at least as traditionally
conceived).[11] Thus, on-going study of the nature of the person must involve
an acknowledgement of the evolutionary character of the development of our
understanding of personhood and a willingness to submit traditional or es-

tablished definitions of the term to critique in light of our expanding awareness of human nature and identity, while also submitting our contemporary
awareness and experience to the critique of tradition.

Each of these issues, to varying degrees, could be said to provide much
of the impetus for the current project, precisely inasmuch as they all imply
the more fundamental question of how we might elaborate a meaningful and
broadly useful understanding of personhood. This must obviously involve far
more than a review of the etymological history of the term "person" in the
theological tradition (or other comparable terms, such as *hypostasis* or *prosopon*), and must also go beyond analysis of the deployment of personalistic
language across a range of subjects by a variety of theologians. Accordingly,
the current project intends to be a more general examination of the nature of
personhood as seen from a particular philosophical perspective, undertaken
with specific theological considerations in mind (especially relative to the
correlation of those areas of theological inquiry most immediately informed
by the concept of the person).[12]

More specifically, our intent herein is twofold. First, we intend to elaborate an understanding of the concept of the person capable of fostering sustained, integrative theological reflection across a range of doctrinal loci (e.g.,
trinitarian theology, christology, pneumatology, anthropology, etc.). Second,
we will allow ourselves to be guided in this effort by the philosophical work
of Michael Polanyi (1891-1976). The theological appropriation of Polanyi's
thought is (as we shall see) by no means a new phenomenon. Particular
attention to the question of Polanyi's understanding of the concept of the
person, however, let alone the potential theological ramifications of just such
an approach to this question, is something that has to date received only
marginal attention. Thus, the current project aims both to move the study of
Polanyi's thought forward (especially by highlighting those elements of his
work that tend in a theological direction), as well as expanding the parameters within which the theological value of Polanyi's work is recognized.

The question naturally arises as to the rationale behind our seemingly
arbitrary selection of Polanyi's philosophical thought for the purpose of
theological reflection. Are there not a wealth of resources within the theological tradition itself to foster the kind of expansive and integrative personalistic theological vision we intend? To this concern we can offer several
responses. First, one of Polanyi's achievements has to do with the integrative
character of his philosophical work; he was able to outline a vision of the
intellective enterprise broadly conceived in a way that invited sustained,

critical reflection not only within particular disciplines, but between different areas of study as well. Second, particular elements of Polanyi's thought (especially his notion of indwelling) offer a relatively unique and fresh perspective from which to examine traditional theological problems. Finally, Polanyi's thought (as we shall see) moves in the direction of the kind of theological vision guiding the current study. Thus, there is much to be gained on both sides from extensive, detailed reflection on the potential correspondence between the theological enterprise on the one hand and Polanyi's more philosophical vision on the other.

Guided by these more general precepts, our efforts will unfold in the following manner. First, we will endeavor in chapter one to present a thorough exposition of Polanyi's epistemological program, which is at the heart of his philosophical efforts. This will involve some initial spadework designed to clarify the parameters of the precise shape of Polanyi's *oeuvre* (which remains something of a contested issue) and to outline his understanding of the contemporary crisis of the Western intellectual tradition. From there we will move to a more detailed analysis of his understanding of the "tacit dimension" and its various components, including the continuity of informal and formal thought, the structures of awareness, the function of conviviality and tradition, and the nonreductivist character of "personal knowledge." This analysis will lead towards those elements of Polanyi's thought that help connect his epistemology to other, less prominent aspects of his thought, such as indwelling and the anthropic tenor of all acts of knowing. We will also briefly examine his views of the nature and status of religious and theological knowledge, and will be able to make an early sketch of an understanding of personhood informed by his thought.

Elaboration of this notion of the person, however, will require further attention to those aspects of Polanyi's philosophical vision that lean in a more ontological, rather than an epistemological, direction. Thus, chapter two will first undertake to examine the implicit linguistic connection between epistemology and ontology in Polanyi's work; this will involve giving attention to Polanyi's five-fold taxonomy of language and his understanding of meaning. From there we will move to a survey of Polanyi's initial attempts to bring the insights of his epistemological program to bear on questions related to the nature of reality, which will lead us into a further consideration of Polanyi's understanding of God.

With this thorough survey of Polanyi's philosophical work behind us, we will in the third chapter further refine our understanding of a Polanyian notion of personhood, and outline the potential value of this working model for the task of theological inquiry. This will involve the identification of two complementary ways that Polanyi's thought evinces a particular understanding of personhood, and will also include the examination of two of the more ambitious efforts to date that have sought to employ a Polanyian understanding of the person in the furtherance of agendas (like our own) not immediately related to Polanyi's own efforts. We will also find it necessary at this point to provide a brief survey of the history of the concept of the person in the Western intellectual tradition; doing so will help prepare the way for our own constructive efforts at drawing together various elements from Polanyi's thought in the development of a positive vision of personhood.

Since Polanyi's work has already received considerable attention within the context of theological studies, it will be necessary for us to outline some of the ways his thought has thus far been employed. This will be taken up in the fourth chapter, and will primarily involve an expositional analysis of the theology of Thomas F. Torrance and his dependence on Polanyi's rehabilitation of faith as an epistemic category, Barbara Dee Bennett Baumgarten's description of visual art as a form of performative theology, and Joan Crewdson's attempt at the development of a far-reaching personalistic theology grounded in Polanyi's thought. This will prompt further analysis relative to the possibility of understanding the related concepts of truth, knowledge, belief, language, and practice in decidedly personalistic terms. We will then be able to move to an examination of a "Polanyian prolegomena" whereby the continuity between Polanyi's understanding of discovery and Christian descriptions of conversion will be developed. Finally, these considerations will also help us recognize more clearly the specific theological loci that will demand further attention; more specifically, the centrality of christology, pneumatology, and trinitarian theology for any theological consideration of personhood will be made manifest, and will spur us on to the constructive doctrinal efforts of the final chapter.

In order to bring our working model of personhood to completion, it will be necessary for us to examine its usefulness relative to a consideration of both divine and human personal being; this will be the superordinate task of chapter five. We will begin with a delineation of the "trinitarian problematic," that series of related questions that taken together are found at the heart of any accounting of the trinitarian life of God. We will then proceed with a closer examination of each of these issues in turn, employing the working Polanyian model of personhood developed in earlier chapters as a heuristic for understanding God's economic relationship to the world, God's transcendence, the personal dimensions of God's immanent life, and the correlation of God's economic and immanent being and action. This reflection will provide us with the decisive opportunity in which to establish the theological viability of our working Polanyian definition of personhood. The broader parameters of the theological vision thus implied by our examination of the trinitarian ground of personal being will be more fully described in the conclusion, which will draw together the central elements of the project and describe opportunities for further study.

One final note of clarification is in order. We noted above that one of our primary intentions throughout this project will be to explore the foundations of a far-reaching mode of theological reflection organized around the concept of the person. In such general terms, we can of course acknowledge that similar efforts have been made by others in the past. The "Boston personalism" of Borden Parker Bowne, Edgar S. Brightman, Albert C. Knudson, and others could stand as one example of a comparable form of inquiry, as could the "French personalism" of Charles Renouvier, Paul Tournier, and Emmanuel Mounier, the "Jewish personalism" of Martin Buber and Franz Rosenzweig, or the "Anglo-American personalism" of William Ralph Inge, Clement C.J. Webb, John Macmurray, Charles Taylor, and Kevin O'Shea. From a more explicitly theological perspective, we might also acknowledge the "Roman Catholic personalism" of Karol Wojtyla, Maurice Nédoncelle, John Cowburne, Charles Winckelmans de Cléty, W. Norris Clarke, and Josef Pieper, or the thought of Austin Farrer or John Zizioulas.[13] We mention these alternatives at this point only to distinguish our efforts from them; given our determination to draw chiefly on the work of Michael Polanyi in our elaboration of a theologically viable form of personalistic inquiry, we will not concern ourselves with exploring the various forms of personalism developed by these individuals.

1
The Mind in Action

Introduction

The first necessary step in any consideration of the philosophy of Michael Polanyi is an examination of his epistemology. Polanyi's philosophical work is dominated by the kinds of questions about the nature of knowledge that motivated to no small degree his move from the practice of physical chemistry to that of philosophy. This chapter examines the structures and dynamics associated with human knowledge as proposed by Polanyi. This will serve to establish in part the conceptual horizon within which the remainder of the present study will be situated and will to varying degrees anticipate the shape of arguments developed in later chapters.

This chapter unfolds in the following manner. First, we will examine several preliminary issues, including the shape of Polanyi's life and work as well as one of the more controversial questions regarding the range of his corpus. Second, we will undertake an exposition of the structure and dynamics of his notion of the tacit dimension. Third, we will outline the broader epistemological implications of the idea of personal knowledge. Fourth, we will develop a tentative sketch of Polanyi's understanding of human personhood. Finally, we will propose some general conclusions regarding Polanyi's epistemological work and the way it potentially elucidates the shape of our own more theological efforts.

Survey of Polanyi's Life and Work

An extensive biographical outline of Polanyi's life is unnecessary within the parameters of the current project.[1] However, a sense of the general shape of Polanyi's professional career will be helpful, if only as a means of providing a framework for the survey that follows of the details of his philosophical program. Richard Gelwick has suggested that Polanyi's career can be seen to have passed through four relatively distinct stages, each representative of

Polanyi's engagement with medicine, chemistry, social theory, and the philosophy of knowledge.[2] This is a useful structure for outlining Polanyi's achievements, for it both demonstrates his far-ranging interests and skills and provides some sense of the areas of inquiry Polanyi sought to bring together under the rubrics of his epistemology.

Polanyi's early studies in medicine and physical chemistry had an enormous impact on his later work in social theory and philosophy. His social, political, and economic views also anticipated many of the themes that would emerge in his later work on epistemology. For example, his explication of the distinction between pure and applied forms of intellectual inquiry anticipated some of what he would later say about the differences between the "focal" and "tacit" dimensions of human thought.[3] Likewise, his early explorations of the relationship between knowledge and the social and historical milieu in which knowledge is pursued revealed patterns which would turn up repeatedly in his later work.[4]

It is not a simple matter to summarize Polanyi's philosophical outlook, or even track the manner in which he developed his ideas. Never content to restrict himself to questions narrowed by the focus of a single means of inquiry, Polanyi sought to engage "the total human situation in an age of science."[5] Furthermore, Polanyi did not always proceed in a systematic manner, and, although specific themes were usually carefully argued, the relationship between major themes was not always elaborated. Rather, he seemed to be about the continual enlargement and refinement of an image that he had in his mind from very early on in his career. Although the priority with which he treated any particular theme at any given point throughout his career was not always consistent, he seemed to have a more or less intuitive sense of where he wanted to go from the beginning, and thereby chose to use his published works to unfold the elements of his thought, making his philosophy a kind of work in progress. Polanyi once observed that one of the elements of successful scientific work was the almost constant alternation between intuition and specification, and he seemed content to let his own work follow this pattern.[6]

Many have already undertaken to outline the contours of Polanyi's thought in and of itself.[7] Further, the potential ramifications of Polanyi's work for various fields of study has also been noted.[8] His recognized authority in the scientific community of his day and his abiding contributions to the practice and understanding of physical chemistry lend exceptional weight to his arguments regarding the philosophical underpinnings of the scientific enterprise and of human knowledge in general. However, there seems to have been only a relatively limited sphere of influence within which Polanyi's philosophical work has exercised any significant, lasting impression; this is especially surprising in light of the extent to which Polanyi's philosophical ideas have been regarded by some as revolutionary.[9] One thing we intend herein is to extend the direction of certain elements of Polanyi's thought with the expectation that doing so will help demonstrate the relevance of his work beyond the parameters he himself envisioned.

The Polanyi Canon

Before proceeding with a more detailed examination of the specifics of Polanyi's epistemology, there is an issue that should be clarified. This issue has to do with what might be described as the shape or content of the acknowledged canon of Polanyi's work. Towards the end of his life, Polanyi collaborated with Harry Prosch in the publication of one of the last works to bear his name, *Meaning*.[10] Since Polanyi's death, there has been some question as to the place of this work within Polanyi's philosophical corpus.

This question took on definitive form in a controversy between, on one side, Prosch, who (naturally) affirmed the place of *Meaning* in the Polanyi canon, and, on the other, Thomas F. Torrance, Polanyi's original literary executor, who denied that *Meaning* is representative of Polanyi's thought. The debate between Prosch and Torrance has been closely aligned to another controversy in Polanyi studies, namely, the question of Polanyi's understanding of the existence of God. In this latter form, the controversy has engaged many others beside Prosch and Torrance.[11] The reason for this association between the canonical status of *Meaning* and the question of Polanyi's understanding of the existence of God has to do with the fact that it is in *Meaning* more than perhaps any other work from Polanyi that we have something approximating a systematic consideration of the implications of his epistemology for non-scientific forms of knowledge, including religious knowledge.[12] While it is not necessary to engage the details of this controversy within the parameters we have established for our study, it is worth noting here because the question of whether or not *Meaning* should be viewed as part of Polanyi's corpus will significantly inform one's understanding of Polanyi's view of personhood.

It can certainly be said that, taken as a whole, *Meaning* reflects a style of thinking consistent with Polanyi's other major works. Themes that appear repeatedly in Polanyi's philosophical writings are in evidence in *Meaning* as well, such as the importance of freedom in intellective inquiry, the modern crisis of the Western tradition, and the correspondence between commitment, understanding, and language (themes that will be explored in greater detail as our own inquiry proceeds). There are, however, several points at which no uncertain tension emerges between the treatment of particular themes in *Meaning* and the treatment these same themes receive elsewhere in Polanyi's philosophical works. For instance, some of what is said in *Meaning* regarding the nature of religious knowledge and the idea of God presents a rather different picture from much of what is said about these issues in *Personal Knowledge*. Such apparent inconsistencies have prompted some to suggest that the final shape of *Meaning* was significantly shaped by Prosch's editorial efforts.[13] Even among those who are in relative agreement regarding the theological direction of Polanyi's thought *Meaning* has a mixed reputation: Torrance rejected *Meaning* outright and never made reference to it in his own work, but Gelwick affirms its place amongst Polanyi's philosophical writings.[14] Gelwick nonetheless stands with Torrance in saying that attempts to minimize the potential relevance of Polanyi's thought for the affirmation of traditional Christian belief represents something of a betrayal of Polanyi's philosophy.[15] Gelwick's position on this matter thus fosters a more expansive understanding of the breadth of Polanyi's thought even as it encourages a close comparative reading of Polanyi's major philosophical works. This is the perspective we will adopt herein; it will be necessary for us to draw on *Meaning* in order to account for the full scope of Polanyi's thoughts on the nature of religious knowledge and the interdependence of knowledge, language, and reality, but our understanding of the message of *Meaning* will require the clarification of Polanyi's thought as developed in *Personal Knowledge*, *The Tacit Dimension*, *The Study of Man*, and his other major uncontested works.

Moral Inversion

All of Polanyi's work, and especially his work in social theory and his early research into epistemology, can be seen to some extent as a reaction against what he believed to be a prevailing and inadequate understanding of the nature of knowledge. Polanyi dedicated significant portions of several of his philosophical writings to explicating the problems that he believed beset much of early twentieth century thought, and retracing his arguments here would be both unwieldy and unnecessary.[16] It is enough for our purposes to highlight the tendencies in late modern thinking that Polanyi believed to be at the heart of what he saw as a very real dilemma in the Western tradition.

Polanyi believed that two areas of conceptual tension had occupied the center of Western thought almost since its inception. The first of these was the tension between "pure knowledge" and "practical knowledge." Polanyi saw evidence of this tension as early as the conflicts between the Pythagorean and Democritian schools of mathematics.[17] The distinction between "pure" and "applied" thought would play itself out in various controversies for much of the history of the Western tradition, and in the nineteenth century, driven by the development of the modern scientific method and rise of industrialization, the balance would shift in favor of the more utilitarian "Democritian" view.

The second area of conceptual tension that Polanyi saw as defining Western thought was that between "Greek skepticism" and "Judeo-Christian messianism." On the one hand, the Western philosophical tradition evinces an abiding concern with the justification of knowledge. On the other hand, Western religious consciousness evinces a belief in the presence and activity of a personal God in history. Whereas the former in some cases suspected the possibility of even the simplest and most direct forms of knowledge,[18] the latter affirmed (to varying degrees and in varying ways) the possibility of knowledge of the highest reality. These two tendencies had repeatedly come into conflict with each other over the course of Western history, and the nineteenth century would again prove to be a decisive moment in the history of the relationship between them as the tendency towards skepticism overwhelmed traditional religious assurances.

It was not so much these two areas of tension in and of themselves that concerned Polanyi. Rather, he maintained that the crisis of modernity sprang from the *combination* of these two areas of tension *with one another*. In short, the commitment to applied thought over pure thought, along with the commitment to critical skepticism over faith as a means to knowledge, were consolidated in the nineteenth century in what Polanyi referred to as a "dynamo-objective coupling."[19] This "coupling" recapitulates the direction of modern thought and thus summarizes the crisis of the late modern mind.

The result of this "dynamo-objective coupling" was a form of "moral inversion" in which the moral passions of humanity were unleashed in a direction in which they could not but self-destruct.[20] The commitment to an epistemology that sought to be both completely pragmatic and objective resulted in the immanentization of truth and reason within history, which Polanyi believed led to a denial of the "reality of reason and equity" and a "sheer love of power."[21] The passions of the modern mind were such that humanity had actually over-reached itself in its efforts to realize its own moral aspirations, and the consequences had been in part evidenced in the rise of various forms of repressive government (especially fascism and socialism) and in various other "pathological" forms of social life.[22] The modern mind, in the pursuit of its own ideals, no longer simply sought to foment revolution for the sake of political and social change, but came to value violent revolution for its own sake. Polanyi believed that the inevitable consequence of this tendency, once it was allowed to perpetuate itself throughout the political, social, and intellectual life of a tradition or a society, could only be a pervasive sense of nihilism. It was against this mindset that Polanyi directed his entire philosophical program.

The Tacit Dimension

Polanyi's understanding of what he termed the "tacit dimension" is at the heart of his philosophical efforts. His explication of the nature and role of tacit thought serves to coordinate his understanding of not only epistemology, but also language and even ontology. We will proceed with an examination of this crucial aspect of his thought by first exploring the continuity Polanyi found between informal and formal knowledge. This will lead to a more detailed consideration of the dynamics of discovery, which Polanyi considered the paradigmatic form of all knowledge. This will include a description of the importance of wholistic perception and awareness within the tacit mode, the structure of awareness, and the collaborative nature of knowledge. Finally, the role of indwelling will be examined as a means of outlining the correspondence between Polanyi's epistemology and his nascent ontology, which will be taken up in the following chapter.

The notion of tacit knowledge can be succinctly described as follows: we always know more than we can tell.[23] Not only does our knowledge exceed our ability to describe it, we are also incapable of explicitly understanding how it is that we have come to hold the knowledge to which we lay claim.[24] Within a strictly objectivist accounting of knowledge and the world, acknowledging the difficulties that attend any description of human knowledge can lead to a pervasive sense of skepticism and eventually a destructive sense of nihilism. From Polanyi's more personalistic perspective, however, acknowledging such difficulties becomes the first step towards affirming the possibility of authentic knowledge of the real world.

The Continuity of Formal and Informal Thought

Rather than attempt to develop an epistemology that presumed a qualitative distinction between various "forms" or "degrees" of knowledge, Polanyi sought to demonstrate the extent to which knowledge of all kinds essentially bears a similar structure, even as he affirmed the differences between them. Objective, formal means of inquiry manifest the same essential tensions as do more subjective, informal modes of experience. Indeed, Polanyi was so impressed with the continuity between formal and informal knowledge that he went so far as to suggest that, in some ways, there is an essential continuity between the knowledge to which human beings might legitimately lay claim and the knowledge we assume an animal might possess by virtue of our observations of the behaviors it manifests. Although he did admit to a qualitative distinction between the conceptual capabilities of humans and those of animals,[25] he nonetheless believed that there exists a notable similarity between the highest levels of abstract thought and the simplest examples of drive satisfaction evident in the behaviors of even the lowest forms of life.[26] This is especially evident, Polanyi believed, in the occasional use animals make of "machine-like contrivances" as well as in the "inventive powers" they occasionally display in their efforts to solve problems put before them using a variety of strategies.[27] Both of these elements suggest a sense of purposefulness and adaptability within the consciousness of animals. The powers of abstraction and articulation that ultimately set us apart from animals are prefigured in their "inarticulate powers" of thought.[28]

In light of the relative distance between human knowledge and the knowledge we might expect animals to have, the distance between informal and formal human thought seems less imposing.[29] Polanyi believed that there are two fundamental human cognitive experiences that portend to some degree all other knowledge: the awareness and organization of our environment through perception and the satisfaction of certain more or less innate drives. The first of these, manifest in our perception of the physical world, anticipates our ability to discover, organize, explore, and elaborate a world of an entirely conceptual nature. The second of these, manifest in our efforts to satisfy the physical demands of our bodies, anticipates the emergence and development of sophisticated skills designed to help us more efficiently and thoroughly explore both the material world and the world of ideas.[30] Within this context, the acquisition and refinement of language becomes the definitive example of that which distinguishes human thought from animal thought, informal experience from formal analysis. The successful acquisition and deployment of language requires the conceptual skills foreshadowed by perception as well as the more practical, sophisticated skills foreshadowed by efforts aimed at satisfying our innate drives. Even at the highest levels of formal inquiry and sophisticated analysis, we realize conceptual powers that find their moorings at the much more primitive level of those efforts aimed at providing us with some awareness of our surroundings and giving us a means whereby we can act effectively within those surroundings.[31]

The Dynamics of Discovery

The search for parameters according to which we can direct our actions provided for Polanyi the paradigm according to which all human epistemic acts can be measured. From our initial intuition of the existence and meaningfulness of a hidden reality, to our most preemptive efforts at clarifying the nature of a reality so perceived, to the more sophisticated means we use to expand our awareness of the entity in question, the structure of the tacit dimension remains consistent; what changes is the range and depth to which we are enabled to engage our environment. The discovery of successive layers of meaning, at once both wider and deeper than we initially expected, was for Polanyi a sure sign that we had reliably grasped the reality at hand. Polanyi explicated his understanding of discovery by way of a number of interdependent themes, including the function of *Gestalten*, the distinction between focal and subsidiary awareness, the dynamics governing the interaction between various levels of awareness, the impassioned nature of the search for knowledge, the convivial relationships supporting all our efforts, and the embodied character of our experience as responsible centers of awareness. It is to a more thorough description of Polanyi's understanding of each of these themes and their interaction that we now turn.

The Function of **Gestalten.** More fundamental to human cognitive capacities even than the conceptual skills portended by perception and efforts to satisfy innate drives is the appreciation of forms or integrated wholes. Polanyi used the language and basic principles of *Gestalt* psychology to describe his understanding of the manner in which the human mind recognizes, retains, and clarifies knowledge. The recognition of a form or a *Gestalt* represents "the outcome of an active shaping of the experience performed in the pursuit of knowledge." It is through such "active shaping" that "all knowledge is discovered and, once discovered, is held to be true."[32] It is important to note that Polanyi is here altering one of the basic premises of *Gestalt* psychology even as he appropriates it. The *Gestalt* theory of Polanyi's time was more inclined to believe that the mind recognized forms that existed independent of itself, but stopped short of saying that the mind participated to any appreciable degree in the formation and development of such forms. Thus, Polanyi's understanding of the process whereby integral wholes are recognized by the mind is much more dynamic and interactive than the *Gestalt* theory of his day.

Affirming that the recognition of forms plays an important role in human perceptual and conceptual capacities anticipates three important elements of Polanyi's thought, each of which will receive more detailed attention below but are worth mentioning at this point. First, the process whereby human beings recognize forms represents an act in which unspecifiable details are integrated into a more or less seamless whole; thus there exists a distinction between the knowledge that we have of the unaccountable particulars of a *Gestalt* and the sense we have of the *Gestalt* itself. "Things that we know and *cannot* tell are parts contributing to a whole, while the whole itself, to which they contribute, is something we know and *can* tell."[33] This insight is the foundation of Polanyi's development of the distinction between subsidiary and focal awareness.

Second, the structure of *Gestalt* awareness anticipates to some degree the hierarchical epistemological, linguistic, and ontological structures Polanyi posited throughout his work. The recognition of a form is not something characteristic of a particular, narrow segment of human conceptual capacities, but is manifest at all levels of cognitive achievement. From the most simple acts of perception, representative of the "most impoverished form of tacit knowing," to the "highest forms of integration," such as "scientific and artistic genius," *Gestalt* awareness is reflected in every degree of mental activity.[34] The continuum of knowledge signified in the perception and appreciation of forms anticipates the integrated hierarchical epistemological, linguistic, and ontological structures that will be more fully explored both later in this chapter and in the following chapter.[35]

Third, although characterizing the recognition of forms in terms of "active shaping" on the part of the observer suggests that knowledge is to a large degree a subjective enterprise, Polanyi's understanding of the dynamics of *Gestalt* awareness provide no accommodation for a strictly individualistic or relativistic view of knowledge. The forms of which we are aware are recognized as valid by us only inasmuch as they help us make sense of our interactions with others and our experience with the world around us. By entrusting ourselves to our understanding of these *Gestalten*, we thereby make definitive claims on ourselves and on others regarding the nature of the shared reality in which we participate.[36] The realism of Polanyi's understanding of human knowledge will also be further elaborated in a variety of ways in the following chapters.

Subsidiary and Focal Awareness. Not all forms reveal themselves to us in the same way. Our awareness of some *Gestalten* is much more immediate than our awareness of others. Polanyi recognized a distinction between what he called our "subsidiary" awareness and our "focal" awareness.[37] Both subsidiary and focal awareness operate in the perception and appreciation of forms of all kinds. The former applies to the general, integrative, less temporally constricted consciousness evidenced in our awareness of the details or components of those forms we perceive; the latter applies to the more specific, discriminatory, and more immediate consciousness of forms themselves. Even though these degrees of awareness are mutually exclusive (that is, we cannot have both subsidiary and focal awareness of the same form at the same time), they operate simultaneously in our perception of both material and immaterial objects.[38] By tacitly integrating (through our subsidiary awareness) the proximal elements of a form, we become conscious (through our focal awareness) of the distal meaning of the form in question.[39] What subsidiary and focal awareness share, however, is a decidedly functional character: just as our subsidiary knowledge serves to guide us to an understanding of that which we perceive focally, our focal awareness carries us beyond ourselves into an encounter with the world around us.[40] "This tacit act of integration is an act of perception, which brings clues (parts), the focal entity (the whole) and the perceiving agent into a relation, which Polanyi called the 'tacit triad'."[41]

Polanyi often used the human capacity to recognize various physiognomies as an example of the simultaneous operation of subsidiary and focal awareness.[42] By attending in a subsidiary manner to the particulars of a given expression, we are aware in a focal manner of the identity or the state of being signified by those particulars (any one or two of which, considered apart from the context provided by the intended *Gestalt*, would be meaningless). A slightly more dynamic example of the simultaneous operation of subsidiary and focal awareness can be found in the successful deployment of a tool, such as a hammer. By attending in a subsidiary manner to the hammer, we are able to use the hammer to drive a nail into a board, the act of which is the object of our focal awareness.[43] In addition to the recognition of familiar patterns and the successful performance of skills, Polanyi also saw subsidiary and focal awareness operative in the "proper use of sensory organs" and "the mastery of tools and probes" (to which we might also legitimately add the mastery of language and concepts).[44]

The Structure of Apprehension. The difference between the subsidiary and focal elements of our awareness further evokes several distinctions intended to describe the means by which the elements of our subsidiary awareness become integrated within our focal awareness. Polanyi suggested that this relationship could be explicated in terms of its "functional" structure, its "phenomenal" structure, its "semantic" aspect, and its "ontological" aspect.[45] The first of these, the functional structure, describes the impetus that moves us from the proximal term(s) of our subsidiary awareness to the distal term(s) of our focal awareness; in other words, it describes our awareness of the difference between ourselves and that of which we are aware. The second, the phenomenal structure, describes our "subception" of the meaningfulness of the proximal elements of our awareness within the distal term they intend; it signifies our intuitive awareness that the disparate elements of our subsidiary awareness can be meaningfully integrated under the rubric of the object of our focal awareness. The third characteristic of the tacit dimension, the semantic structure, affirms that the meaningfulness of the proximal elements of our awareness is to be found in the more integrated elements of which we are focally aware; it involves the transposition or displacement of the meaningfulness of the elements of our subsidiary awareness to some point "outside" or "away" from ourselves. Finally, the fourth characteristic of tacit thought, its ontological aspect, involves two things: first, that the elements of our subsidiary and focal awareness taken together represent a comprehensive entity or event that cannot be reduced to either the elements of our subsidiary or our focal awareness; and second, that our awareness of this comprehensive entity or event implicitly affirms a particular way of looking at the world, one that necessarily accommodates the existence of the entity or event of which we are aware.

This understanding of the structure of tacit thought would have significant ramifications for Polanyi's understanding of both knowledge and language. What is particularly worth noting at this point is that by explicating
the tacit dimension in terms of its functional, phenomenological, semantic,
and ontological coordinates, Polanyi advocated a view of knowledge (and,
implicitly, reality) that is profoundly relational and interactive. These coordinates each implicitly affirm both a radical independence as well as a radical
interdependence between subject and object: neither can be entirely subsumed within the other, nor can either exist entirely apart from the other.
Further ramifications of this perspective will be explored later in this chapter
and in the following two chapters.

Dual Control. The interaction between subsidiary and focal awareness provides a exemplary illustration of another important element of Polanyi's
thought, that of dual control. Just as our tacit awareness of the distal meaning
of a form depends on our subsidiary awareness of the proximal elements of
that form, so too the "principles controlling a comprehensive entity would be
found to rely for their operations on laws governing the particulars of the
entity in themselves." Accordingly, just as "unbridled lucidity" relative to the
particulars of a form will destroy our comprehension of the form, so too "the
laws governing the particulars in themselves would never account for the
organizing principles of a higher entity which they form."[46] Rather, each
form is subject to dual control, that is, organization according to the laws that
govern the subsidiary elements of the whole as well as those that govern the
"comprehensive entity formed by them."[47]

The principle of dual control thus subsumes two other dynamics employed by Polanyi in his explication of complex forms or systems, namely,
boundary conditions and marginal control. The former, boundary conditions,
refers to the conceivable parameters within which a given form or system
may manifest itself, given the arrangements or limitations of the manner in
which it is instantiated.[48] The latter, marginal control, refers to the "operational principles not manifested in inanimate nature," but which nonetheless
exercise a determinative influence on the structure and dynamics of the form
or system in question.[49] The principle of marginal control is evidenced by the
"functions of all comprehensive entities having a fixed structure," including
(especially) living beings.[50] Such structures result from the influence of
higher principles of organization acting on the system, rather than from any
inherent impetus within the system that might push the system towards

greater levels of sophistication: "no level can gain control over its own boundary conditions and hence cannot bring into existence a higher level, the operations of which would consist in controlling these boundary conditions. ... [A] higher level can come into existence only through a process not manifest in the lower level, a process which then qualifies as an *emergence*."[51]

It is worth noting that Polanyi's understanding of the dynamic correlation of subsidiary and focal awareness suggests something of his understanding of the correspondence between knowledge and reality. The correlation of subsidiary elements within the horizon of a meaningful whole perceived via focal awareness intends not only a particular identity or state of being, but an operational principle.[52] Such a principle suggests in itself both a particular class of objects capable of manifesting this principle as well as a fundamental dynamism representative to some degree of the nature of reality. Hence inasmuch as the objects of our focal awareness are representative of the integration of any number of subsidiary elements, their meaning cannot be reduced or even approximated in terms of those more fundamental or subsidiary elements (or, it follows, according to the methods of inquiry appropriate to those elements as themselves objects of focal awareness).[53] It is ultimately the significance or meaningfulness of a given form or system, as understood by our relationship to it, that points to the reality of that form or system. For example, the "skillful conduct" of a task, "knowable by our tacit act of comprehending it," may be said to be more real than certain elements caught up in the performance of the task or certain tangible elements associated with the task.[54]

What is particularly interesting about Polanyi's understanding of dual control is that he followed the logic of this schema to its apparently inevitable conclusion: not only do the elements of human knowledge and experience manifest a certain dependence on the "lower" principles of life (as evidenced by the study of physics and chemistry), but they also manifest a certain dependence on "higher" principles of life (such as those more often explicated within a philosophical or religious context). This also provides yet another proleptic image of the stratified models of knowledge, language, and reality manifest in Polanyi's work, each of which will be more fully explored in the following chapter.[55] Additionally, the notion of dual control suggests a dynamic and relational ontology, given that complex systems or forms both manifest an "upward and outward" direction, intending increased sophistication, and require an "downward and inward" acting force to draw them on to greater convolution.[56]

This summary of the concept of dual control and the manner in which it is evidenced in the recognition of complex forms thus provides us with an initial sense of Polanyi's development of the hierarchical epistemology on which his understanding of both language and reality is based, and also provides an important foundation for elaborating a Polanyian view of personhood. Before going on to a focused consideration of these themes, it is necessary to exposit further the dynamics that condition the structure of knowledge. What remains to be seen is how dual control facilitates the emergence of sophisticated forms of thought and how these forms of thought evoke an elaborate matrix of relationships within which the possibility of accurate knowledge of reality is pursued. The means by which Polanyi was able to justify the correlation of epistemology and ontology will also require further consideration. These questions can now be explored in turn through an examination of Polanyi's understanding of intellectual passions, the convivial nature of knowledge and the importance of tradition, and the importance of indwelling as a mediating category in Polanyi's thought between epistemology and ontology.

Intellectual Passions. Despite being impressed by the continuity between formal and practical knowledge and even the continuity between human knowledge and the knowledge we might reasonably ascribe to animals, Polanyi was even more taken by the richness and sophistication evidenced in the intellective strivings of humanity. He believed it was therefore important to account somehow for the flowering of the kind of highly complex efforts manifest in pure mathematics, theoretical physics, philosophy, ethics, the arts, and other forms of learning and study. Why would human beings, alone among the forms of life on earth, not only pursue the fulfillment of their fundamental needs and appetitive desires, but go on to create a panoply of skills and disciplines the pursuit of which signified concerns far beyond those related to the survival of the species?

Polanyi referred to the skills and disciplines manifest in the mental life of humanity as intellectual passions, which he imagined to be different from appetitive passions in several ways. Whereas appetitive passions represent an element of the human experience more or less common to all forms of life, tend to be more or less subjective in nature, and can be readily fulfilled, intellectual passions distinguish the human experience, are much more public (or relational) in nature, and perpetuate themselves by their very fulfillment, drawing those who pursue them further on in a quest to clarify both the shape of the desire and the means by which the desire might be fulfilled.[57]

Intellective passions intend a hidden sense of being that draws human persons out of themselves into a wider awareness of reality.[58] They serve not only a "selective" function, but "heuristic" and "persuasive" functions as well. In other words, intellectual passions not only motivate inquiry and help focus investigation, they condition our interpretive efforts as we consider our experience in light of the question before us, and also encourage us to assert our conclusions for consideration and subscription by others.[59] Each of these functions further signifies what may be described as the "givenness" of the human situation, or, perhaps more accurately, the human dilemma.

Our intellectual passions serve as evidence of the inescapable uncertainty with which humans are faced and the inevitably incomplete nature of their knowledge. Human beings are required to commit themselves to beliefs and responsibilities that can never be fully justified from a critical perspective,[60] nor can humans escape from the limitations to which they find themselves subjected on a regular basis, limitations that condition not only their ability to accurately understand that to which they have committed themselves but also to follow through on those commitments.[61] Polanyi noted the similarities between his own sense of the human experience and certain elements of the existentialist tradition even as he sought to go beyond the nihilism and meaninglessness he saw manifest in existentialist philosophy.[62]

Although humanity's efforts to satisfy their intellectual passions are met with any number of challenges and limitations, these passions nonetheless represent an important element in Polanyi's thought. The "persuasive" function of intellectual passions in particular, more than the "selective" or the "heuristic," best facilitates the next several steps in the logic of Polanyi's philosophy. This is because this function points more directly to two important elements of Polanyi's thought to which we have thus far only made indirect reference: first, the collaborative or social shape of knowledge; and second, the inter-relatedness of epistemology and ontology.

Conviviality. Polanyi developed his understanding of the social context within which knowledge is made possible through two related but distinct themes: conviviality and tradition. The first of these Polanyi characterized as the mutuality expressed in a given society committed to the common pursuit of truth. Convivial relationships manifest the sharing of fundamental convictions, the active pursuit of fellowship, cooperation in common undertakings, and the exercise of whatever authority is necessary to maintain stable community structures.[63] It is worth noting that Polanyi saw the denigration of convivial communities as a consequence of both positivism and romanticism to be a chief symptom of the crisis of the modern mind; thus he intended, in recovering the grounds for personal knowledge, also to recover the foundation necessary for the development of convivial societies of all kinds.[64]

It is also worth noting that Polanyi saw conviviality to be a necessary precursor to the emergence and development of any sophisticated means of formal inquiry. Not only does overcoming the absence of "logical antecedents" and "logical derivatives" in any field of study require the kind of pluralistic collaboration manifest in convivial societies,[65] but it is impossible for any single individual (or any single community) to engage the range of problems that must be faced in any attempt to realize a simultaneously comprehensive, creative, and critical view of the human experience.[66] The convictions and commitments of a society are formed across *"chains of overlapping neighborhoods"* of expertise within which "the *principle of mutual control*" helps guarantee that "marginal contributions" are accorded their proper place within the life of the society.[67]

Tradition. The relationships maintained in any given convivial society necessarily extend across time as well as space. "A society which wants to preserve a fund of personal knowledge must submit to tradition."[68] Commitment to the creative renewal of tradition is representative of a more fundamental obligation to help foster a greater awareness of the truth of reality within the culture.[69] Socialization within a given community could be characterized as an apprenticeship in learning how to recognize, accept, and creatively perpetuate the commitments manifest in that community.[70] As such, this apprenticeship "may be regarded as a much simplified repetition of the whole series of discoveries" and insights upon which that community was originally established and has since extended itself.[71] Commitment to the standards of the tradition and to the tradition itself entails a kind of "devotion," acting not only as a "guide to intuition, but also a guide to conscience; they are not merely indicative, but also normative."[72] They are, in other words, held with the expectation that they are binding for all within the community, as well as (in a slightly different manner) for those outside the community. Furthermore, tradition serves as the "common ground" between the members of a community in instances of disagreement; those who disagree will appeal to the traditions of the community in the hopes of convincing the other of the rightness of their own views.[73]

Commitment to tradition thereby necessarily evokes a certain tension within the life of a society. On the one hand, the community finds itself beholden to the standards manifest within the life of the culture; on the other hand, the standards of the culture are constantly being reconsidered by individuals within the culture who seek to apply the standards of the culture to novel circumstances. The authority of the tradition may be judged "competent," but cannot be considered "supreme" or else both additional discoveries and the adaptation of the culture to unanticipated situations becomes impossible.[74] The members of a society can successfully renew their tradition only by exploring that which has thus far been outside the realm of their experience. This process will likely involve a certain amount of "moral struggle" as members vie with one another for the most adequate interpretation of the culture, but nevertheless helps guarantee that the boundary conditions and plausibility structures manifest in the community are better equipped for successful ongoing deployment.[75] The "creative renewal" of a tradition always involves an appeal "from a tradition as it *is* to a tradition as it *ought to be*. That is [sic] to a spiritual reality embodied in tradition and transcending it."[76] If the members of a society have fulfilled a certain number of basic expectations in their process of mutual inquiry, then it can be assumed that their conclusions or commitments are appropriate within the context in which they find themselves.[77]

Having reviewed Polanyi's understanding of the role of intellectual passions, conviviality, and tradition in human knowledge, it is now possible to understand how Polanyi brought these three elements together under the common rubric of discovery. The process of discovery is the context within which the heuristic nature of Polanyi's epistemological program becomes most evident.[78] It is within the context of a discovery that an essential element of Polanyi's understanding of reality is revealed, namely, that human rationality mirrors and manifests a rationality evident in reality itself. The process of discovery and verification in science includes the "sensing" of the scientist within himself those "hidden gifts" which equip him to the task, as well as the "hidden" complexity and rationality of nature.[79] For example, a potential "discovery may be thought to attract the mind which will reveal it–inflaming the scientist with creative desire and imparting to him a foreknowledge of itself; guiding him from clue to clue and from surmise to surmise."[80] For this reason it may appear that it is "perhaps more appropriate to

regard discovery in natural sciences as guided not so much by the potential-
ity of a scientific proposition as by an aspect of nature seeking realization in
our minds."[81] The process of discovery, in other words, assumes both the
existence of a reality existing to some degree independent of human experience and the possibility that human beings can nonetheless connect with that
reality. Such connection invests the process of discovery "with a compelling
sense of responsibility for the pursuit of a hidden truth" which both demands
the services of human beings for revealing it and requires their obedience
once they have found it.[82] As noted above relative to the necessary role of
tradition in knowledge, there can be no hard and fast rules or laws about the
means by which new discoveries are introduced into existing structures, nor
can there be any hard and fast rules about the shape of existing structures
themselves other than their own ongoing viability.[83] Thus the process of
discovery becomes for Polanyi paradigmatic for all forms of self-
transcendence realized when human beings find themselves in contact with a
rationality and a reality larger than themselves.[84]

Indwelling

It is necessary to round out this survey of Polanyi's understanding of the
mind in action with a brief review of the means by which the connection
between knowing and being is made in his philosophy. Polanyi used the term
"indwelling" to describe the vehicle whereby the personal knowledge held
by humans facilitates in them particular modes of existence. The notion of
indwelling "overthrows centuries of dichotomies that have separated mind
and body, reason and experience, subject and object, the knower and the
known" and instead seeks to bring such categories together into a pattern of
interdependent relationships.[85]

   In short, indwelling describes a process in which we direct our focal attention towards a particular object or event by way of a subsidiary process
that involves the interiorization of the means whereby our focal awareness is
directed. By means of a subsidiary commitment, we agglomerate or assimilate[86] objects, skills, or concepts[87] into ourselves in order to deploy them as
the means whereby we might become focally aware of other objects, skills,
or concepts.[88] That to which we attend focally is perceived at some relative
distance to ourselves (that is, as a distal object), whereas the means whereby
we perceive the object of our focal attention is, relatively speaking, so much

closer to us that we find ourselves *inside* it (that is, as a proximal object). We have, in other words, incorporated it into our body.

It is, however, possible to bridge the distance between ourselves and the object of our focal awareness until we find ourselves dwelling in the object itself, at which point we are no longer focally aware of the object, but have shifted our awareness of it to the level of our subsidiary commitments; from this vantage point, the object has become the means whereby we are able to perceive other objects perhaps previously hidden from us.[89] This description of Polanyi's notion of indwelling thereby harks back to the earlier review of his understanding of *Gestalt* psychology: inasmuch as we are able to indwell objects, skills, or concepts, we thereby signify our awareness of them as integral wholes that themselves signify particular operational principles, and it is these principles that we seek to realize *in ourselves* through the process whereby we indwell the object, skill, or concept in question.[90]

The notion of indwelling also recalls Polanyi's insistence on the continuity between informal and formal knowledge: the manner in which we conceptually indwell nonspatial objects is immediately related to our experience of embodiment. "Our body is the only assembly of things known almost exclusively by relying on our awareness of them for attending to something else. Parts of our body serve as tools for observing objects outside and for manipulating them."[91] This experience is paradigmatic for our experience of conceptual or intellective indwelling.

The notion of indwelling has important ramifications for a Polanyian understanding of personhood, as will become more apparent within the context of the review of Polanyi's hierarchical understanding of knowledge, language, and reality presented later in this chapter and in the following chapters. For now, it is enough to note that Polanyi himself recognized the significance this idea could have for understanding human identity and existence. At a very basic level, Polanyi's notion of indwelling opens up our awareness of the somatic character of human knowledge. "Our own body is the only thing in the world which we normally never experience as an object, but experience always in terms of the world to which we are attending from our body. It is by making this intelligent use of our body that we feel it to be our body, and not a thing outside."[92] Thus our sense of embodiment becomes the means whereby we shape the strategies we use to incorporate objects, skills, and concepts into ourselves so as to indwell them. Our knowledge and the extension of ourselves into the world via our language is thereby representative to some degree of our awareness of the world as it has come to us through our physiological and kinesthetic experience.

At a more complex level but in a similar manner, the notion of indwelling offers a novel perspective on the question of the nature and operation of the human mind. Polanyi acknowledged that a strictly physical or chemical analysis of the brain cannot support the possibility of the existence of anything resembling a mind (if "mind" is understood to be something that transcends physiochemical processes); he believed this to be representative of the limitations of physical and chemical analysis as well as the absurdity of a strictly empirical accounting of human experience.[93] Instead, he insisted on talking about the mind, not as an "aggregate of its focally known manifestations," but as "that on which we focus our attention while being subsidiarily aware of its manifestations."[94] Both strictly positivistic and behavioristic accounts of learning and intelligence are thus ruled out, for "it is not possible to keep track of a mind's workings except by comprehending them, so that a focal observation of the particulars of intelligent behavior is impossible" apart from their being situated with a meaningful context that is itself representative of the mind. In other words, by attending "comprehensively" to the elements that intend intelligent behavior, "we are in fact focusing not on the behavior, but on the mind of which they are the workings. We are reading the mind at work in these particulars."[95]

Both the somatic character of knowledge and (more especially) the nature of the mind as revealed in light of the notion of indwelling raise the further question of the nature of personal identity. The process whereby we indwell objects, skills, and concepts is very much one in which we come to identify ourselves with and in accordance to the objects, skills, and concepts we interiorize or assimilate.[96] Our indwelling thus both extends our identity into and through the means by which we attain focal awareness while simultaneously subjecting our identity to the influence of those same means. This further highlights the profoundly relational nature of Polanyi's thought and sharpens the question of the nature of identity as realized by a "centre of unspecifiable intelligent operations," that is, by a person.[97]

Finally, the notion of indwelling also further illuminates the process of self-transcendence that human beings realize through the process of discovery. Consistent with his appreciation of the continuity between informal and formal knowledge, he sought to demonstrate the extent to which human intellectual powers are realized not merely in the development and manipulation of symbols, but in the latent ability such symbolic representation fosters to extend ourselves beyond the realm of our immediate experience or awareness.[98] As they reach beyond themselves through the objects, skills, and concepts they indwell, human beings are enabled to aspire to an "ecstatic vision" in which the distinction between the subject and the object disappears, thereby allowing for the unmediated participation of the subject in the object of contemplation. Such an experience is unlike a discovery inasmuch as it is not expected to continue to reveal itself in new and surprising ways; rather, there no longer exists any sense of incompleteness or separation.[99] Indwelling thus provides the means whereby human beings can aspire, not only to the successful performance of menial tasks, but to realizing both their highest intellectual strivings and their deepest religious longings.

Summary

Polanyi's explication of the mind in action provides a striking corrective to what he believed to be the corrosive effects of the modern mindset. Through his excavation of the roots of human knowledge in intellectual passions oriented towards the recognition and appreciation of *Gestalten*, in his description of subsidiary and focal modes of awareness and the nature of dual control, in his appeals to conviviality and tradition as the necessary preconditions for all knowledge, and in his examination of the manner in which the process of indwelling signifies the existence of a reality beyond that evidenced by the empirical sciences, Polanyi outlines an epistemology that both affirms the possibility that human beings can aspire to reliable knowledge of material and immaterial realities even as it establishes responsible personhood as the center of all knowledge. As noted at the beginning of this chapter, this is an epistemological program with far-reaching implications, one that is still being absorbed in many fields of study.[100]

Within the context of the current chapter, two essential tasks remain to be completed. First, it is necessary to examine the way Polanyi's explication of the tacit dimension serves to organize his approach to broader questions having to do with the nature of knowledge. Second, some initial conclusions need to be outlined regarding what might be best described as the anthropic shape of Polanyi's philosophy and the consequential understanding of personhood that can be gleaned from his program taken as a whole. The detailed elaboration of a Polanyian view of personhood will have to wait until after an examination of the incipient ontology evinced in Polanyi's thought, which is the subject of the next chapter.

The Hierarchy of Knowledge

Given the nature of the issues and questions that most engaged Polanyi's attention throughout his philosophical career, it should not be surprising that his work in epistemology became for him the starting point from which he organized his approach to problems in other areas of study, such as language and ontology. His tendency to use epistemology as a model for his studies in language and ontology was likely only encouraged by his understanding of the extent to which his notion of personal knowledge enabled him to recapture some sense of confidence that human beings could claim to have reliable knowledge of the real world. Furthermore, the fact that knowledge revealed itself to him as something that is best understood as manifesting a hierarchical structure, it comes as no surprise that his elaboration of a hierarchy of knowledge proleptically contains an image of his understanding of language and of reality itself. Finally, given the extent to which he organized (albeit often implicitly) his understanding of knowledge around the reality of the person, it is not surprising that we should find that the direction of Polanyi's studies in language and ontology also reveal a decidedly personalistic, even anthropic tone.

Recovering the Anthropic Principle

That there is in Polanyi's thought the expectation of a strong correlation between the structure of our awareness, the structure of our knowledge, and the structure of the object(s) of our awareness should by now be obvious. At this point, it is only necessary to bring to the fore a theme that will both help further clarify the consonance between epistemology, language, and ontology as well as anticipate the themes of the following chapters. This theme could be described as the "anthropic" character of Polanyi's thought.

Polanyi suggested that our awareness of the difference between higher and lower forms of life will involve varying degrees of personal investment on our part. As "we proceed to survey the ascending stages of life, our subject matter will tend to include more and more of the very faculties on which we rely for understanding it. We realize then that what we observe about the capacities of living beings must be consonant with our reliance on the same kind of capacities for observing it."[101] In other words, as we affirm the reality of increasingly "higher" forms of life, we are thereby acknowledging that we are recognizing forms of life that more closely resemble ourselves. The capacities on which we rely for knowing and understanding the world respond most profoundly to the presence and behavior of entities that manifest those same abilities. Thus, personhood becomes the measure of all things, for it is our experience of personhood (that is, our indwelling of ourselves as responsible centers of self-consciousness) that is the most fundamental experience we have by which we are enabled to make sense of ourselves and our environment.[102] This, however, does not mean that our knowledge is subjective, nor does it intend a relativistic epistemology, for truly *personal* knowledge is always simultaneously "objective" and "subjective."

The anthropic character of our knowledge is perhaps most evident when we consider that the linchpin that binds the various elements of human knowledge together is, quite obviously, the human person. Especially in his earlier philosophical writings, Polanyi displayed a marked tendency to justify his arguments regarding the nature of knowledge in personalistic terms. Rejecting both "medieval dogmatism" and "modern positivism," he asserted that the only criterion we have for assessing our knowledge is our own self-reliance, itself "lacking any fixed external criteria, to say on what grounds truth can be asserted in the absence of such criteria."[103] Within this context, the purpose of philosophical reflection can be nothing other than "bringing to light, and affirming as my own, the beliefs implied in such of my thoughts and practices as I believe to be valid" and then deploying these beliefs successfully in the search for truth.[104] As noted above, Polanyi's later philosophical work and his examination of the structure and dynamics of the tacit dimension allowed him to back away somewhat from what might be called the fideism of his earlier work, but the role of commitment in knowing remained a crucial element of Polanyi's thought throughout his career.

The reality of human personhood was for Polanyi not only the motif by which he organized his understanding of knowledge, but also the means by which he began his inquiry into questions of language and reality. Indeed, he saw no other way to approach such questions: humanity stands at the apex of the natural order, and thus it is not only appropriate but necessary that personhood become the standard according to which the whole spectrum of life should be measured and understood.[105] One of the chief concerns Polanyi had with the rise of objectivism and strict materialism is that neither were able to account for the reality of personhood, and thus opened the way to the possibility of "complete metaphysical nihilism."[106] It was in part to stem the tide of such nihilism that Polanyi sought to reassert the prevalence of commitment in all acts of knowing and, concomitantly, the reality of the person as the center of all knowledge (and, by implication, all being).

Nonreductivism and Interdisciplinarity

One of the examples to which Polanyi would refer when explaining his understanding of the existence of stratified levels of meaning was our experience of language. Speech signifies a hierarchical system in which a range of interdependent levels of meaning are brought to be bear in an effort to make sense of our experience of the world. The fundamental elements of basic vocalization are combined and given meaning according to the higher principles governing the formation and deployment of concepts as manifest in distinct words, which are in turn subjected to the organizational principles manifest at the higher level identified with the construction of phrases and sentences, which again in turn find themselves coordinated relative to the still higher levels of style and narrative.[107] The elements of the lower levels find themselves subject to the coordinating powers of the higher levels, even as the higher levels depend upon the lower for support and existence.

This kind of stratification is manifest to some degree or another in every distinct act of knowing and in every conceptual system taken as a whole. Human knowledge reveals an "interpreted universe ... the particulars of which we have interiorized for the sake of comprehending their meaning in the shape of coherent entities."[108] It is through our indwelling of discrete levels that we are enabled to perceive the meaning manifest at other levels and are thus able to direct our awareness in efforts to clarify that which is yet unknown to us.[109]

In a very general sense, Polanyi suggested we could distinguish among four types of knowledge, each of which identifies varying degrees of meaningfulness, comprehensiveness, and precision. At the most basic level, we find a form of knowledge that is rather utilitarian, manifesting as it does no significant sophistication of terminology or standards for validation or verification; this level represents the most ordinary, everyday manner in which we exercise our powers for recognition and understanding. By bringing a greater degree of sophistication to bear on our terminology, by being more responsive to past experience and expectations for the future, and by systematizing to some degree our concepts, we are enabled to move from mundane forms of knowledge to more advanced, meaningful forms of awareness; such developments herald the emergence of the "descriptive sciences," which also marks the beginning of our ability to explore the ramifications of our knowledge apart from immediate experience. From here we can ascend to the "exact sciences," which are characterized by even greater terminological

sophistication and more profound consideration of the systematic organization of our knowledge, and which rely even less on the need for immediate
experience as a correlate of cognition. Finally, we recognize the possibility
for purely "deductive" inquiry, having so refined our terminology and methodology that reference to experience is no longer necessary. The move from
descriptive to deductive inquiry thus represents a process of "increasing
formalization and symbolic manipulation."[110]

Despite the fact that the rational order or operational principles manifest
at each level are salient largely at their respective strata, there exists also a
necessary interpenetration between the elements manifest within the varying
levels of the hierarchy of knowledge. The elements of the lower orders of
awareness can serve as subsidiary elements in which we dwell with the intent
of capturing an increasingly expansive vision, up to and including an understanding of the whole of reality. At the same time, the expansive and integrative levels of awareness associated with those more meaningful horizons
within which we situate our most important commitments and most serious
questions provide a necessary framework within which we can pursue detailed efforts aimed at clarifying the specific elements manifest at lower
levels of meaning.[111] Polanyi provided a description of what he imagined the
hierarchy of human knowledge would appear to be, and modeled this hierarchy on our awareness of the evolutionary history of the world. Since there is
in Polanyi's description of this hierarchy a close association between "levels
of meaning" on the one hand "levels of reality" on the other (both organized
around the emergence and development of personal centers of consciousness
capable of sustaining rational commitments), a more thorough description of
this hierarchy will be undertaken in the following chapter.[112]

Polanyi's Understanding of the Theological Enterprise

Polanyi understood religious faith to be representative of a valid and distinct
heuristic vision, and he compared it to "mathematics, fiction and the fine
arts," all of which are "validated by becoming happy dwelling places of the
human mind" in the quest for truth.[113] As in the practice of the empirical
sciences (or, for that matter, any intellective endeavor), the necessary first
step in reflection on religious experience is a commitment to indwell a particular frame of mind. Within the framework of belief, systematic reflection
becomes the means of elucidation whereby the perspective engendered by
the framework one inhabits is enabled to reveal a more expansive vision of

reality than was possible apart from such indwelling. Systematic reflection on religious experience or awareness, which Polanyi considered to be constitutive of theological inquiry, thus involves the attempt to bring one's understanding of the question of God to bear to the issues and challenges of life. It involves the attempt to construct an integrated vision of nothing less than the entirety of all that is.[114] Thus, the theological vision potentially signifies (depending on the relative success with which it meets) the highest or fullest level of intellective indwelling possible for human beings.

Such a vision, however, cannot function in a vacuum. One of the primary challenges facing the theological enterprise is the need to make itself understandable within the broader social and cultural context in which it exists, a context that may be in no way beholden to the religious commitments that inspire and support any particular theological vision. Polanyi saw this as one of the problems facing religion in the late modern Western world, namely, its inability to present its claims credibly in and to a culture(s) that had for all intents and purposes learned to do without religious commitment.[115]

In order for this task to be accomplished, Polanyi believed that there needed to be a manifest correlation between the elements present in a theological vision and at least some of the more salient elements of the secular vision characteristic of the wider culture. Such correlation, along with a demonstration of the intellective appeal of the theological vision and its ability to account better for the human experience, would help encourage the kind of conversion (that is, commitment to religious faith) that would then enable others to participate meaningfully (or rather, to indwell) the theological vision.[116] Apart from such indwelling, religious claims appear to be nothing more than meaningless doctrinaire assertions.

There is also a subtle but dangerous tension that attends the theological enterprise, perhaps more than in any other intellective endeavor. Even as a particular theological worldview attempts to make known the viability of its religious commitments in the wider world, it must not only make itself understandable to those outside the religious community or tradition that supports it, but must also resist the tendency to absolutize the content of its vision. By making the elements of its vision intractable, it immediately marginalizes itself within its broader social and cultural milieu; even more damaging is the extent to which such ossification represents a betrayal of the implicit purpose of a heuristic vision, that is, the ongoing effort to understand better a reality that is expected to continue to reveal itself in new and unforeseen ways.[117] When the "object" of one's heuristic vision is the Origin and Ground of Being, this expectation can never be exhausted.[118]

The best way, Polanyi thought, for the theological enterprise to pursue its efforts at making itself intelligible to the world within which it exists, while at the same time avoiding descent into meaningless dogmatism and idolatry, would be for those engaged in theological inquiry to undertake dialogue with those dedicated to intellective inquiry in other heuristic fields. This strategy follows as a natural consequence of Polanyi's understanding of human knowledge as existing within a unified horizon of experience while also manifesting stratified levels of meaning.[119] Since this issue has already been examined, and since the development of a specific strategy for interdisciplinary dialogue between Polanyi's thought and the contemporary theological enterprise will be taken up again in the following chapters, it does not require further elaboration at this point.

Approaching a Polanyian Understanding of Personhood

It is at this point still too early to consider whether or not Polanyi's philosophy provides a stable foundation on which to pursue our own distinctly theological ambitions. It will first be necessary to examine the extent to which Polanyi's epistemological perspective fosters a broader understanding of the world and reality in general; this task is taken up in chapters two and three. It will also be necessary to examine the way Polanyi's thought has been both critiqued and appropriated within the context of contemporary theological studies; this task will be taken up in chapter four. However, we are by now able to draw some initial conclusions regarding Polanyi's understanding of personhood. This will also allow us to set forth some clarifying observations regarding the extent to which the perspective engendered by Polanyi's philosophy moves us closer to the goals we have set for ourselves.

Given the extent to which personalistic categories appear throughout his philosophy, it is somewhat surprising that Polanyi did not devote more attention to elucidating the nature of personhood.[120] It is possible that he felt his work set forth his understanding of personhood in such a forthright manner that a systematic explication would be redundant. It is also possible that he felt that his understanding of the tacit dimension presented unique challenges for modern notions of personhood. Whatever the reason, it can reasonably be said that we do not have anything from Polanyi laying out in great detail his understanding of personhood (with the possible exception of some of the material in the last section of *Personal Knowledge*). Simply put, providing a metaphysic of the person was not Polanyi's intent.

Despite the relative lack of attention Polanyi devoted to this issue, we can readily glean several insights from his epistemology that point to a particular understanding of personhood at work in his thought. For example, his recognition of the importance of *Gestalten* suggests that human beings are predisposed to the apprehension of integrated, meaningful wholes. This raises the question of how it is, relative to the evolutionary history of our species, we are to account for this capacity, as well as the much more interesting question of the relationship between the meaningful integrations sought by human beings and the dynamics manifest in the natural order; this latter question also invites a consideration of the possible implications of Polanyi's understanding of intellectual passions and his characterization of knowledge as an essentially heuristic endeavor. All of these suggest that Polanyi intuited that the intelligibility of the natural order itself presents an interesting problem relative to the question of human knowledge and identity. Furthermore, the notion of integrated complex systems governed by the principle of dual control suggests a general model for understanding the organization of human awareness and identity. Polanyi's insistence on the importance of conviviality and tradition in every act of knowing suggests that he recognized that human personhood is in some way essentially relational. Similarly, the emphasis he placed on the importance of conscience and commitment suggests that he believed individuals are, in addition to being caught up in a web of interdependent relationships, also radically independent in some ways. Given that so much of Polanyi's thought is indebted to personal categories, it is not unreasonable to conclude even at this early point that development of his wider philosophical oeuvre will continue to reveal itself in profoundly personalistic terms. Such development would first require closer examination of other details of Polanyi's philosophy, which is precisely the task of the following chapter.

Conclusion

Early in his essay dedicated to explicating Polanyi's understanding of personhood, David Rutledge suggests that Polanyi's philosophy does not so much provide a complete theory of knowledge in itself, let alone a theory of being or reality, so much as it clears the way for the development of a broader postcritical worldview.[121] Although we have yet to complete our survey of the chief elements of Polanyi's philosophical program, the insights garnered even from our initial review of his epistemological theories are enough to suggest that Rutledge's observation is indeed a fair one. We can certainly expect, given the amount of time Polanyi spent exploring issues related to questions of knowledge more than questions of reality or being, that the accuracy of Rutledge's comment will be even more evident by the end of the following chapter. At the same time, it should also by now be apparent that Polanyi's epistemological program presents a more expansive and integrative alternative not only to those philosophical perspectives against which he directed his efforts, but also to many other contemporary notions of knowledge and action. In his attempt to overcome the restrictions of late modern thought, Polanyi ended up recasting epistemology, absolving it of the constricting preoccupation with the justification of knowledge and making it a wider concern, one profoundly attentive to the quest for meaning. It is to the ramifications of this view of knowledge for our understanding of reality that we now turn.

2
Contact with Reality

Introduction

Having in the first chapter surveyed the specifics of his epistemology, we can now broaden our analysis to include the insights and implications of Polanyi's wider philosophical program. This chapter does not attempt to provide an exhaustive accounting of the many consequences that follow from Polanyi's work relative to the task of philosophical inquiry. Rather, it is intended to demonstrate two things: first, that Polanyi's thought encompasses much more than questions of epistemology, and could be said to provide a starting point for a far-reaching philosophical system (one largely unrealized by Polanyi himself); and second, that the perspective engendered by Polanyi's thought has much to recommend it to both the personalistic and theological ambitions of the current study.

This chapter proceeds in the following manner. First, we will examine the application Polanyi made of his epistemology to questions of meaning, and will within this context outline his multimodal taxonomy of language. Second, we will explore Polanyi's less extensive but no less important efforts at bringing the concepts and categories employed in his epistemology to bear on questions of the nature of reality. Third, we will explicitly engage the question of Polanyi's understanding of the reality of God. Finally, we will clarify several general conclusions regarding the value of Polanyi's philosophy as a foundation for our own more theological ambitions. These conclusions will also serve to orient us towards the work of the following chapters.

Knowledge as a Model for Language

Polanyi considered the human tendency towards articulation and our ability to extend our awareness and experience through the manipulation of language to be what distinguished human beings from other forms of life.[1] The term "language" here is best understood as the matrix within which our meaningful interpretation and understanding of the world is manifest, as well as within which we see manifest most clearly the play of our intellectual passions and heuristic endeavors. It is through language that personal obligations are first perceived and comprehended, and through language that commitments are manifest. Articulation of any kind thus becomes representative of both our belief in the commensurability of our experience and awareness as well as an acknowledgement of the imperfection and instability of our interpretive and expressive efforts.[2] In other words, the study of language bridges the study of knowledge and that of reality, just as the commitments (tacitly) signified by language bridge knowing and being.[3]

The Logic of Commitment

Polanyi's expectations regarding the anthropic shape of knowledge followed from his understanding of the nature of the commitments implicitly signified in and by human knowledge. In light of the epistemological indeterminacies that attend human knowledge, he suggested that we should not be surprised to find that similar indeterminacies accompany our use of language, which further evinces the necessary role of commitment in every act of knowing.[4] A strictly mechanistic, deterministic account of life and knowledge could not but fail to account for human identity and experience because it would lack all reference to the committed striving manifest in the emergence and development of life, a striving that continues to be manifest to varying degrees in every human articulation and every heuristic act.[5] It is impossible to hold that a set of ideas or beliefs are true and yet to assume we are not thereby committed to them: "[a]ccording to the logic of commitment, *truth is something that can be thought of only by believing it.*"[6]

Because it represents an extension into the unknown, commitment necessarily entails an effort to stabilize belief. Polanyi perceived three ways in which our commitments operate in attempts to actualize our heuristic efforts. First, commitments are defended from the critique and challenges presented by competing belief systems. Second, attempts are made to expand the range of specific commitments as more and more heuristic effort is brought to bear in the clarification of the understanding of the world signified by them. Third, commitments entail an implicit attempt to deny the rationality (that is, the commitment) according to which competing systems might appeal.[7]

It was in light of the logic of commitment that Polanyi was able to make sense of the relationship between particularity and universality. All acts of commitment necessarily intend personal action within a particular context;

such acts involve, within their respective milieu, the deployment of articulation that is itself representative of commitment but ultimately directed towards a transcendent ideal that signifies a higher level of reality than that immediately (or, perhaps better, subsidiarily) apprehended.[8] Polanyi used these coordinates to distinguish between the subjective, the objective, and the universal. Subjective experience is by definition private and thus no sure foundation for reliable knowledge, even though it plays a role in all acts of knowing. Responsible fulfillment of the obligations arising from that which is seen to be objectively true is what enables one to move beyond mere subjectivity to fully personal forms of knowing and being, provided that which is seen to be objectively true is grounded in a convivial tradition intending a range of commitments held with universal intent (that is, the expectation that such commitments could in principle be seen to be universally valid).[9] Polanyi summarized the tension between the particular and the universal thus:

> We have seen that the thought of truth implies a desire for it, and is to that extent personal. But since such a desire is for something impersonal, this personal motive has an impersonal intention. We avoid these seeming contradictions by accepting the framework of commitment, in which the personal and the universal mutually require one another. Here the personal comes into existence by asserting universal intent, and the universal is constituted by being accepted as the impersonal term of this personal commitment.[10]

What is especially worth noting at this point is that it is precisely the reality of the person that bridges the distance between the subjective and the objective. In keeping with his understanding of complex emergent realities representative of levels of achievement, Polanyi avoids both the relativism of strict subjectivism as well as the determinism of strict objectivism (and thus also avoids the nihilism of both). We will explore this element of Polanyi's thought in greater detail in the following chapter.

Given the stratified epistemological scheme Polanyi elaborated in his philosophy, it is not surprising to find that he believed that the dynamics of commitment also manifest a potentially hierarchical pattern. Our commitment to a particular way of viewing the world or a particular way of life is immediately related to the heuristic success with which such efforts meet. As we find our knowledge affording us greater insight into reality and our experience, we become more committed to viewing the world in such a way. As we become increasingly invested in our beliefs, we indwell them to a more significant degree, thus participating in them with more and more of ourselves. Since reliable knowledge not only signifies subjective beliefs but also entails some measure of involvement in an objective reality, any increase in our commitment to a particular way of viewing the world is coterminous with our participation in the object(s) intended by our knowledge. This movement signifies a shift in our perspective, one in which we move from seeing the world in reductionistic or atomistic terms (that is, as a series of discrete objects) to viewing the world in increasingly personal terms; we become more inclined, in other words, to see the world as signifying the heuristic strivings of other persons.[11] Thus, the mutuality manifest in our interactions with complex living systems observes a pattern of ascent in which, at the lower levels, there need be only some recognition of mutual interaction and perhaps mutual influence, while at the higher levels this interaction and mutual influence is seen to be much more profound; the "I-It" perspective is replaced by an "I-Thou" perspective.[12]

The "medium" through which one commits oneself, while itself "blind" to the transcendent ideals guiding all heuristic efforts, both provides the possibility for such commitment even as it delineates the available forms of expression of this commitment. Understood in this sense, our context determines our calling.[13] To deny one's call is to neglect one's responsibility and choose, not freedom, but an illusory sense of liberty that in truth involves nothing other than self-assertion. Human beings have "no other power" than that of recognizing and submitting themselves to the transcendent obligations and responsibilities contained in their calling; apart from obedience to the standards and responsibilities to which they are subject, or if they attempt to observe critically and objectively these standards "in a detached manner," human beings will find that the "law is no more than what the courts decide, art but an emollient of nerves, morality but a convention, tradition but an inertia, God but a psychological necessity. Then man dominates a world in which he himself does not exist. For with his obligations he has lost his voice and his hope, and been left behind meaningless to himself."[14]

Polanyi believed that commitment requires conversion, itself understood as a radical, comprehensive process through which one is brought to a new level of awareness, a new way of dwelling in the world. Reasoned argumentation is insufficient to convince others of our point of view; we must enable them to see the totality of our position and trust that the elegance, simplicity, and profundity of our position will win them over; we must, in other words, believe that they will recognize in our position one better able to account for their experience of reality than their own position.[15]

The Multimodal Structure of Language

One of the primary witnesses to our knowledge is our language, for our language is one of our most fundamental heuristic enterprise. Languages represent "conceptual frameworks," providing alternative ways of viewing and understanding the world and our experience therein.[16] Taken as a whole, a particular language can be said to represent a kind of grand unified theory, a dynamic and evolving effort to circumscribe the parameters within which all human experience might be understood.[17] Because of the variegated nature of human experience, it can be said that one language evokes another; as we reach the limitations of a given means of expression without thereby exhausting our experience, we anticipate the possibility of another "kind" or "degree" of expression. To the extent that we are aware (either as individuals or as a society) of the degree to which our language manifests our commitments, we find ourselves living "*in thought*," that is, quite literally inhabiting (indwelling) our heuristic endeavors.[18]

There exists a noticeable parallel between our use of language, Polanyi suggested, and the structure of our (tacit) awareness. At the most basic level, we can distinguish between the "denotative" or "representative" meaning manifest in language events, in which one thing is seen to signify another, and the "existential" meaning seen in other language events, in which a thing is seen to signify only itself.[19] This simple distinction suggests a series of slightly more sophisticated distinctions which describe the different ways in which our encounter with language evokes different interpretive responses. "Receptive" interpretation describes those instances in which we learn to understand particular forms of language. "Intermediate" interpretation describes those instances in which we successfully deploy these forms of language in established forms of parlance. "Innovative" interpretation describes those instances in which we perceive some limitation or inconsistency within established forms of parlance and attempt to overcome this perceived deficiency through a novel or creative use of a particular form of language.[20] Both the distinction between denotative and existential meaning as well as the distinction between receptive, intermediate, and innovative modes of interpretation are representative of the broader outlines of Polanyi's understanding of the tacit dimension, wherein knowledge simultaneously manifests a phenomenal, a functional, a semantic, and an ontological character.[21]

Because he thought that language recapitulates the dynamics of personal knowledge, Polanyi, not surprisingly, elaborated a stratified view of language in keeping with his hierarchical epistemology. His earlier efforts at developing a view of articulation that captured the nuances of his epistemology eventually gave way to a more far-reaching taxonomy of language that recognized a variety of distinct modes of expression and interpretation.[22] Within this taxonomy, Polanyi recognized five forms of language: signs, symbols, metaphors, art, and myth. Each of these forms of language are distinguished according to the manner in which the subsidiary elements of an event intend the object of focal awareness, as well as the extent to which they allow for various forms or degrees of indwelling.

The first of these forms of language, the sign, is both the most straightforward of the five as well as the most sterile. Regarding the relationship between the subsidiary elements and the focal object that they signify, we find that the former possess no intrinsic interest; our attention is entirely occupied by the meaning (that is, the object of focal awareness) to which the subsidiary elements point. Regarding the range and depth of indwelling made possible by a sign, we find that signs admit to little or no opportunity for significant personal participation in the language event (or rather, in the meaning of the integration signified by the sign). Such "self-centered integrations" are useful within a considerably wide range of heuristic efforts, but their very facility makes them superficial in nature.[23] Examples of these kinds of language events would include maps and schematic drawings, directional signs, and certain mathematical formulae.

Symbols, however, allow for greater participation and therefore evoke a potentially greater range of comprehension and meaning than do signs. Regarding the relationship between the subsidiary elements manifest in a symbol and their focal object of intension, we find that it is the subsidiary elements more than the connoted focal object that manifest some degree of intrinsic interest. This is what distinguishes a symbol from a sign: the distal meaning of the proximal particulars is embodied in those particulars to an extent that does not readily allow for this sense of meaning to be embodied in some alternative manner. What this means relative to our participation in the interpretation or expression of a symbolic language event is that we find ourselves surrendering to this more pervasive integration of the subsidiary elements and their focal meaning; thus, in our surrender to a symbol "we accomplish the integration of those diffuse parts of ourselves that are related" to the elements of the symbol. "Our surrender to these symbols is thus at the same time our being carried away by them."[24] Examples of this kind of language event, Polanyi suggested, include nationalistic images such as flags, memorials such as tombstones, and awards of recognition.

Metaphors, the third kind of language event in Polanyi's taxonomy, are indicative of those instances in which we find both the subsidiary elements of the event as well as their focal meaning to possess equal measures of intrinsic interest. This is so because a metaphor represents a novel or creative integration of these elements. "The tenor bears on the vehicle, but, as in the case of a symbol, the vehicle (the focal object) returns back to the tenor (the subsidiary element) and enhances its meaning, so that the tenor, in addition to bearing on, also becomes embodied in the vehicle."[25] This means that with metaphors, as with symbols, we find ourselves (via the associations we have with the elements of the metaphor) embodied in and carried away by the event.[26] What distinguishes metaphors from symbols is the distinctly creative or imaginative vision implied by the former; Polanyi chiefly employed poetry and literary images as examples in his explication of metaphor.

The shift in perspective necessary to recognize those language events Polanyi characterized as examples of art requires greater elaboration than did the differences between signs, symbols, and metaphors; there is no single element or characteristic that makes them readily identifiable. Polanyi includes in his initial exploration of the nature of art descriptions of dramatic theater, poetry, and both representational and nonrepresentational visual art.[27] By working through examples of each of these various forms of art, he is able to glean a number of characteristics that distinguish artistic forms of expression and interpretation from other, less sophisticated forms. For example, whereas signs, symbols, and metaphors are representative of a singular event, works of art often contain such a range of both subsidiary and focal elements that they evince a dramatic or narrative structure. Within the context of this structure, neither the subsidiary elements nor the objects of focal awareness can be said to "bear on" or connote one another; rather, both embody each other (in much the same way that the subsidiary and focal elements of a metaphor mutually evoke some degree of intrinsic interest).

This interdependence of the elements of an artistic work gives the work as a whole a somewhat more formal, perhaps even a more artificial or abstract, manner of self-presentation than can be found in signs, symbols, or metaphors; thus, works of art can be said to take on a life of their own, cut off to some degree from both those who first envision and execute them and from those who relate to them as observers. Polanyi described this sense of removal in terms of "framing," and suggested that it allowed for a form of participation in the event in a way and to a degree that could not be had with less expansive forms of language: by virtue of the formality of a work of art and the integrity it manifests, we become interested in it for its own sake rather than engaging it with the expectation that it signifies something else. The formality and complexity of a work of art also requires repeated intellective effort on our part in order to recognize the integration of its elements into a comprehensive whole: our awareness of signs, symbols, and metaphors is relatively irreversible (that is, having perceived them once, we are not likely to require the same intellective effort to perceive them again), but our apprehension of a work of art may prove to be rather recalcitrant and may require us to exercise our imagination again and again in an effort to understand the meaning manifest in a given work.[28]

By noting what he saw as the parallels between scientific discovery and artistic creation, Polanyi was able to outline some of the means by which we can speak constructively about the validity of art. The development of sophisticated forms of scientific connoisseurship became for him a model for understanding the refinement of aesthetic sensibilities, with all the concomitant implications that follow regarding the possibility of speaking objectively about the value and meaning of art. For example, just as the standards of specifiability, applicability, and intrinsic interest help govern the direction of scientific inquiry, so too can they be said to provide a foundation for the development of an objective aesthetic.[29]

In keeping with another important aspect of his earlier work, Polanyi also engages the question of "visionary art," or nonrepresentational artistic language that has no bearing on experience. The corollary in Polanyi's earlier philosophical work to the pursuit of visionary art would be the practice of pure science or inquiry along the lines of pure mathematics. Like these rarefied forms of abstract, intellective endeavor, visionary art pushes us to reconsider our understanding of the boundaries of reality, moving as it does beyond the conventional, the acknowledged, the mimetic, towards the unknown, the hitherto unimagined, the poetic. Visionary art, like pure mathematics and pure science, intuits a hidden reality that cannot but reveal itself in radically unconventional forms of expression.[30]

Despite the complexities involved in understanding artistic forms of language, it is possible to summarize the manner in which they facilitate a particular form of linguistic indwelling relatively succinctly. By situating ourselves within a work of art (that is, by attempting to find ourselves embodied therein and thereby to live within and according to its meaning), we find ourselves caught up in a comprehension that is markedly different from that of our ordinary experience. When we respond to a work "by surrendering from our own diffuse memories of moving events a gift of purely resonant feelings," then the "total experience is of a wholly novel entity, an imaginative integration of incompatibles on all sides."[31] In other words, the narrative structure of works of art, the expansive range of their elements, and the profundity of their depth, if balanced so as to reveal an integral work, quite literally can serve to transport us to another world.

For the most part, the structure and dynamics manifest in myth is largely the same as the structure and dynamics manifest in works of art. What distinguishes mythic language from art is its greater profundity: whereas works of art represent more or less self-contained meaningful events or entities, myth aims to envision the "world as a whole." This effort amounts to a "daring speculation," extending far beyond the "mere reaching for further observable events" manifest in lower levels of language, "transcending all observable objects and extending the imagination far beyond any possible experienced horizon."[32] Thus, myth explicitly and necessarily seeks a transcendent horizon, a perspective within which universal intent can be extended to the furthest possible limits. Following Mircea Eliade, Polanyi suggests that cosmogenies are particularly significant given that they provide a foundation for other myths (such as the exploits of superhuman heroes or the emergence of a particular culture).[33]

Consistent with his conclusions regarding the continuity evident in all forms of human knowledge, Polanyi suggests that the only difference between the mythic tenor of the "primitive" mind and the scientific tenor of the "modern" mind is that the former naturally gravitates towards "more far-reaching integrations than are acceptable" to the latter.[34] The mythic mind is inclined to apprehend the meaningful integration of subsidiary elements in a way that the scientific mind finds unjustifiable or even absurd. This is because the mythic mindset reaches towards integrations that go far beyond the ability of the scientific mindset to establish or even perceive. The essential structures and dynamics of both (that is, their reliance on the tacit dimension and personal knowledge), however, are largely identical.

Mythic language, like metaphor and art, is able to incorporate elements that are normally thought of as incompatible or even mutually exclusive. However, whereas metaphoric or artistic integrations can be considered natural, mythic integrations are necessarily "transnatural." Polanyi's definitive example of a transnatural integration would likely be his mention of the idea of "agencies existing outside the world and before its existence, but nevertheless operative on and therefore in the world."[35] The logical conclusion of this line of thought (i.e., the definitive "transnatural integration") would, it seems, be the idea of *a* supernatural, omniscient, and omnipotent "Agent" that transcends the world while also exercising power over it.

The tension manifest in any transnatural integration must be an enduring tension in order for the myth that embodies this tension to maintain its viability as a myth.[36] Apart from this abiding sense of tension, a myth risks collapsing into one or another of the various forms of natural integration; if a myth should be seen to fall to a level comparable to works of art or perhaps even metaphors, it may retain some solvency, though not as a myth, for it has lost the power proper to it as a myth. That which constitutes a myth and grounds its legacy as a myth is its ability, like works of art, to enable us to transcend our ordinary experience by indwelling their framework or their perspective. But myths are different from works of art in two important ways. First, the range of elements they seek to incorporate within their structure is much more far reaching than are those typically found in works of art; myth is "an all-encompassing work of art, which like any other great work of art, fills its subject with inexhaustible significance."[37] Second, myths are understood to communicate a more significant measure of truth than do works of art, that is, they speak of events "*recollected*" and not merely "*represented*."[38] Myth involves not only the "commemoration," but also the "reiteration," a "'doing-again' of what was done 'once upon a time'." This act of recapitulation serves much the same function as does the "framing" of a work of art, that is, it sets it apart and so enables us through our participation therein to transcend our daily routine.[39]

Polanyi's explication of myth and his affirmation of the value of myth led him into a consideration of the nature of religious belief, which he acknowledged involves "a form of 'acceptance' much more complex" than any manifest in the surrender to signs, symbols, metaphors, art, or even myths.[40] Religious awareness, like myth, facilitates a forms of indwelling in which "we dwell for the moment in Great Time and are one, not only with one another and with our fathers, but also with the All. We participate in the ultimate meaning of things."[41] Like myths, too, religious awareness involves the reconciliation of a range of apparent incongruities, and Polanyi identifies a number of these, many of which could be understood as some version of what is sometimes referred to in theological inquiry as the (so-called) scandal of particularity.[42] Polanyi concludes that the idea of God must be seen as that horizon, comprehended only by indwelling (i.e., admitting to no "logical, scientific, or rational" argument), within which we find not only the incongruities of religious awareness reconciled, but all the inconsistencies of our lives potentially brought into some measure of harmony.[43] Like visionary art, religious myths affirm that "[i]f not this story exactly, then *something like this* is somehow true–in fact, is somehow the highest truth about all things."[44] In other words, the truth of religion does not have to be seen as actual or even plausible, but only as meaningful.[45]

As noted above, Polanyi's taxonomy of language, incorporating as it does signs, symbols, metaphors, art, and myth, serves within the broader context of his thought to bridge the distance between epistemology and ontology. From Polanyi's perspective, it is in language perhaps more than anywhere else that our commitments and aspirations are brought into being and through the refinement of language that we strive to actualize all our personal, intellective endeavors. What is particularly worth noting at this point is that Polanyi's taxonomy of language as described above observes a pattern that was first manifest in the hierarchy of knowledge and that will be manifest again in the hierarchy of being. If we confine our observations for now to the taxonomy of language, we could say that this pattern suggests that the greater the degree of sophistication evident in a particular language event, the more likely it is to signify the intentionality of personal agency; this would apply to both the one who indwells it by speaking and the one who indwells it by hearing. The more expansive and more profound the meaningfulness of a given language event, the more personal it will be.

Martin Moleski has noted that "Polanyi understood 'articulation' in the widest possible sense."[46] If this is accurate (as it seems to be), then it is no exaggeration to suggest that Polanyi's taxonomy of language points the way to an even more expansive view of articulation, one that goes beyond the distinction between sign, symbol, metaphor, art, and myth. This more expansive view of articulation would include not only the explicitly linguistic utterances of speech and script, but also the less explicitly linguistic but no less articulate demonstrations of expression and interpretation contained in virtually every form of human awareness and action. Several obvious examples of certain behaviors provide an intuitive sense of what this expanded taxonomy might include: for example, gestures, ritualized patterns of movement, and even patterns of social organization could each be said to represent nonlinguistic forms of articulation.[47]

Having said that, we need to acknowledge that Polanyi affirmed the difference between what he described as natural and artificial meanings. By the former term, he meant those meaningful integrations "achieved by our trained powers of perception or by our productive skills." By the latter term, he meant those meaningful integrations "contrived by man." Natural integrations he referred to simply as perceptions or skillful actions; "artificial" meanings he referred to as "semantic" integrations.[48]

Furthermore, it is also necessary to recognize that Polanyi's analysis of articulation includes a number of linguistic "laws," such as the law of poverty, the law of grammar, the law of iteration, and the law of manageability. These laws can be succinctly described in the following terms: first, the "law of grammar" suggests that a language must operate according to recognized standards; second, the "law of poverty" determines that the range of words in a language must be limited to what can practically be employed; third, the "law of iteration" affirms that words must be identifiably repeated to be useful; fourth, the "law of consistency" holds that words must be consistently applied relative to their referents; finally, the "law of manageability" maintains that the elements of a given language must be easily reproducible.[49]

These "laws" suggest that a view of language any more expansive than that identified by Polanyi via his explication of signs, symbols, metaphors, art, and myths (or other comparable descriptions) risks so inflating the notion of "language" as to render it meaningless. Thus, in order to elucidate Polanyi's understanding of meaning as revealed in language, we must establish the connection between articulation and reality, a connection that exists in the concept of the person; this is a task that will be taken up in the following chapter. What is also necessary for this task is the elaboration of an ontology in which meaning is itself seen to be an emergent property arising from the dynamic relations of mutually indwelling complex entities. This is precisely one of the ambitions of the current project, as is demonstrating that such a vision is best grounded in a trinitarian understanding of God. These expectations orient us to the goals of the following chapters. For now, it is enough to note that Polanyi's understanding of language serves as the bridge between his epistemology and his nascent ontology.

Summary

Polanyi's development of a stratified taxonomy of language serves as an essential bridge between the more narrow epistemological issues that predominate his work and those broader ontological questions implied by his explication of knowledge. By grounding his understanding of the meaningfulness of language in the heuristic act of discovery, itself anchored within the wider context of his notion of personal knowledge, he thus provides an implicitly personalistic image of the clarification and extension of personhood via the communication of meaning into new forms of being. The importance of Polanyi's views on language relative to the question of his understanding of personhood will be taken up again in the following chapter, and will have important ramifications for our approach to several of the theological problems that motivate our efforts. However, we must first turn our attention to an examination of Polanyi's treatment, scattered and incomplete as it is, but no less important for understanding the scope of his thought, of questions of a more ontological nature.

Knowledge as a Model for Reality

Even though Polanyi did not claim to have provided "any definite theory concerning the nature of things,"[50] he recognized that his theories about knowledge carried implications for our understanding of reality. His work contains a number of intriguing observations regarding his view of the world, but he was never able to formalize his observations into anything resembling a complete system.[51] It is, however, possible to sketch in rather broad strokes an outline of the nature of reality as Polanyi understood it, for those instances in his work in which he does make reference to questions of a more ontological nature are numerous enough to merit consideration. Furthermore, Polanyi's ontological musings suggest that he expected there to be a correlation between the contours of our knowledge and the structure of that which we affirm as known.[52] Having examined both Polanyi's development of a stratified epistemological perspective admitting a variety of levels of meaning as well as his hierarchical taxonomy of language admitting a variety of levels of articulation, it is no surprise to find that he expected the universe itself to be "filled with strata of realities, joined together meaningfully in pairs of higher and lower strata."[53] Polanyi's philosophy opens the way to viewing reality as a series of interlocking complex entities or events.[54]

The Necessary Realism of Knowledge

From Polanyi's core idea that discovery is at the heart of knowledge, we can infer with him that a mind "uninformed by intuitive contact with reality" will "place unreal and fruitless interpretations on the evidence before it."[55] In light of the dynamics governing personal knowledge, it is easy to see how the "from-to" structure of the tacit dimension contains in itself an "ostensive definition" or understanding of the objects of our awareness.[56] We should expect that the reliability of our knowledge will have to be judged against the independently existing objects of our awareness. Any given statement is true "to the extent to which it reveals an aspect of reality, a reality largely hidden to us, and *existing therefore independently of our knowing it*."[57] It is thus necessary for us to exhibit a certain amount of passivity in the exercise of our awareness, for we must submit ourselves to the demands and obligations revealed to us by the comprehensive entity towards which our focal awareness is directed if we hope to have reliable knowledge of it.[58] At the same time, we cannot be entirely passive in our intellective endeavors; it is necessary that we prepare ourselves to recognize the opportunities provided by a given heuristic outlook so that we might be able to fulfill the opportunities our efforts may reveal.[59]

This tension between the passivity and activity of the agent in the act of knowing provides some indicator of Polanyi's intent to overcome some of the expectations typical of the late modern mind regarding the relationship between "mind" and "matter." On the one hand, there is a tendency to see "mind" as entirely passive, responding to the stimulus impinging on it from the "outside" world; this view results in an entirely materialistic account of "mind," and cognition is reduced to neurophysiological function following from sensory perception. On the other hand, there is a tendency to see "mind" as active, imposing patterns of meaning on random events; this view results in a more idealistic account of knowledge and finds it difficult to account for the embodied character of human experience. By placing the mind in matter and by making matter subject to a degree to the workings of the mind, Polanyi proffered a more expansive and integrative view of knowledge (and, by implication, reality) than was possible from either a materialist or an idealist perspective.[60]

Alongside his belief in the correspondence between the structure of reality and the shape of our knowledge, Polanyi also expected that purely formal or abstract forms of knowledge, even when not initially associated with any immediate observation or experience, could decisively shape our experience of reality. Just as our intuition of a "hidden" or previously unknown aspect of reality motivates us forward in our efforts to clarify the nature of the event at hand, so too does abstract knowledge sometimes sug-

gest an image or a direction that, almost by accident, illuminates in an unforeseen manner our understanding of some aspect of our experience.[61] Polanyi referred to theoretical physics, pure mathematics, and abstract art as
forms of knowledge that, while having no necessary reference to any aspect
of our immediate experience, nonetheless had demonstrated their capacity to
lead us into new avenues of awareness and understanding.[62] This further
highlights the inescapable tension manifest in Polanyi's thought regarding
the relationship between knowledge and reality:

> Why do we entrust the life and guidance of our thoughts to our conceptions? Be-
> cause we believe that their manifest rationality is due to their being in contact with
> domains of reality, of which they have grasped one aspect. This is why the Pygma-
> lion at work in us when we shape a conception is ever prepared to seek guidance
> from his own creation; and yet, in reliance on his contact with reality, is ready to re-
> shape his creation, even while he accepts its guidance. We grant authority over our-
> selves to the conceptions which we have accepted, because we acknowledge them as
> intimations–derived from contact we make through them with reality–of an indefi-
> nite sequence of novel future occasions, which we may hope to master by develop-
> ing these conceptions further, relying on our own judgment in its continued contact
> with reality. The paradox of self-set standards is re-cast here into that of our subjec-
> tive self-confidence in claiming to recognize an objective reality.[63]

Polanyi was aware that many in his day had given up on the possibility
of talking meaningfully about "reality" and "things as they are in themselves." Given the difficulties attending efforts to establish strictly objectivist
accounts of being, a retreat from ontology was more or less inevitable, but
was not justifiable. Polanyi considered the various means some employed to
get around metaphysical and ontological problems to be more than a little
intellectually dishonest; the "pseudo-substitution" of standards of convenience, or economy, or simplicity, or convention as descriptors of the nature
of knowledge was thought by Polanyi to be an example of unacceptable
philosophical gerrymandering. "The purpose of the philosophic pretense of
being merely concerned with grammar," he suggested, "is to contemplate
and analyse reality, while denying the act of doing so."[64] Such efforts would
fail to account for the resolution of controversies that often attend revolutions
of thought, for they ignore the fact that such controversies are inevitably
solved, not through arguments over which theory is more convenient, or
economic, or simple, but over which theory better accounts for our experience of the world. "We may properly ascribe convenience only to a minor

advantage in the pursuit of the major purpose. ... Our choice of language is a matter of truth or error, of right or wrong—of life or death."[65]

Knowing Life

Even though he did not provide a comprehensive or even a systematic means of explicating questions of ontology, Polanyi did provide some useful suggestions for approaching the question of the nature of reality in light of our understanding of knowledge. Two examples of his efforts at delineating a nascent perspective on ontological questions are particularly worth noting at this point. The first, in keeping with the description of Polanyi's views on language provided earlier in this chapter, is found in the midst of Polanyi's analysis of articulation, and also bears on his consideration of intellectual passions, connoisseurship, and the practice of morphology.[66] Against the objectivism and positivism of his day, Polanyi argued that we need to acknowledge and affirm our ability to recognize "real entities," and to admit that the way we organize our knowledge is itself an image of a world populated by interdependent comprehensive integrations. The classifications whereby we organize our understanding of entities and events signify the indefinite range of properties we expect the members of each distinct class share with one another. The greater the correspondence manifest between a given classification and the members of that classification, "the more rational should be as a rule the identification of things in its terms and the more truly should such classification reveal the nature of the classified objects."[67] Given this expectation, Polanyi suggested that we can discern at least three different levels of intension manifest in our knowledge. The first includes those attributes held in common by the members of a given classification in addition to the attributes or features that distinguish them as members of that classification. The second includes those attributes we expect the members of a given class may share, but of which we are at best only marginally aware. The third includes attributes of which we are at present entirely unaware but that we may expect will become evident at some indeterminate future point.

What is particularly worth noting relative to this brief outline of Polanyi's understanding of the correlation between knowledge and reality is that the more intensional our awareness, the greater is our expectation that the objects of our awareness can be said to manifest in themselves the kind of heuristic passion we see manifest in our own efforts towards understanding. It might, in other words, be fair to say that the greater the intension manifest in our language, the more likely we will expect we are faced with a personal entity or an event signifying personal intention.

This expectation is borne out later in *Personal Knowledge*, wherein Polanyi provides something of an extended dénouement outlining the implicit ontological vision that follows from (and supports) his exposition of knowledge. He sought to incorporate in this vision the ambitions of his philosophical program (i.e., the retrieval of the person, the recovery of meaning, etc.) within the evolutionary history of the world in general and humanity in particular; thus he presents a panoramic reading of the history of life, hoping to demonstrate thereby that the dynamics manifest in the history of the world should be thought of in personal terms. Even knowledge of the inanimate, the static, that which admits entirely to physical and chemical explanation, is measured only in light of our knowledge of the living, the dynamic, that which signifies a comprehensive, complex entity of which no form of epistemological reductionism can make sense. A brief sketch of this vision will help round out our survey of Polanyi's philosophical work.

Even at the lowest or most simple level, the operation of what can be described as a primitive form of heuristic striving is manifest. The emergence and development of embryonic biotic systems open to the organizing tendencies of higher operational principles marks the appearance of a form of being that anticipates the emergence of stable centers capable of pursuing self-interest.[68] There followed the appearance of "living machinery," that is, complex systems of interdependence in which the whole is seen to be representative of a series of interlocking systems each of which is relatively less sophisticated than the system as a whole. This was first manifest in the "appearance of a nucleus within a bed of protoplasm," and was further realized by more sophisticated forms of "internal organization" and purposeful action, representing the "aggregation of protozoan-like creatures to multicellular organisms" that further expanded the physiological sophistication of living creatures and facilitated new means of reproduction and the development of a "major ganglion" situated in that part of multicellular forms of life "which first meets and tries out the unknown world." Thus was established a hierarchy of functions within such life forms, a hierarchy that further conditioned the coalescence of a center capable of acting intentionally.[69]

The advent of purposeful action that went beyond simple function served as the harbinger of a hierarchy of intentionality, one representative of a range of efforts to maximize life through the exercise of commitment. Polanyi distinguished between three degrees of commitment: *primordial* commitment, signifying the vegetative commitments of an active center intent on maintaining function and growth; *primitive* commitment, signifying the rudimentary efforts and behaviors of an active center that itself signifies a comprehensive entity comprised of any number of lower-order levels of organization; and *responsible* commitment, signifying the self-aware conscious decisions of the deliberative person.[70]

The introduction of the possibility of activity based on committed striving opens the way for a recognition of the possibility of learning. This includes the development and elaboration of standards of authority and evaluation according to which one's expectations regarding the satisfaction of intellective endeavors may be measured. This also includes a need to refine one's capacity to "form expectations based on necessarily insufficient evidence," a need which both heightens the importance of commitment in knowing and becoming and which also further facilitated the development of a distinction in awareness between subject and object, both of which influence the continued coalescence of conscious centers of intention.[71]

What eventually emerges from these rudimentary matrices of achievement is any number of paradigms, each describing some measure of intellective excellence. The concomitant refinement of language and social organization that attends the development of these more rarefied standards is representative of "noogenesis," and as such signifies a definitive evolutionary step forward, manifest as the appearance of the "noosphere," a "lasting articulate framework of thought."[72] Within this context it becomes possible for the first time for individuals to recognize one another *as persons*, that is, as responsible centers of commitment joined together in patterns of mutual influence, rather than radically distinct centers of activity, competing with one another for limited resources.[73] This awareness of mutuality further opens the way towards the development of "superior knowledge," represented by those "transcendent" standards and obligations to which not only individuals but whole cultures and traditions find themselves committed. Intellectual exchange at this level thus involves yet another "grade of knowledge, not appraised critically by those who recognize it, but accepted by them largely unseen, on the authority of those whom they believe to possess it," knowledge that is not itself subject to appraisal but to which we submit ourselves "for our own guidance." The standards and authority of such knowledge is that to which "we surrender our person for the sake of becoming more satisfying to ourselves ... This act is irreversible and also a-critical, since we cannot judge the rightness of our standards in the sense in which we judge other things in the light of these standards."[74]

This "second revolution" in the emergence of sophisticated standards of intellective achievement directs human beings towards a realm of transcendent ideals that take them beyond the apparent meaninglessness of a life destined to end in death. While this perspective is itself conditioned by the abiding reality of finitude in all of its forms, it is at least capable of providing a sense of meaning within the context of humanity's brief existence. This fragile sense of meaningfulness is not, however, merely an ephemeral self-delusion, for it points to an unimagined future in which the aspirations and standards of excellence of human beings may be realized. It suggests that the ultimate fruition of the world itself is a kind of archetype for the many ways our knowledge always points to a hidden reality more expansive and more meaningful than we can even guess, but which we can have some reliable hope of moving towards provided we responsibly fulfill the commitments engendered by our sense of calling.[75] Polanyi ends his description of the means whereby we are enabled to understand life as follows: "We may envisage then a cosmic field which called forth all these centres by offering them a short-lived, limited, hazardous opportunity for making some progress of their own towards an unthinkable consummation. And that is also, I believe, how a Christian is placed when worshipping God."[76]

Joan Crewdson rightly points out that the ontological perspective effected by Polanyi's philosophical program is one that leaves aside the language of substance or essence and opts instead for the language of commitment, indwelling, and achievement.[77] These dynamics are manifest in hierarchical patterns signifying increasingly committed efforts at indwelling particular perspectives, both on the part of the objects of our awareness and on our own part as subjects determined to understand the world.[78] Crewdson, however, makes a subtle but critical error in saying that Polanyi's philosophy advances an ontology in which "mind" is seen as the ultimate "ordering principle in matter and as having been at work in the evolutionary process from the beginning."[79] There are, it seems, two ways of making sense of this statement. On the one hand, we might say that "mind" is a wholly natural phenomenon operative in the universe since the beginning of time. On the other hand, we might say that Crewdson is thinking chiefly of the "mind" of a transcendent divine being. Neither of these options are attractive; the former devolves into a form of idealism (or pantheism), while the latter implies a certain determinism.

What is needed instead is a way of affirming the ontological vision afforded by Polanyi's thought while avoiding the problems that follow from
Crewdson's suggested interpretation. Here we may again have recourse to
the concept of the person. The notion of personal being affirms the centrality
of commitment, indwelling, and achievement for both epistemology as well
as ontology. Further, it preserves the integrity and independence of individual entities even as it affirms their dynamic relationality and interdependence. A more fulsome exploration of this proposal will be taken up in the
following chapters; this will involve, first, clarifying in Polanyian terms the
ontology of the person and, second, describing the necessarily theological
foundation ultimately needed to support such a vision.

Summary

That Polanyi's philosophical work bears significant implications not only for
our understanding of knowledge, but also language and reality, should by
now be obvious. The structure and dynamics of the tacit dimension describe
not only the character of our ways of knowing, but also analogously signify
our efforts at articulation, and even the embodied strivings of complex entities. This correspondence between knowledge, language, and reality should
not, of course, be taken to mean that we can collapse ontology into epistemology. But neither can we posit a hard line of demarcation or separation
between them; the horizons of knowledge, language, and reality overlap one
another considerably. It is, then, both the structure and dynamics of the tacit
dimension on the one hand and the overlap between knowledge, language,
and reality on the other that provides us with a starting point for articulating
an ontology of the person from a Polanyian perspective. What is also evident
at this point is the extent to which Polanyi's work, despite its profundity and
its reach (or perhaps *because* of its profundity and reach), requires a significant degree of completion before it can be considered a more or less comprehensive philosophical system. Our efforts henceforth are intended as a step
towards the realization of both of these ambitions.

The Reality of God in Polanyi's Philosophy

The fact that Polanyi's philosophical efforts generated a range of implications, not to mention a host of questions, regarding the nature of religious
knowledge was something he himself recognized even while still pursuing
his epistemological investigations.[80] Likewise, the reception of his work

almost immediately evoked a striking interest in exploring the ramifications of his thought for the practice of theology; this tendency has continued almost unabated up to the present day, and it is probably fair to say that Polanyi's work has had greater exposure and influence in the realm of theological studies than in any other area of intellectual endeavor, even (perhaps surprisingly) epistemology. This section provides an outline of those instances in Polanyi's work that explicitly engage religious or theological issues. It is expected that, by surveying these representative examples, we can come to a greater awareness of the sense of promise seen by those who have sought to expropriate Polanyi's work for the task of theological inquiry. Further, by situating those instances in Polanyi's work in which theological issues are brought to the fore within the broader context of Polanyi's philosophy, we will hopefully be able to anticipate somewhat the tenor of a distinctly Polanyian approach to focused theological reflection.

The Theological Direction of Polanyi's Philosophy

In order to highlight the distinctly theological trajectory of Polanyi's thought, we should distinguish this tendency from other comparable tendencies in his work taken as a whole. What we are here calling the theological direction in Polanyi's thought follows largely from the more fundamental ontological, metaphysical, and religious tenor of his work. Although our use of these terms at this point somewhat abuses their more commonly acknowledged and technical philosophical meanings, the variance between them and the importance for the distinctions they signify will become evident. In brief, we can say that these perspectives represent increasingly expansive horizons of meaning, and that Polanyi's thought allows for reflection on the highest or most expansive level (i.e., the theological).

What is meant by saying that Polanyi's thought manifests an implicitly "ontological" perspective? Quite simply, it means that his philosophy allows us to claim to have reliable knowledge of the real world, and that the parameters of Polanyi's view of knowledge largely correspond to his view of reality itself. A kind of fundamental ontological perspective can be seen in Polanyi's thought in light of the realist tenor of his epistemology; this has already been reviewed, so it is only necessary to mention this theme here in order to set it off from the alternative perspectives considered below.

Recognizing the shift from this "ontological" perspective to the "metaphysical" perspective implied in Polanyi's thought only requires recalling that Polanyi included a certain open-endedness in the elaboration of his stratified epistemology. When this is seen (as Polanyi intended it to be) alongside his expectation that the shape of our knowledge and awareness corresponds with the shape of that of which we are aware, then we have taken the first step from ontology to metaphysics. When we further recall Polanyi's belief that those entities that are most real are those that transcend the realm of our physical experience, then we have completed the shift in our perspective from the "ontological" to the "metaphysical." We can aspire, in other words, not only to reliable knowledge of empirical realities, but of immaterial ones as well.

The further shift from an implied metaphysical perspective to an incipient religious perspective likewise needs only a little elaboration of themes that are by now familiar. It was not unusual for Polanyi to suggest that certain details of his philosophical program bore a striking similarity to religious awareness. For example, he believed that the pursuit of the achievements towards which people strive are designed to serve as starting points for the realization of shared "cultural and social purposes," which will eventually "reveal to us God in man and society." God is seen here as the actualization of the highest ambitions to which human beings might aspire.[81] At the same time, Polanyi suggests that human beings "need a purpose which bears on eternity" because the challenges and crises facing humanity cannot be resolved "on secular grounds alone."[82] It is not unreasonable to think that Polanyi believed religious awareness potentially offered the most expansive and integral vision available to humanity: religion "can transpose all intellectual experiences into its own universe, and has also served, in reverse, most other intellectual systems as their theme."[83] In short, Polanyi recognized that his philosophical program elicited religious questions.

However, it is perhaps also possible to suggest that Polanyi's philosophical program also evokes an even broader horizon of meaning, namely, a distinctly theological one. In order to address this possibility, we must first ask what it is that distinguishes a "theological" perspective from a "religious" perspective. If it is fair to characterize a religious perspective in terms of the efforts of human beings to recognize and honor the divine, then it could be said that a theological perspective represents a human response to divine self-revelation; in more colloquial terms, we might say that whereas religious reflection moves in a "bottom-up" direction, theological reflection necessarily involves a prior "top-down" movement. If this distinction holds, then by suggesting that Polanyi's work moves in a theological direction we may be moving beyond the boundaries that Polanyi himself recognized. This move, however, seems legitimate if we recall that Polanyi insisted that, in all areas of knowledge, we find ourselves obligated to a truth that exists independent of us, and which, in light of the more or less accurate understanding we have, continues to reveal itself to us in new and unforeseen ways. When we further recall that Polanyi believed that this dynamic is manifest along the entire spectrum of knowledge, from our awareness of the "lowest" forms of insentient being to the "highest" forms of mystical indwelling,[84] then it becomes possible to see how what might be characterized in Polanyian terms as the "objective pole of religious or mystical awareness" could find a significant connection to the idea of divine self-revelation. If what has already been said about the extent to which his thought intends a direction that is at once ontological, metaphysical, and religious, then it is not hard to conclude that there is room within the context of Polanyi's philosophy for the elaboration of a nascent theological stance. We are at this point perhaps further from the explicit details of Polanyi's program than he himself would have been comfortable with, but this nonetheless seems like a reasonable extension (if not completion) of some of the more open-ended elements of his thought.[85]

Polanyi's Near Miss

Given both Polanyi's understanding of the theological enterprise and its potentially expansive and integrative vision along with the overall tenor of his thought, it is something of a mystery that he did not more fully engage the question of religious knowledge. We have already noted the extent to which efforts aimed at clarifying Polanyi's religious convictions and his intentions for the application of his thought to theological questions have resulted in controversy rather than clarity.[86] Therefore, a few summary observations are necessary to account for this lacuna in his work.[87]

The tension manifest in Polanyi's thought regarding religious and theological issues is quite profound. On the one hand, his philosophical writings increasingly acknowledge religious themes, such that whereas an early work like *The Logic of Liberty* exhibits a paucity of references to religion or God, a later work like (the admittedly contested) *Meaning* includes extended reflection on questions of a more religious nature. On the other hand, Polanyi also admitted to there having been a shift in his thought such that by 1963 he was comfortable describing as a "belief in the reality of emergent meaning and truth" what he had in 1946 described as a "spiritual reality."[88] Given this

adjustment in his language, it is perhaps especially surprising that he engaged religious and theological questions more fully in his later work than in
his earlier work. As noted in the previous chapter, the question of Polanyi's
religious beliefs has been hotly contested, with some suggesting that Polanyi
intended that his work be directed in part towards the renewal of religious
belief and others suggesting that Polanyi held to no particular religious beliefs of his own. What is to be made of this tension?

William Scott has suggested three reasons as to why there appears to be
such inconsistency in Polanyi's thought regarding the question of "religious
realities."[89] First, it is not inconceivable that Polanyi suffered at points from a
"failure of articulation," that is, he was unable to make clear the precise
nature of some his own ideas.[90] Second, it is likely that Polanyi, who manifest a marked diffidence even towards those closest to him to discuss the
question of his religious commitments, would never have felt comfortable
elaborating the details of his faith in his work (possibly because he was
concerned doing so would cause people to lose sight of the broader thrust of
his efforts).[91] Third, it is possible that Polanyi changed his mind between the
late 1940s, during which time he worshipped in the Church of England, and
the late 1960s and early 1970s, during which time he was pulling together
many of the ideas that would constitute much of *Meaning*.

Without greater attention at this point to the details of Polanyi's life and
character, it is probably impossible to decide such questions in any kind of
ultimately convincing manner. Establishing a determinative answer is, however, thankfully not necessary. We are, of course, obligated to deal fairly and
critically with the details of his work in our own efforts to appropriate his
thought for the purpose of constructive theological inquiry. However, we can
also acknowledge that it would be something of a betrayal against the whole
thrust of Polanyi's efforts to fail to acknowledge the new vistas of awareness
opened up by his philosophy, vistas he himself could not have foreseen.[92] In
saying this, we need not presume to proffer a judgment about Polanyi's own
beliefs, but rather need only recognize the direction of his work and the need
for a distinctly theological foundation for its fulfillment.

Conclusion

If our earlier observations are accurate regarding the novel alternative Polanyi's epistemology provides to many late modern perspectives on the
question of knowledge, then it also seems fair at this point to say that the

ontological horizon implicitly supporting Polanyi's wider philosophical perspective also represents a relatively unique and creative alternative to many contemporary notions of reality and being. Relative to our own ambitions, we can in particular note here the extent to which Polanyi's emphasis on the personal character of knowledge supports a view of reality that is in some sense equally personal, given the correlation in Polanyi's thought between knowing and being. However, in light of the fact that Polanyi was not able to explore fully the wider ramifications of his epistemological theories, we must also acknowledge that the ontological perspective suggested by Polanyi's work is incomplete at best. What is required in order to begin constructing a more comprehensive accounting of knowledge, language, and reality (as well as the correspondence between them) is the further extension of some of the trajectories manifest in Polanyi's thought. Relative to our own primary goals, this would involve an examination of the extent to which a dialogue between Polanyi's philosophical program on the one hand and the Christian theological tradition on the other would result in the clarification and edification of both.

However, we have also seen that any appropriation of Polanyi's work for the purpose of theological reflection requires some care. Throughout this chapter we have sought (among other things) to elucidate Polanyi's understanding of the nature and reach of religious knowledge, and have found that we cannot unreservedly appropriate his work for theological inquiry; rather, it must first be selectively refined.[93] This is consistent with suggestions made by others who have sought to demonstrate the potential theological value of Polanyi's thought. As Thomas Torrance has noted, "[o]ur concern with Michael Polanyi's philosophy is not simply with what he himself taught, but with what we, learning from him, may do in carrying further the kind of … inquiry which he has taught so many of us."[94] Richard Allen offers an even more specific proposal when he suggests that Polanyi's philosophy needs a full-blown trinitarian theology in order to be brought to completion.[95] Torrance and (especially) Allen thus further orient us to the particular tasks we will take up throughout the remainder of our study.

3
Post-Critical Personhood

Introduction

The preceding chapters have largely been expository in nature, exploring the dimensions of Polanyi's philosophy and describing the details of his program. Beginning with this chapter, we turn our attention towards a more constructive enterprise, namely, critically adopting and employing elements of Polanyi's thought in an attempt to examine questions he himself did not address but which nonetheless are implied by his efforts. More specifically, we are now ready to begin narrowing our focus to the particular issue of Polanyi's understanding of personhood and its potential value for theological inquiry. Engaging this issue will require several steps, including identification of exactly what can be said about Polanyi's understanding of the person, the interface between Polanyi's philosophy and theological studies, and how a Polanyian rendering of the concept of the person can be applied to particular theological questions. The current chapter takes up the first of these tasks, leaving the other two for the following chapters.

We will begin by identifying two complementary ways that Polanyi's thought evinces a particular understanding of personhood, and will then examine two of the more extensive efforts made to date that employ a Polanyian understanding of personhood in the furtherance of ambitions not immediately related to Polanyi's own project. We will then briefly examine the various ways the concept of the person has been described in the Western tradition with an eye to the particular challenges presented by modernity, and will attempt to respond to these challenges by developing a working model of personhood responsive both to contemporary concerns and the dynamics of Polanyi's thought. What we will find throughout is that, as David Rutledge has suggested, for Polanyi the concept of the person "is best understood not as a mysterious metaphysical entity, as a disposable synonym for other 'man' words, or as self-authenticating *praxis*, but as an indispensable metaphor for the unique event that comes into being when a man owns himself."[1] In many ways, the work of this chapter involves nothing other than the elucidation of this observation.

Personhood in a Post-Critical Horizon

Before turning to an examination of some of the ways others have used Polanyi's work as a starting point for developing projects of their own organized around the concept of personhood, we first need to establish what can reasonably be said about Polanyi's own views on this matter. How did he conceive of the concept of the person? Given that, as we have noted, Polanyi did not undertake anything like a systematic anthropology, we are forced at this point to work in a somewhat constructive fashion, weaving together insights drawn from the tapestry of his thought as a whole. However, given the thoroughly personalistic tenor of his efforts, we find many resources suitable to this task close at hand.

All of the elements of Polanyi's philosophy that we explored in the previous two chapters can be said to varying degrees to provide key insights into Polanyi's understanding of personhood. The moral dimensions of knowing and being (including the moral and intellectual crisis of the late modern period), the continuity between formal and informal thought, the dynamics of the tacit dimension and of indwelling, the vital importance of tradition and conviviality—all of these can and should be brought to bear in an attempt to excavate the understanding of personhood on which Polanyi tacitly relied. Further, it is possible to recognize that there is not one, but two general characterizations of personhood evident in Polanyi's thought, the first of which can be called an "existential" approach and the second of which can be called an "emergent" approach. We will examine both of these in turn, keeping in mind that they do not represent developmental stages or dissimilar forms of personhood, but rather complementary perspectives on the phenomenon of the person.

Existential Personhood

One of the tenets of classic existentialist thought is that meaning, and to a large degree life itself, begins in the experience of anxiety. Whether or not he intended to follow existentialism in this particular insight is not our concern at this point, but we find in Polanyi's work several observations that lean in this direction.[2] The precondition for all forms of personal knowledge, and thus for the appearance and development of the responsible knower, is the experience of anxiety that results from individuation, a process whereby one differentiates oneself from one's environment. Differentiation from the world, Polanyi suggests, is the only means by which we can "achieve a personhood capable of committing itself consciously to beliefs concerning the world," even though this differentiation necessarily incurs "a fiduciary hazard."[3] Apart from such differentiation, responsible personal being is not possible, and all our knowing and acting remains imprisoned within a realm of solipsistic self-delusion.[4] Nor does this act of differentiation ever cease: we commit ourselves repeatedly, on a moment by moment basis, to ways of knowing and acting that could never be justified on wholly objective, impersonal grounds.[5] It is this act of regular, responsible commitment in the face of the anxiety that attends existence that human beings transcend both strictly subjective and strictly objective modes of knowing and being and move towards realizing a form of knowing and being that is distinctly *personal*.[6]

With this in mind, we can see how it is possible to say that the moral and intellectual crisis of the late modern period represents nothing other than a subversion of the person. Both in its prioritization of instrumental knowledge over pure knowledge as well as in its preference for skepticism over commitment, late modern culture undercuts the conditions that are necessary for responsible knowing and being. The "dynamo-objective" coupling of these two tendencies fosters, not the flourishing of a culture within which people are able to discern and pursue their distinct vocations, but rather the appearance of isolated individuals each acting towards the satisfaction of their perceived private interests divorced from any responsibility to society.[7] This further results in the destabilization of all forms of knowing and being aimed at perpetuating constructive cultural effort, for from this perspective follows a belief in the "intrinsic righteousness of unscrupulous revolutionary power." The transformation of self and society is thus directed towards the unmitigated rejection of everything that is perceived to restrict the potential limits of individual and social change. Over and against the constructive but more tenuous stability afforded by tradition, conviviality, and commitment, late modern culture retreats in desperation to the more destructive but "acidproof" security of objectivism and perpetual violent revolution.[8]

Polanyi's work can thus be read as an attempt to supplant forms of individuation that lead to such destructive, nihilistic tendencies, and to retrieve an understanding of personal differentiation that allows for and even encourages both personal and cultural flourishing. Whereas late modern existentialism, tending as it does towards untrammeled individualism, results in a general collapse of meaning, Polanyi sought to outline the means whereby persons could apprehend the world and their place therein in an integrated, purposeful, and meaningful fashion.[9] His is an existentialism that seeks the on-going renewal of culture through the combined efforts of a "society of explorers" who respect and submit to the authority of tradition and community even as they strive towards greater levels of achievement.[10]

When we inquire after the specific factors that contribute to the process of existential differentiation, we find three specific elements of Polanyi's thought at play more so than others. Specifically, tradition, conviviality, and calling each offer distinct but related insights into the development of the person. In and of themselves, each signifies a particular form of interdependence, so it is not surprising to find that these three taken together are likewise interdependent throughout the process of individuation. The first, tradition, speaks to the interdependence that exists between a given culture at a particular point in time and the historical heritage of that culture (a heritage that also implies a future). Conviviality similarly speaks to the necessary reciprocity that exists between the individuals active within a culture at any given point in time. Finally, the notion of calling suggests the appearance of a distinct form of being that is to some measure dependent on these other two dimensions without being reducible to them even as it simultaneously serves as the means through which they are renewed and perpetuated.

There is a considerable degree of similarity between, on the one hand, Polanyi's exposition of the process of differentiation and the formation of personal identity and, on the other, the tacit triad. Just as the subject, the object, and the subsidiary horizon that binds them together are united in the latter, so too does the one seeking a responsibly differentiated sense of self employ in turn their temporal and spatial relationships as a means of apprehending the identity and vocation to which they themselves are called.[11] Polanyi thus envisions the appearance of distinctly personal forms of being in terms consistent with H. Richard Niebuhr's description of the "responsible self." Human association, Niebuhr suggests, is less a matter of "atomic individuals" entering into partial or contractual social arrangements "for the sake of gaining limited common ends or of maintaining certain laws." Rather, human beings tacitly presume relations with one another "in which unlimited commitments are the rule and in which every aspect of every self's existence is conditioned by membership in the interpersonal group."[12]

A further consequence of this understanding of existential differentiation has to do with the way that the individuation of the responsible person coincides with the apprehension of a wider, transcendent firmament of both obligation and opportunity. Here we hear echoes of Polanyi's analysis of the role of universal intent in the furtherance of personal knowledge: such intent "establishes responsibility," not through the exercise of compulsion nor the indulgence of obsession (both of which exclude responsibility), but by positing the recognition of a range of moral imperatives to which the person is subject. Personal freedom is positively correlated to the apprehension of and submission to these imperatives: the "strain of responsibility" is greater when there is a "wider range of alternatives left open to choice," but so too is this strain a direct measure of one's relative freedom.[13] Fulfilling these transcendent imperatives is how one actualizes one's destiny, not according to a deterministic pattern, but rather by exercising the commitment whereby one continues to achieve their calling to personal being.

So compelling is this vision of the responsible exercise of commitment in the fulfillment of universal obligations that Polanyi suggests, as we noted in the previous chapter, that human beings ultimately have "no other power than this." The attempt to deny these imperatives cannot but result in the loss not only of individual identity and purpose, but also any coherent sense of shared meaning and purpose as well. Stripped of meaningful social, political, and cultural boundaries within which to pursue their calling, individuals find themselves tacitly committed to a worldview in which they ultimately have neither the means nor even the hope of breaking out of the nihilism that pervades their experience.[14] The consistent actualization of these imperatives, by contrast, opens up a range of transcendent opportunities the likes of which could not be guessed from the primitive boundary conditions of the human experience. This last observation moves us towards a more explicit consideration of the second perspective on the phenomenon of personal being evident in Polanyi's work, namely, emergent personhood.

Emergent Personhood

In one sense, it is entirely accurate to say that the notion of emergence is just as much a factor in the foregoing existentialist analysis of personal being as it will be in what follows in this section. The exploration of a distinct calling, itself seen as a unique vocation appearing within the context of a tradition of convivial relationships, could very much be described in terms of emergence. The question can thus rightly be asked as to whether or not we are justified in positing by way of the descriptor "emergent personhood" a distinct perspective on the concept of the person in Polanyi's thought. What distinguishes this perspective from existentialist personhood, especially if the dynamic of emergence can in some sense be said to be operative in both?

Our use at this point of the term "emergent personhood" is intended to highlight the necessary connection that exists in Polanyi's thought between the concept of the person and his nascent stratified cosmology of complex entities. If existentialist personhood provides us with a perspective on Polanyi's thought that is especially sensitive to matters of phenomenology, then emergent personhood provides us with a perspective attuned more so to matters of ontology. Thus, we will in this section be doing some initial unpacking of the suggestion offered at the end of the previous chapter, namely, that we need to avoid both the idealism and the determinism that seem to follow from Joan Crewdson's proposal that Polanyi's philosophy proffers an ontology in which mind is said to be the ultimate "ordering principle in matter and as having been at work in the evolutionary process from the beginning."[15] The notion of emergent personhood, in other words, is intended to help us recognize the centrality of commitment, indwelling, and achievement for understanding being as much as for understanding knowing, and to provide us with a perspective that affirms the integrity and freedom of individual entities even as it acknowledges their interdependence.

We need to recall at this point that Polanyi's description of the appearance and development of increasingly complex forms of life employs two related ideas, heuristic passion and embodiment: the tentative and primitive exercise of the former leads to the appearance of more complex forms of the latter, which in turn allows for more sophisticated and focused examples of the former. Thus, the appearance of increasingly complex and meaningful heuristic integrations follows apace with the appearance of increasingly complex forms of embodiment, and the primitive strivings of animals prefigures "noogenesis" and the appearance of the "noosphere."[16]

What is most significant about this relative to the issue at hand is that embodiment need not (and, indeed, should not) be understood in a reductionistic manner, that is, in such a way that the concept of the body is thought to be coterminous with the physical apparatus of an organism. Within the context of Polanyi's thought, embodiment can be said to include not only the physical, chemical, biological, anatomical, and physiological structures and operations of an organism, but also its capacity for and exercise of the symbolic means whereby it seeks to expand the horizon of all its heuristic endeavors. Embodiment, in other words, includes the exercise of articulation.[17]

Indeed, articulation may be said to be the chief means by which distinctly human forms of embodiment are manifest and evolve. This is so, first, because it is chiefly articulation that distinguishes human beings from other animals and, second, because it is articulation that facilitates the means by which we can be said to dwell in the minds of others.[18] Articulation thus signifies a fundamental mode of human relationality, a mode in many ways even more primitive than material or physical relationality. Additionally, it is chiefly through our efforts at articulation that all of our shared cultural endeavors proceed; it is precisely this unfolding of our articulate achievements that is signified by the concept of the "noosphere," one of the more significant (but largely tacit) consequences of which involves a commitment to the relative correlation of our experience and knowledge on the one hand and reality itself on the other.[19]

We can elaborate further on the connections between articulation and embodiment by recalling the dynamics of indwelling. Involving as it does the experience of simultaneous externality and internality, indwelling helps specify what it means to speak of embodiment in terms of articulation. Every act of indwelling involves the interiorization of the subsidiary elements of our awareness of a particular event.[20] At the same time, it is precisely this act of interiorization that enables us to recognize the event as something external to us, as something of which we are focally aware and that is distal to us.[21] It is, of course, this focal awareness itself that evokes our interiorization of those subsidiary elements of the event that cause us to be aware of the event in the first place.[22] Further, those subsidiary elements on which we (tacitly) rely in our apprehension of the event are chiefly those that define the operational principle(s) of the event at hand: understanding is achieved through a "purposive effort envisaging an operational field in respect of which the object guided by our efforts shall function as an extension of our body."[23]

Highlighting in this way the correspondence between articulation and embodiment helps clarify what we intend by the notion of emergent personhood. It is in and through the body that personal being is born, and it is in and through embodiment that personhood comes into its own.[24] By incorporating within itself not only physical, chemical, biological, and physiological operational principles, but also (through the refinement of its powers of articulation) psychological, sociological, and even theological ones, the body becomes the locus wherein the person apprehends and pursues their unique calling within the matrix of relations in which they both subsist and exist (that is, in which they achieve both independent and interdependent being).

Indeed, the appearance of a distinctly *personal* form of embodied being implicitly signifies a horizon of transcendent obligations and opportunities: the more personal a particular form of being, "the more involved is its plan of action and ... the more fully is the living body committed to comprehensive governing principles of universal standing."[25]

With this in mind, we are able to revisit Polanyi's description of a hierarchically ordered universe consisting of interdependent complex entities and recognize how the distinct form of existence signified by the concept of the person fits within that framework. We see now that embodiment can act as something of a heuristic key for unlocking the logic of this cosmology: what recognizing the correspondence between articulation and embodiment (or, perhaps better, what recognizing the former as an instance of the latter) provides us with is a concrete way of affirming the affinity between the most primitive forms of integration and achievement and the highest levels of human aspiration and achievement. This helps illuminate Joan Crewdson's suggestion that Polanyi's thought intends an ontology grounded in commitment, indwelling, and achievement rather than one grounded in concepts of nature, essence, or substance. However, this perspective also helps us avoid the error into which Crewdson falls when she proposes that some form of "mind" can be said to have been at work throughout the entirety of the evolutionary process. Reading the history of the universe via the rubric of embodiment rather than that of mind helps us recognize both the distinct character of the latter as well as its contingent development as a particular instance of the former. This, in turn, helps clarify the anthropic tenor of Polanyi's thought: the decisive clue to the meaning of reality is to be found precisely in the appearance of that form of existence we associate most closely with mind, namely, the person.

Thus, the notion of emergent personhood, like that of existential personhood, involves affirming both the contingence of the means by which persons come into existence as well as the integrity and reality of the level(s) of achievement manifest in their existence. Despite the misgivings we may have about the freedom and dignity of human beings owing to their evolutionary history, their identity as persons orients them towards a horizon of transcendent obligations and opportunities that serve to distinguish them from the rest of the natural order. It is the resolve to make good on these opportunities through the fulfillment of these obligations, despite the uncertainties that necessarily attends this enterprise, that clarifies both the particular nature of personal being and the meaning of life in general.[26]

Summary

The two approaches to personal being that we have explored in this section are, we can readily admit, somewhat constructive proposals aimed at excavating ideas that are largely implicit in Polanyi's work. However, they seek to draw together various strands of his thought rather than to emphasize one or two elements to the detriment of others. They provide complementary perspectives to the question of how we are to understand the appearance and development of that distinct form of life that we recognize as personal. They also provide us with a starting point for thinking about how this distinct form of existence intend a horizon of meaning and purpose that in some way transcends the contingent means by which personhood comes into being. They thus provide us with a useful means of encapsulating the insights Polanyi offers relative to the concept of the person and allow us to employ these insights in the pursuit of our own, more theological ambitions. Before we engage these questions directly, however, we will first examine what others have proposed with regard to Polanyi's understanding of personhood, and will then supplement our efforts by weaving together the insights we have gleaned in this section with theirs.

Studies in Polanyian Personhood

Given Polanyi's insistence on the necessarily personal shape of knowledge (and thus, albeit implicitly, of being), it is not surprising that some have sought to elaborate further this tendency in his philosophy; indeed, what is perhaps surprising is that more people have *not* done so. Bruno Manno and David Rutledge both provide helpful introductions to Polanyi's understanding of personhood, and both have likewise explored some of the potential theological implications of Polanyi's view of persons. Their respective efforts are reviewed here in turn, beginning with Manno's earlier work and following with Rutledge's more detailed and farther reaching efforts.

The broader purpose of Manno's *The Person and Meaning* is to apply Polanyi's post-critical epistemology to questions and issues in the realm of education, specifically religious education.[27] In pursuing this goal, Manno also provides an insightful description of Polanyi's recovery of personal categories of thought and being. Manno opens with a review of Polanyi's analysis of the crisis of modern thought and then moves, as one would expect, through an exposition of the details of Polanyi's thought before settling in to his examination of the implications of Polanyi's post-critical philosophy for educational formation.

Manno's summary of Polanyi's explication of the modern mind is detailed and accurate, but he does not, surprisingly, highlight the extent to which the modern mindset (as Polanyi understands it) signifies a loss of any real sense of the personal nature of knowledge or reality; given the thrust of Manno's project, one would expect that he would have perhaps focused more on the understanding (or, perhaps more accurately, misunderstanding) of personal knowledge and personal being fostered by the modern outlook. Instead, Manno restricts his reading of Polanyi's analysis of the modern period to the emergence of mechanistic, deterministic, and reductionistic modes of thought.[28] Manno does point out, as many do not, some important nuances for understanding both modern thought and Polanyi, such as Descartes's desire to overcome skepticism, not belief, through his deployment of the *cogito*,[29] and Polanyi's desire to recontextualize, not reject, modern thought within a wider epistemological horizon.[30]

The bulk of Manno's efforts are taken up with his delineation of the epistemological details of Polanyi's philosophy. Manno is careful in his description of the details and logic of Polanyi's thought, and he does a better job than most at showing the connections between the various elements of Polanyi's thought he engages. Beginning with a consideration of Polanyi's description of the relationship between intellective and pre-intellective forms of knowledge, he moves through an analysis of the dynamics of discovery, the structure of the tacit dimension, the emergence of personal forms of knowing and being, and the notion of a hierarchically stratified understanding of both knowledge and reality.[31] Working from the unpublished lectures Polanyi delivered at the University of Texas in 1971 and the University of Chicago in 1969 (all of which would later be used in the construction of *Meaning*), Manno also provides one of the first detailed expositions of Polanyi's understanding of the experience of meaning as manifest in his taxonomy of language.[32] As before, although he acknowledges at several points along the way some of the implications of Polanyi's thought for an understanding of personhood, the concept of the person is not a central concern in Manno's analysis. However, what may seem to be a weakness should probably be read as a strength, for it indicates that Manno intends to stick close to the shape of Polanyi's arguments (for example, Manno does not overextend his claims regarding the extent to which the question of personhood was a controlling issue for Polanyi relative to his understanding of language).

By correlating certain elements of Polanyi's thought with the work of Erik Erikson, Jean Piaget, and others, Manno is able to outline a psychosocial developmental scheme that serves as a road map for his description of the task of religious education.[33] He finds Polanyi's notions of calling, the heuristic character of knowledge, and the commitment to and renewal of tradition within a society of explorers particularly suited to his task. Religious education also provides the context within which Manno further elaborates his understanding of human personhood along Polanyian lines.[34]

Manno focuses his description of human personhood by way of the human capacity for comprehension and understanding.[35] Comprehension and understanding are manifest in the intellectual passions and strivings of agents, actively and collaboratively reaching towards universal standards.[36] Within the hierarchical pattern of living and being signified by these strivings, the individual is seen as an organizing center or entity that responsibly provides direction to the pursuit of calling (or irresponsibly neglects the obligations implied in calling).[37] The acquisition of language as the means whereby acknowledged standards of belief and practice are transmitted becomes a definitive instance of the process whereby identity is shaped and perpetuated.[38] Seen thus, personhood involves a process of increasing simultaneous individuation and socialization: as the individual becomes more open to relationships, the integrity of their identity becomes more stable and better suited to the pursuit of further intellective strivings.[39]

While it is true that Manno did not go as far as he could have in his analysis of Polanyi's understanding of personhood, his project represented a good first step in that direction.[40] David Rutledge recognized the need for further examination of this issue and sought to extend the study of this aspect of Polanyi's thought with his *The Recovery of the Person in the Post-Critical Thought of Michael Polanyi*, which is the most extensive study of this subject completed to date. Rutledge draws on Polanyi's epistemology and identifies three ways that Polanyi characterizes personhood: in terms of knowing, in terms of speaking, and in terms of acting. All of these point to the more fundamental dynamic representative of personal being, that is, commitment, which Rutledge takes up in the latter stages of his investigation.

Rutledge also offers some relatively singular qualifications regarding the lens through which he believes Polanyi should be read. For example, he suggests that many have misunderstood Polanyi as intending to provide a general theory of knowledge or, even more mistakenly, a theory of existence or being. Rutledge believes instead that Polanyi himself saw his own work as a kind of first step, a sketch of the parameters of a theory of knowledge, but not complete in and of itself. Significantly, Rutledge admits that Polanyi's work manifests some ambiguity regarding this issue: whereas Polanyi's earlier work (up to and including *Personal Knowledge*, which Rutledge considers Polanyi's "central achievement") might have been intended to be more peremptory, his later work appears to involve the application of his earlier work *precisely as a theory* to specific areas of inquiry. Nonetheless, Rutledge advises that approaches to Polanyi made with the expectation that a comprehensive system will be found must end in disappointment.[41] Furthermore, he points out that the task of theologically appropriating Polanyi's philosophy is an ambiguous enterprise. This follows somewhat naturally from his qualification regarding the incompleteness of Polanyi's thought: if Polanyi was not about the construction of a full-fledged system, then it would be a mistake to approach his philosophy as if all it needed was to be "baptized" by recontextualization within a theological horizon.[42] What is instead needed in any theological effort determined to make use of Polanyi is an effort to clarify the extent to which the structure of Polanyi's philosophy may be of use in exploring fundamental theological questions; our own efforts are intended as a further step in that direction.

By beginning his study with an examination of the challenges the modern mind presented to the idea of the person, Rutledge intends both to provide a more accurate reading of the modern period than supplied by Polanyi as well as to situate his own understanding of the extent to which Polanyi's thought (despite his imperfect grasp of the history of modernity) recaptures the possibility of affirming the personal nature of knowing and being. Rutledge takes it as self-evident (although he also supplies abundant citations in support) that late modern thought is characterized in part by its relative inability to deal effectively with the category of personhood and the displacement of the person effected by the rise of objectivism. His analysis of the crisis of modern thought is more expansive than Polanyi's, more closely wedded to other scholarly treatments of the history of modernity than Polanyi's, and more focused in terms of the question of personhood than Polanyi's.[43] By arriving at many of the same conclusions as did Polanyi, Rutledge gives the lie to those critics who suggest that Polanyi's understanding of modernity is fatally flawed.

As with Manno's work, the majority of Rutledge's time is spent explicating the details of Polanyi's philosophy. Rutledge uses his three-fold taxonomy of Polanyian personhood (i.e., person as knower, speaker, and actor) to organize his approach to Polanyi's thought. In his description of the person as knower, Rutledge specifies five broad themes that distinguish Polanyi from other contemporaneous philosophers of knowledge: first, his emphasis on the historical context of the scientific enterprise; second, his concern with the "process of discovery" rather than the "codification of discovery"; third, his generally realist outlook; fourth, his appropriation of *Gestalt* psychology; and fifth, his elaboration of the relationship between intellective and pre-intellective thought.[44] The remainder of Rutledge's description of the person as knower is built around his interpretation of Polanyi's notion of the tacit dimension, taking particular note of the dynamics of discovery, the distinction between focal and subsidiary awareness, the commitments entailed in knowledge, the convivial order that supports all knowing, and the stratified epistemology inherent in Polanyi's view of knowledge.[45]

Exploring the idea of "person as speaker" provides Rutledge with an opportunity to bring Polanyi's thought into dialogue with others who have devoted attention to the question of language and its relationship to personhood. Prior to explicating Polanyi's view of articulation and its place within the realm of personal knowledge, Rutledge provides a summary description of several ways in which late modern thought devalues language; he thereby anticipates the conclusion that Polanyi's post-critical philosophy necessarily includes a renewed sense of the importance of language. Rutledge notes four related but distinct ways in which language is devalued by an objectivist worldview: first, cognition is granted precedence over language as the primary horizon within which rationality is manifest; second, language is thus thought to be meaningful only inasmuch as it conforms to the more rigid, abstract standards of rationality according to which cognition is thought to operate; third, language is reduced to being a system of representations intending cognitive states or propositional statements, rather than being seen itself as a heuristic act; and fourth, the expressive, cultural, and historical contexts implicitly manifest by language that lend it intelligibility and meaning are ignored, thus heightening the perception that language is more or less vacuous apart from its reference to cognition.[46]

Having thus set the stage, Rutledge then sets out to demonstrate how it is that Polanyi's characterization of articulation recaptures a more accurate and meaningful understanding of language. Working primarily off Polanyi's description of the necessary conditions for language (i.e., the laws of poverty, grammar, iteration, consistency, and manageability), Rutledge argues that language represents the "primordial world of meaning" out of which our critical perspective emerges and within which all our analytic efforts take place. Thus, the heuristic character of knowledge as manifest by the operations of the tacit dimension of thought is itself representative of the more fundamental dynamics of language, which is also a heuristic enterprise manifesting a structure comparable to that of the tacit dimension; what appears in the ambit of epistemology to be posterior is actually anterior. Language can thereby be said to become representative of the many ways in which we, through indwelling, engage simultaneously in the extension and reception of meaning within the wider interpersonal, cultural, and historical horizons within which we find ourselves.[47] Rutledge's arguments in this section are convincing, but there is a rather large hole in his description of Polanyi's understanding of language: he neglects all mention of the various modalities of language set forth in *Meaning* (i.e., signs, symbols, metaphors, art, and myth), the point at which Polanyi (via Prosch) explored some of the implications of his understanding of articulation (contrary to Rutledge's assessment that Polanyi never pursued these ideas).[48]

Because he misses Polanyi's later engagement with the question of language, Rutledge is forced to turn to the work of George Steiner in order to extend his own line of argumentation. He is sympathetic to Steiner's claim that "*language* and *man* are correlate" (that is, they "imply and necessitate each another"), and finds agreement between Steiner and Polanyi regarding, first, the inadmissibility of both a strictly behaviorist and a strictly empiricist accounting of language, second, the essentially contextualized or situated nature of all language, third, the tacit manner by which meaning is brought to bear in and by language, and fourth, the importance of tradition in perpetuating and renewing language.[49] Rutledge is particularly impressed with Steiner's explication of language in terms of temporality, alternity, privacy, and orality. The first of these, temporality, involves the way in which language both exists within time and is itself a determining factor in our awareness and understanding of time. The second of these, alternity, recognizes the extent to which language, in its affirmations, simultaneously offers concomitant patterns of negation, and by this apparently paradoxical deployment renews itself. The third of these, privacy, emphasizes the tension between the individual (idiosyncratic) use of language and the more universal context of meaning out of which individual usage emerges. Finally, orality signifies the dependence of textuality (and thus textual rationality) on speech (Rutledge suggests that we might view "chirographic" rationality as a bridge between "typographic" and "oral" rationality, but does not explore this idea). Rutledge sees Polanyi's understanding of articulation as a foundation for a view of language in which the conflicting demands evinced by the polarities mani- fest by the temporality, alternity, privacy, and orality of language may be successfully managed.[50]

Focusing his attention on the extent to which Polanyi's view of language opens the door to a much wider understanding of knowledge than can be had from epistemological accounts strictly wedded to cognitive states or activi- ties, Rutledge moves into his analysis of the "person as actor." He highlights the work of B.F. Skinner and J.J.C. Smart as representative of a broader tendency in late modern thought to devalue the notion of "action," and notes the implications this outlook has for an understanding of personhood. Skin- ner's behaviorism and Smart's identity theory, both of which Rutledge finds to be materialistic and reductionistic in their respective ways, both denigrate the reality of personal being, preferring instead to speak of the dynamics of personhood in terms of (per Skinner) conditioning (i.e., "person" as a set of stimulus-response relationships) or (per Smart) the brain (i.e., "person" as neurophysiology). Rutledge, borrowing a term from Polanyi, picks up on the "pseudo-substitution" endemic to both perspectives, and points out that Skinner and Smart have illegitimately extended their anthropological obser- vations into a full-blown metaphysic, one which cannot do justice to human experience or even consistently live up to its own standards and expecta- tions.[51] Working off Polanyi's notion of a stratified epistemology, Rutledge argues against such reductionistic attempts to characterize human identity. He instead proposes that Polanyi's redefinition of the mind and the body enables us to look scientifically at human behavior and experience while avoiding the materialism and reductionism of behaviorism and identity the- ory. For Polanyi, Rutledge suggests, "mind" is seen as the organizing princi- ple of the body, the higher level of explanation that integrates the activities of the body. As such, the "mind" is not so much an entity or a substance unto itself (thus, the dualism that Smart especially despises is avoided), but rather displays a "conative" aspect, and is thus representative of the commitments and acts of a unified center of (self) consciousness. The body, from this perspective, cannot be thought of in terms of "extension in space," for even the concept of space is problematized within the ambit of Rutledge's inquiry; rather, the body signifies the means whereby we (through indwelling) present ourselves to the world, the means whereby we extend ourselves meaningfully in relationships with other acknowledged centers of consciousness. Since it is the mind that organizes and coordinates such efforts, the mind represents a higher level of reality than the body, but is at the same time always necessarily embodied. It is thus in terms of the commitments and intentions of the mind, manifest through the body, that the possibility of affirming meaningful action is recovered, which thereby also affirms the real existence of responsible persons.[52]

Rutledge concludes his project by introducing what he sees to be some of the theological implications of the insights garnered throughout the previous sections. He draws together his various observations about Polanyi's understanding of personhood and boils them down to something approaching a viable definition of Polanyian personhood: the "person" is that which is manifest in both "appropriation" and "reliance," the former signifying the means whereby we, guided by our intellectual passions, "responsibly claim something as our own," and the latter signifying the dependencies we have on our evolutionary history as a species, our embodiment, and the givenness with which we experience our language and culture. Both appropriation and reliance further signify (to varying degrees and in slightly different ways) a more fundamental dynamic seen to be constitutive of personhood, namely, commitment. The notion of commitment introduces the possibility of characterizing interpersonal dynamics in terms of covenant, which Rutledge finds to be an important first step in exploring not only Christian ethics but also a Christian understanding of the relationship between God and the creation.[53] Furthermore, Rutledge sees the recovery of the possibility of affirming the reality of personal being as an essential first step in the broader cultural renewal of the Western tradition that he believes must take place before the Christian gospel can be brought to bear in any significant or even meaningful manner. Finally, Rutledge closes with several observations regarding the difficulties attending efforts to bring Polanyi's philosophy to bear in a theological milieu, difficulties that follow from the fact that Polanyi's philosophy does not, as Rutledge understands it, provide in itself any definitive markers for theological inquiry. Nonetheless, he believes that the profoundly personalistic outlook Polanyi provides has much to offer for efforts that strive to understand God, humanity, the world, and the relationships between them within a unified conceptual horizon.[54]

Given Rutledge's concerns about the difficulties involved in bringing Polanyi's thought to bear in a theological context, and given the pedagogical concerns driving Manno's efforts, it is not surprising that neither of them attended more thoroughly to specific areas of theological inquiry. However, they both successfully demonstrate the extent to which Polanyi's thought is conditioned by concerns close to the heart of an explicitly personalistic agenda. Before we shift our attention to a more explicit engagement with the task of theological reflection, we need to draw together the insights offered by Manno and Rutledge along with our own earlier examination of existentalist and emergent descriptions of personhood in Polanyi's philosophy.

Accounting for Personhood in the Western Tradition

In order to orient ourselves to the task at hand, we need to consider briefly the history of the concept of the person in the Western intellectual tradition. We cannot hope to provide anything like a comprehensive survey of this issue, and more thorough treatments are readily available.[55] What we do need to do, however, is attempt to account to some degree for the influences that condition the milieu in which we currently find ourselves, for we will find in doing so that our efforts are representative of a much wider movement in contemporary thought. More specifically, what we will see in the following survey, cursory though it may be, is that the question of personhood is close to the heart of a number of problems (not only theological and philosophical, but cultural as well) currently being considered by a number of people from a range of perspectives.

At a very general level, Western notions of personhood can be said to have emerged historically from two main sources, the first of which is the religious experience of the Hebrew people. Within this context, the concept of the person appears chiefly via the people's being confronted by the reality of God, who is himself understood as being personal. Over and against contemporaneous polytheism and idealism, Judaism bore witness to a God who reveals himself precisely in terms of personal identity, passionately involved in the ebb and flow of human experience.[56] The push for clarity regarding the nature of personhood is part and parcel of the Jewish worldview, and the tension between the idea of a personal God and the possibility of personal human identity is a consistent element in Western monotheism.

Alongside its understanding of a personal God, Hebrew monotheism also contained within itself a dynamic view of human nature. Rather than proffering an anthropology organized around the idea of a relatively fixed fundamental structure or substance, Jewish thought characterized human nature as a series of "coordinates interpenetrating one another in function to form a single whole."[57] More precisely, human nature was understood in terms of the interaction of *nephesh* (soul), *basar* (flesh), *ruach* (spirit), and *leb* (heart).[58] There is a corresponding tendency to avoid abstracted, formal analysis, with an emphasis placed instead on examination *via empiricus* of the human experience; theory is here always bound to practice.[59]

These anthropological tendencies turn up in Jewish reflection on the creation of humanity, the origins of human evil, and the possibility of human redemption. Humans are seen as being an integral part of the created order, not as an immaterial substance encased by matter, but as flesh animated by a spirit given by God, with no part of human nature pre-existing any other part; neither (at least in earlier Jewish thought) is any dimension thought capable of surviving the loss or death of its corollary components. Having been created in the image of God, human beings are necessarily related to their Creator, an idea that enabled Jewish thought to proffer a vision of "the integration of the person, body, and soul in a way and to an extent unknown among both Stoics and Platonists."[60] Given this picture, the experience of evil and sin would naturally be seen as a rupturing of both the relationship with God as well as that with the rest of the created order, including even one's relationship with oneself.[61] Redemption would come to be characterized by the reintegration or restoration of these relationships, a tendency that would eventually find its logical conclusion in the hope of resurrection after physical death.[62] Thus human nature itself provided something of an anthropic template according to which the entire narrative of God's work in creation could be organized; the basic scheme of "creation, fall, redemption, consummation" became an important means for interpreting not only human identity but the world as a whole.

The second major source for Western notions of personhood is Hellenist thought and culture. As opposed to the Jewish religious heritage, the traditions of Greek philosophy offered a very different range of resources. It has long been observed that, for the Greeks, personhood more often signified impermanence and imperfection than anything else.[63] Early Christian speculation on the nature of personhood was profoundly impacted by Stoic notions of the relationship between infinite and finite forms of being.[64] Aristotelian metaphysics also provided a significant point of departure in the later elaboration of Christian notions of personhood. Aristotle's understanding of a substance as the unifying, distinguishing character of a given thing, something that is seen to inhere in itself and which enables us to recognize it over time (i.e., through change), became an important conceptual resource.[65] At the same time, his emphasis on the "whatness" of a thing as opposed to its "towardness" or relationality reinforced an essentialist mode of thought.[66]

The fact that John of Damascus would include in the "philosophical chapters" of his *Fount of Knowledge* a veritable laundry list of Greek philosophical concepts and their importance for theology testifies to the enduring significance Hellenism had for Christian thought.[67]

Hebrew and Hellenistic thought came together in a new way during the development of the early Christian theological tradition. It is often said that the christological and trinitarian controversies of the fourth and fifth centuries served as the context within which hitherto unprecedented reflection on the nature of personhood was undertaken and a new level of sophistication achieved.[68] Whether or not this is strictly accurate cannot concern us at this point.[69] However, in light of the theological developments that occurred throughout much of the first six hundred years of the common era, we can certainly affirm that the early Christian theological tradition was engaged in a process of exploration and clarification that culminated in a view of personhood largely unseen in the ancient world, one that has since exercised a determinative influence in Western civilization.[70]

Throughout the patristic and medieval periods, Christian reflection on the problem of personhood was situated within an expansive and synthetic conceptual framework.[71] Despite the differences between the various philosophical and theological schools, there existed a relative consensus as to the parameters of the conversation, one that took place around a consideration of the correspondence between particulars and universals. For both Thomas Aquinas, whose realism signifies one response to this question, and for William of Ockham, whose nominalism was a very different response, the parameters of the discussion were largely the same. It was thus a sea-change in Western thought when, during the early modern period, people began thinking more so in terms that were quantitative rather than qualitative. The accession of mathematics and the appearance of the modern empirical sciences signaled the displacement of classical models for understanding entities, the relationships between them, and reality as a whole.[72] The perspective afforded by modern thought would decisively impact the question of personhood (though it seems that more often the question of personhood itself was not so much a matter of consideration as were related issues having to do with knowledge, causality, and ethics). Western views on personhood were decisively influenced throughout the modern period by the unfolding of a worldview that was characterized by materialism, secularism, instrumentalism, idealism, and an abiding preoccupation with consciousness and subjectivity. We will briefly explore each of these in turn.[73]

The tendency manifest in modern thought towards an increasingly materialistic view of the world arose largely as a result of the appearance of the modern scientific method. As early as the fourteenth century, William of Ockham was reconditioning the received view of the idea of a first cause, and his studies in ætiology and causality helped pave the way for the rise of a new way of looking at the physical world.[74] The astronomical and discoveries of Copernicus, Galileo, and Kepler amounted to nothing less than the introduction of a new science, one both methodologically and conceptually at odds with much of the received scientific wisdom of the time.[75] The later appearance of Newtonian mechanics and Darwinian evolutionary theory would in different ways contribute to the decisive entrenchment of the modern materialistic worldview.

Throughout the modern period, philosophers found themselves taking many of their cues from the empirical sciences. Descartes can be said to have initiated this tendency when, in keeping with his distinction between mind (*res cogitans*) and matter (*res extensa*), he offered a description of the material world in which matter was seen to be subject to impersonal, deterministic laws of probability.[76] The thought of Thomas Hobbes marked the emergence of a far-reaching form of materialism that sought to apply the developing scientific methodology of his day to questions of a more social, political, and philosophical nature. The legacy of modern philosophical materialism expanded throughout the modern period, from the empiricism of Feuerbach and Dühring to the positivism of Comte and Mach, and continued to be evident well into the twentieth century.

Because modern science eschewed metaphysical descriptions of both nature and of causality, the tendency to characterize phenomena more so in functional or instrumental terms became another hallmark of modern thought. What this would mean for the concept of the person is the eventual displacement of metaphysical attempts to characterize human identity by biological, psychological, and sociological efforts. Jeremy Bentham's determination to account for human behavior strictly in terms of the avoidance of pain and the pursuit of pleasure is an early exemplar of this tendency. Similarly, J.S. Mill extended a utilitarian line of thinking, both expanding on Bentham's views and making significant contributions of his own in the area of political theory, ethics, and logic. In a slightly different vein, the advent of psychology and the work of Wilhelm Wundt, Franz Brentano, William James, and others signified a new way of looking at human beings, one much more preoccupied with the observation of behavior than with reflection on the nature of personhood.

Both empiricism and functionalism helped shore up another trend characteristic of modernity, namely, that of secularism. Although secularism was not directly indebted to the scientific theories and practices of the time, it probably would not have taken hold quite as strongly as it did had there been an alternative means of describing the world and human experience that did not involve recourse to classical metaphysics. Fueled by the perception that critical, empirical thinking had rendered the metaphysical enterprise unworkable, the advent of modern protest atheism considerably advanced the secular outlook of modern thought.[77] Arthur Schopenhauer, Kasper Schmidt (a.k.a. Max Stirner), David Strauss, and Friedrich Nietzsche, as well as several of those figures mentioned earlier, all championed in various ways a view of the world in which the idea of a personal God was seen as not only unnecessary, but was deliberately and explicitly rejected.[78]

Undoubtedly, the most influential development of the modern period relative to the question of personhood was the exposition of self-consciousness. We have already mentioned the impact of Descartes's distinction between mind and matter relative to modern views of matter; his distinction had equally profound implications for the modern view of mind.[79] This distinction, along with its epistemological correlate, the famous "*cogito*," provided the foundation for a new way of both pursuing knowledge and characterizing personhood. Whereas matter signified an entirely mechanistic and deterministic order that did not manifest the intention or activity of mind (or, perhaps more accurately, "a Mind"), mind came to signify an order in which reason, guided by logic, was thought to hold sway. By attempting to unite these two ideas, that of impersonal physical law alongside that of rationality, Descartes initiated a philosophical trajectory that would eventually "bring about the decline and fall of reason in European thought."[80]

Subsequent notions of subjectivity can be seen in different ways in the work of John Locke, Jean-Jacques Rousseau, Immaneul Kant, and Johann Fichte. Locke espoused a view of personal identity in which neither matter nor mind were the means by which individual identity was perpetuated; rather, consciousness became the center of identity.[81] His uncertainties about the category of substance and his consequent polite agnosticism led to the more radical skepticism of David Hume, whose work would lead to a wholesale reconsideration of the possibility of reliable knowledge.[82] Meanwhile, Rousseau's celebration of liberty and the exercise of the will impacted the modern understanding of humanity, even as his views on natural theology impacted modern awareness of God. His distinction between the "organic general will" and the "mechanical will of all" influenced Kant's understanding of the difference between pure reason and practical reason.[83]

Kant inherited the legacy of early modern thought and thus found himself concerned not only with overcoming the deterministic materialism of his time (exemplified by Newtonian mechanics), but also with avoiding the philosophical skepticism that had emerged in the wake of Hume.[84] Kant's determination to recover the possibility of both belief in God and of reliable metaphysical (moral) knowledge led him to invert the relationship between the subject and the object. "Instead of beginning with the claim that an external (or noumenal) objective reality contains structures that are grasped by the mind, he proposes that the human subject itself provides the structural categories by which 'objects' that appear (as phenomena) in human consciousness are 'thought'."[85] This reversal of the traditional way of describing the relationship between the subject and the object carried with it significant ramifications for understanding the nature of personal identity and the means by which the subject comes into being and pursues knowledge of the world. Kant also built on modern notions of the self in such a way that human beings could be seen as ends in and of themselves, and not just the means to some other, ostensibly higher ends; persons neither had nor required any external point of reference that served to ground their identity and value as persons. Furthermore, his work in ethics and his emphasis on intention as the means by which virtue may be measured likewise enhanced the modern image of an autonomous subject.[86]

The prioritization of subjectivity also resulted in a new emphasis on the importance of relationship in the formation of the person (understood now chiefly in terms of the "self"). When applied (as it was by Fichte) to the question of God, this led to a reconsideration of the nature of divine personhood. Fichte elaborated his entire philosophical program on the foundation of self-awareness; any consideration of our knowledge of the world, he held, must begin with a analysis of our awareness of ourselves. Fichte believed that subjective consciousness signifies an activity more so than a substance; one's awareness of oneself constitutes one's act of existence. However, self-awareness also necessarily involves awareness of that which is "not-self," which circumscribes the self to some degree. Thus, the relationship between "self" and "not-self" assumes a dialectical character.[87] This bore significant ramifications for Fichte's understanding of metaphysics, not the least of which was a relative rejection of the notion of a personal God.

Kant in particular is a figure whose impact on modern philosophy goes beyond that of many other figures of the period. Not only did he bequeath to the modern tradition a sophisticated view of the subject, his work also contributed to the development of another trajectory in modern philosophy, that of idealism. Kant's distinction between noumena (existents considered in and of themselves) and phenomena (existents considered relative to our experience of them) helped him establish a form of transcendental idealism grounded in certain unifying categories, especially space and time (the first of which were thought to organize all external or physical experiences, and the second of which organized all internal or mental experiences). This form of idealism provided Kant with a foundation for overcoming both the determinism and the reductionism implied by the prevailing materialist worldview; it reasserted the freedom of the mind, and did so in a manner compatible with the secular tendencies of the time.[88] Kant's work would be elaborated in different ways by a variety of others, and modern idealism would reach its zenith in the thought of G.W.F. Hegel, who understood history to be nothing less than the unfolding of reason, freedom, and being itself manifest in and as self-consciousness.[89] Common to all forms of modern idealism is the idea that all that exists can be attributed to the exercise of self-consciousness.[90] The legacy of modern idealism can be seen in the work of Arthur Schopenhauer, Henri Bergson, and the emergence of philosophical personalism, and Hegel in particular has exercised a significant influence on late modern theology.[91]

In light of the fact that the rise of modern thought resulted in the fragmentation of the more unified worldview of the pre-modern world, it was probably inevitable that reactionary movements would emerge. Such movements could be described either as an attempt either to recover something that was sensed to have been lost or to reassert in an altogether new way an aspect of the human experience that mainstream modern thought neglected. Probably the most influential reactionary movements to have emerged are the related fields of phenomenology and existentialism.[92] Both movements carried within them significant consequences for the modern understanding of personhood. Both rejected to some degree the strict empiricism manifest in modern thought; similarly, both resisted reductionism and the modern predilection to characterize human experience and awareness "objectively," that is, apart from the matrix of relationships within which human beings found themselves. Both were thus determined to recapture the importance of meaning and significance as qualifiers of human knowledge and experience.

Phenomenology came into its own under the guidance of Edmund Husserl, who sought to elaborate a way of knowing the world and oneself through an "eidetic" methodology that strongly asserted the existence of a transcendent or autonomous self. By "bracketing" (that is, artificially or conceptually setting aside) the natural order, Husserl thought it possible to achieve an immediate apprehension of the essence of a given reality, including oneself. Husserl's methodology and insights were appropriated by Martin Heidegger, who, despite his appreciation for Husserl's work, rejected his description of the possibility of knowledge of the transcendent self. Concerned as he was with the contextual or situational nature of human experience (i.e., the *Dasein*, the "being-in-the-world"), Heidegger suggested that one could know oneself fully only by way of the actions through which invests oneself in the world of relationships. Gabriel Marcel, another of Husserl's students, followed Heidegger in his attack on Husserl's notion of a transcendent self as well as in the explication of a philosophical method very much concerned with the situational character of human knowledge and experience. Heidegger's decisive influence is evident in the work of Emmanuel Levinas, Maurice Merleau-Ponty, and Paul Ricoeur.

Heidegger's concern with "being-in-the-world" also made a significant contribution to the development of existentialism. Existentialism shares much of the philosophical perspective of phenomenology, but goes beyond phenomenology in asserting the importance of the individual. Here we find an emphasis on the importance of commitment in faith that can be traced back to Søren Kierkegaard, although many late modern existentialists committed themselves to forms of faith that Kierkegaard would have found appalling. The problems and challenges of the modern period in particular and the human experience in general (especially death) provided a framework for existentialist thinkers to scrutinize the nature of faith, commitment, and authentic personal existence. The realization of individual freedom came to be seen as the means by which meaning, value, and truth could be clarified and actualized. These tendencies are found in the thought of Karl Jaspers, Jean-Paul Sartre, and Albert Camus, among others.

Phenomenology and existentialism had a further significant influence on the Western intellectual tradition inasmuch as they can be said to have established the conditions that made it possible for the appearance of distinctly "postmodern" forms of philosophical reflection. Postmodernism draws not only on phenomenology and existentialism, but also on the practice of hermeneutics pioneered by Wilhelm Dilthey and further refined by Hans-Georg Gadamer. The postmodern mindset fosters a propensity to accentuate difference and "otherness" alongside a desire to encourage solidarity and overcome the estrangement that can result from the unmitigated social and even psychological fragmentation that attends the dissolution of the "metanarratives" against which postmodernism aligns itself. Within this context, there follows a radical reconsideration of the nature of subjectivity, denouncing the modern notion of the autonomous individual and advancing in its place an understanding of individual identity in which the self is seen more or less as something of a conglomerate of forces, both personal and impersonal, interacting within a particular milieu; the idea of the "subject," it is said, is a fiction developed by those who would "subject" others to their control. Exemplars of postmodern thought include Theodor Adorno, Michel Foucault, and Jacques Derrida.

In general, it seems fair to say that, if the pre-modern world view was dominated by a conceptual synthesis in which reflection on God, humanity, and the world took place within a unified horizon, by the end of the modern period (if indeed the modern period can be said to be over) this possibility had been not only displaced but nearly destroyed. The shift in perspective manifest in Western thought had been such that the notion of rationality itself is suspect: the world is no longer expected to exhibit or signify the will of a divine Sovereign, human beings are understood less as rational creatures bearing the image of their Creator and more as competing subjects driven by both rational and irrational motives, and the idea of God is more often than not thought to be a matter best left to private preferences. Our concern throughout this rapid survey has been less a matter of the details of these historical developments and more with attempting to describe something of the legacy with which contemporary engagements with the problem of personhood must reckon. Probably the most significant lingering consequence of developments during the modern and late modern period for this issue is the need to demonstrate the connection between ontological and existential concerns; a personalistic metaphysic divorced from the contingencies of human experience will be hard pressed to find an audience.[93] Fortunately, we find both in the theological tradition and in Polanyi's thought a number of resources that can help us engage this challenge head-on. Our earlier analysis of existentialist and emergent accounts of personal being in Polanyi, as well as our review of Manno's and Rutledge's respective attempts to build on

Polanyi's work, have given us a point of entry into this problematic, one that we can follow by drawing together the various strands of this chapter before turning to the more theological work of the following chapters.

A Polanyian Ontology of Personal Being

In our earlier consideration of Polanyi's understanding of personhood (at the end of the first chapter), we noted in passing that Polanyi may have pre-scinded from directly addressing the question of the nature of personhood because his notion of tacit thought may have seemed to him to be somewhat unsuited for the task. While there is nothing in Polanyi's writings to suggest that this was necessarily the case, it seems a reasonable possibility, given the "from-to" structure of awareness that is at the heart of the tacit dimension. An epistemological scheme organized around the principle that awareness always moves along a kind of "from-to" axis would find it difficult at best to address the question of personhood because our experience of personhood can never be wholly "objectivized," that is, made an object of focal aware-ness; we can never entirely attend "to" it, but must always attend "from" it. In other words, personhood must be, even as it becomes to some degree or another an object of awareness or inquiry, the horizon from which we attend to the objects of our focal awareness. Thus, within the context of the question of personal being our own personhood itself is always both a proximal *and* a distal term; we indwell it even as we seek to clarify its form.[94] That Polanyi recognized human awareness and experience as the definitive example of "life reflecting on itself" is attested to in his work.[95] That he recognized the inherent problems this caused relative to the question of personhood is not.

Polanyi recognized the distinction between the experience of personhood we have that follows from our engagement with impersonal dimensions of reality as opposed to the experience that follows from our encounter with other persons. Relative especially to the latter, he emphasized that any con-sideration of personhood proceeds by way of analysis of actions, or, in other words, by way of analysis of those instances that lead us to believe that we are confronted with a personal entity. This pattern of analysis is not totally dissimilar from that of our engagement with impersonal realities, for both can be said to be grounded in reflection on the operational principles. How-ever, the operational principles of persons, intending as they do a transcen-dent horizon, are qualitatively different from those of impersonal realities. Contrary to behaviorists and materialists who would collapse the mind into its workings (and thereby lose sight of the reality of the mind), Polanyi insists that what we know in our indwelling of meaningful entities and events (that is, in our subsidiary comprehension of them) is the mind behind them.[96] Just as we are aware of and seek to comprehend other personal entities by interiorizing and indwelling their expressions (which themselves signify the person's mind), so too we become aware of ourselves as persons through responsibly indwelling the commitments to which we are called, thereby extending our sense of personhood. Thus is established a pattern of mutual indwelling that is representative of persons in relation, that is, a convivial society of explorers.[97]

David Kettle has extended this line of thinking in Polanyi's philosophy relative to the question of the interdependence of individual self-awareness and awareness of others.[98] Kettle suggests that, in general terms, our awareness of ourselves as embodied beings and our awareness of the world as having an existence apart from ourselves represents a "dual indeterminacy." It is the "interanimation" of these two horizons of awareness that brings us both to knowledge of ourselves and knowledge of the world: awareness of one arises simultaneously with awareness of the other, although we can at any one time focus only on one or the other.[99]

Kettle uses three bipolar images to explicate his thesis. The first of these is the experience of movement around a vertical axis, in which our position along this axis serves as a "still point" that helps us coordinate the movement of elements further away from ourselves. The second image Kettle uses is the experience of movement along a horizontal axis, in which our awareness of a more stable or fixed horizon serves as a "still point" wherein we can relativize our own experience of motion. The third image Kettle uses is the experience of movement within a zero gravity environment, in which case both location and orientation arise simultaneously (that is, awareness of both a stable point of reference and a range of indeterminate elements in motion relative to the fixed point).[100] Kettle suggests that it is this third image of bipolarity more than the first two that describes our fundamental experience of self-awareness as persons: *we do not first exist as persons, and then indwell this life; our indwelling, our habitation constitutes us as persons.*[101] Thus, the "dual indeterminacy" of personhood involves the uncertainty each person faces with regard to both the question of the world and the question of their own identity. This indeterminacy is resolved in a pattern of mutuality and interdependence such that our awareness of ourselves as persons is contiguous to the apprehension and understanding we have of the world around us in personal terms.[102]

Kettle's analysis suggests a tripartite understanding of personhood consistent with Polanyi's thought. The idea of an indeterminate center and a range of indeterminate coordinates "outside" that center suggest two of the three elements of this conceptualization; the need for some accounting of the relationship between these two poles of indeterminacy suggests a third element, as well. Our consideration of them here observes a logical order only, for if Kettle's analysis is accurate (as it seems to be), then we must recognize that it is impossible to prioritize our experience or awareness of any one of these loci over the others. Our strategy will be to move from the more "interior" elements of personal being to the more "exterior." This move will also entail a increasingly expansive view of the ways in which the coordinates of personhood can be said to manifest themselves; in other words, the shift from relative interiority to relative exteriority will mark a concomitant shift from in awareness from singularity to plurality.

Polanyi's idea of an "organizing center" from which we attend to our experience and coordinate our heuristic endeavors suggests the existence of what might be referred to as an "indwelling self." This phrase signifies that sense of ourselves that does not admit to any objectification. If we adopt Polanyi's language as a way of making sense of our experience as persons, then our understanding of the "indwelling self" can be said to be that perspective that we must always indwell but which can never become the object of awareness from some other vantage point. It is not the object of our awareness, nor the particular perspective we have adopted in order to heighten our focal awareness of an object or afforded by a particular perspective, *but is itself the experience of indwelling a particular perspective and being oriented towards a given object*. Recalling Polanyi's insistence on the importance of the conscience, which he understood to have both an intellective as well as a moral function, is helpful here. The "organizing center" or "indwelling self" we are at this point describing can be seen as that perspective from which our deliberations are conducted and our decisions and commitments are made.[103] It is worth noting that this characterization of the "indwelling self" leans decisively in the direction of function than in the direction of form; in other words, we are not so much describing a nature or a substance as we are an action, or, perhaps more accurately, a nature that is best understood in terms of structured action.

The possibility that we objectify from what might be called a more or less transcendent point of reference some aspect of our experience as self-aware beings introduces a second locus of personhood. More accurately, it describes a horizon within which we see situated a potentially wide range of coordinates, each signifying a different form of objectivized self-awareness (that is, each signifying a different pattern of indwelling). By recognizing that we are inclined to value some forms of self-understanding (that is, self-objectification) over others, we affirm the possibility that this horizon within which the objectification of self-awareness is manifest is potentially hierarchical in nature. In Polanyian terms, we might describe this horizon in terms of a series of increasingly expansive and integrative forms or *Gestalten*, each signifying some measure of self-awareness or identity. As we both seek and are enabled to indwell the "higher" and more meaningful of these forms, we find ourselves coming to a greater awareness and understanding of ourselves. As with our understanding of the functional structure of what we are here calling the sense of an "indwelling" self, an "organizing center," so too our understanding of the horizon signifying our objectified, "indwelt" sense of self should be understood in dynamic terms: the breadth and width of the horizon of objective self-awareness describes a process of coming into being rather than a static, pre-existing structure.

The extension of oneself through committed, meaningful action, manifest chiefly in our heuristic efforts, brings us to the third coordinate of personal being. By combining our examination in the previous chapter of Polanyi's stratified taxonomy of language along with our review in the first chapter of his understanding of indwelling, we find the means whereby we can reflect on the great variety of ways in which we seek to interiorize the subsidiary elements of our experience in our efforts to make contact both with others and with reality.[104] What is particularly relevant for our immediate purposes is to note the extent to which this process of indwelling, this subsidiary integration and interiorization, opens us up to a horizon of meaning within which we find ourselves integrated and even interiorized within a wider frame of reference.[105] We must recognize, in other words, that the meaningful acts whereby we objectivize and extend ourselves in forms of indwelling opens us to further measures of reciprocity and mutuality essential for personal being. Inasmuch as we think of indwelling and the actualization of ourselves through meaningful action as the imposition of our own sense of subjectivity onto a passive, essentially meaningless (i.e., impersonal) world, we will have failed to grasp the radically relational character of personal being. Neither, however, should we take the opposite view that would essentially collapse the personal knower into the experience of knowing; if our explication of personal being avoids the trap of thinking of

persons as radically isolated and autonomous subjects, so too does it avoid
the trap of thinking of persons as radically enmeshed automatons.

Our consideration of these three coordinates of personhood, that is, the
indwelling self, the indwelt or objectified self, and what we might call the
extended self or the "horizon of the other," leaves us with an image of personal being bearing no small (or accidental) resemblance to Polanyi's notion
of the "tacit triad." The coordination of the three dimensions of personhood
manifests an isomorphic affinity to the coinherence of the acting agent, the
subsidiary clues, and the object of focal awareness that Polanyi suggests one
finds in every act of knowing. Further, we have seen that, just as Polanyi's
explication of knowledge recognizes a variety of stratified fields of knowledge, so too does a Polanyian explication of personal being recognize that
persons themselves exist as comprehensive entities subject to the dynamics
of dual control.

Having tracked the shape of personhood from its more interior to its
more exterior coordinates, we need only briefly mention those elements of
personal being that signify movement more so in a direction from the exterior to the interior. Polanyi's understanding of the influence of dual control
on complex, stratified systems can be brought into play as a means of organizing our understanding of the interdependence of what we have been
here referring to as the "indwelling self," the "indwelt self," and the "extended self."[106] It is the simultaneity of motion in both an "outward" direction and an "inward" direction that enables us to affirm that personal being
transcends subjective experience.[107] This simultaneity of motion, that is, the
interplay between the more objective and the more subjective out of which
emerges the personal, recalls Kettle's imagery of the interdependence of
form and background, each arising only relative to the other as the twin
indeterminacies anchoring a meaningful horizon or perspective.

In keeping with Polanyi's understanding of the "molar" achievement
signified by the coalescence of personal identity,[108] we can thus acknowledge
that the notion of personhood involves each of these coordinates, that is, the
"indwelling self," the "indwelt self," and the "extended self."[109] By further
exploring the implications of a fully molar view of personhood, we can see
how the idea of personhood necessarily involves a perspective that strives to
account for the entire life of the individual, and does not admit to definitive
moments or events within which one's personhood could be said to be clarified or completed.

One of the ramifications of the emergence and development of person-hood as outlined above has to do with our understanding of our knowledge of other persons. In keeping with Kettle's explication of the "dual indetermina-cies" that come into play in our awareness of our own identity and existence as persons, we should expect that our awareness of other persons will follow much the same pattern. In other words, we rely in our awareness of other persons on the interdependence of the points of indeterminacy that establish the relation(s) we share with them. Inasmuch as we indwell in a subsidiary manner the particulars of the horizon within which we encounter other per-sons, we can thereby be said to apprehend in a focal manner the personal reality signified by such particulars; we do not so much deduce the existence of other persons based on observation of their actions as much as we en-counter persons themselves by dwelling in the particulars of the extension of their own personal being.[110] We noted earlier Kettle's conclusion regarding the interdependence of our "habitation" and our identity as persons: *we do not first exist as persons, and then indwell this life; our indwelling, our habitation constitutes us as persons.* We can rephrase this statement relative to the reality of interpersonal relations (and in such a way as to further draw out the decisively personalistic tenor of our existence) in the following man-ner: we do not first apprehend the reality of other persons and then enter into association with them, but are rather enabled to recognize those forms of personal being with which we share communion solely by dwelling in our mutually determinative relations.

It may seem that the Polanyian notion of personal being we have out-lined in this section is not all that different from other recent attempts aimed at delineating the key coordinates of personhood; W. Norris Clarke and Joseph Bracken immediately come to mind as two others who have sug-gested insights bearing some resemblance to what we have proposed here.[111] Thus, the question arises as to what a Polanyian understanding of person-hood offers that may not be found in alternative formulations. The particular value of approaching the concept of the person by way of Polanyi's thought can be found in the notion of indwelling, the concept that serves as a primary component in the structure of his philosophy. Every aspect of Polanyi's explication of personal knowledge either points to or clarifies the dynamic of indwelling, from the continuity of informal and formal intellective effort, to the awakening and eventual satisfaction of heuristic passions, to the unity-in-distinction of subsidiary and focal awareness and the four-fold structure of the apprehension of meaning (understood in terms of the functional, phenomenal, semantic, and ontological significance of *Gestalten*, concepts, and language). The notion of indwelling also plays a central role in understanding the emergence and development of complex hierarchical systems governed by dual control and the continuity between knowing, valuing, acting, and being. Even Polanyi's description of the importance of conviviality and tradition (signifying in part the reciprocal indwelling of minds in one another) can be understood in terms of the relative mutuality of indwelling. Indwelling is the operative dynamic at work in all instances of personal being, whether considered epistemologically, axiologically, or ontologically.[112] In short, the concept of indwelling must be at the heart of any Polanyian understanding of personal being, as it offers a means of articulating an expansive and integrative vision in which the reality of personal being exercises a determinative influence on all forms of reflection on questions of knowledge, values (both moral and aesthetic), and reality. It will be primarily by way of an exploration of the potential theological value of the concept of indwelling that our later efforts will proceed.

In sum, then, our understanding of Polanyi's view of personhood admits to both singularity and plurality, individuality and relationship, dwelling in and breaking out. Recalling again Kettle's understanding of the "dual indeterminacy" of personal being and the extent to which these indeterminacies develop interdependently, we see that it is impossible to say whether "substance" precedes "relationship" or vice versa, for *they both arise together*. We cannot postulate the existence of an *a priori* substance that makes relationship possible. Likewise, we cannot say that personal being within a Polanyian perspective is fundamentally or exclusively relational in nature. Finally, we must acknowledge that some degree of uncertainty necessarily attends the question of personhood: a definitive understanding of any instance of personal being would require comprehensive knowledge of the entity at hand, and such awareness is impossible for us (even relative to our understanding of ourselves).[113]

Having now elaborated an initial understanding of the dynamics of personal being, we should note that we have provided very little in the way of what might be called the ontological content of this vision. For example, our analysis of the interpenetration and interdependence of the coordinates of personal being did not identify in anything other than functional terms how we might understand the precise character of the indwelling self. Similarly, we have not established the specific relations that would likely prove essential in the emergence and development of a robust instance of personal being.

Polanyi himself, not having given extensive attention to the question of personhood, might be of some help here, but whatever insights we might glean from his work would likely only lead us back to one or another of the themes of his work we have explored thus far. Further, the direction of our efforts thus far requires that we give attention to examples within the theological tradition to explicate just such themes. We will then see better how the task of theological reflection can contribute to the fulfillment of Polanyi's thought, and how Polanyi's philosophy can in turn offer new insights into theological problems.

Conclusion

We have now completed the first of the three tasks mentioned at the beginning of this chapter, namely, the development of a working model of personhood in terms consistent with Polanyi's thought. We are thus now prepared to move closer to the theological ambitions of our study, and will proceed in the following chapter to examine the way that others have attempted to adopt a Polanyian post-critical perspective in the furtherance of theological inquiry. This will pave the way for our engagement with the particular issues that will occupy us in the concluding chapter, namely, an examination of the way a Polanyian understanding of personhood potentially informs our understanding of issues related to the doctrine of God. We can already expect, given our efforts to this point, that just such a personalistic interpretation of the trinitarian life of God will open up the possibility of elaborating a fulsome cosmology of interpersonal relations.

4
From Philosophy to Theology

Introduction

When we turn to a consideration of the contribution Polanyi's philosophy has to offer for the task of theology, we find that the ground has already received a good deal of tilling. Even while Polanyi himself was still working out some of the details of his program, it was recognized that his thought potentially carried significant ramifications for the practice of theology. Richard Gelwick and Richard Prust were among the first to explore the possibilities that existed for the development of a far-reaching theological perspective based on Polanyi's ideas, and they have been followed by a significant number of others who have sought to elaborate one or another of the various elements of Polanyi's work within a specifically theological context.[1]

Our task in this chapter will be two-fold. First, we will explore some of the more representative examples of theological projects that have been shaped to a significant degree by Polanyi's thought. Second, we will outline an approach to theological reflection that is suited to our own particular ambitions, building when appropriate on the foundations laid by others. We can expect that the superordinate question guiding our study (i.e., the question of the nature of the person) will help delimit our efforts and prevent us from becoming distracted by any of the number of legitimate but for our purposes more marginal concerns that would require attention in a more thorough exposition of theological method. Rather than attempting something as ambitious as the delineation of an expansive and integrative methodology, we will instead be aiming for nothing other than the articulation of a prolegomena to personalistic theological inquiry.

The Theological Reception of Polanyi's Philosophy

The projects outlined below illustrate the various ways theological studies influenced by Polanyi's thought have proceeded. The notion of personal knowledge emphasizes the role of faith in knowledge, the correlation between knowing and action, and the essentially personal nature of all knowing and being. Polanyi is often seen as one who intended to recover these themes, rescuing them from the neglect to which they had been subjected during the modern period. Thus, the recovery of faith, the recovery of the relationship between knowing and acting, and the recovery of personalistic thought are three of the trajectories along which theological efforts dedicated to appropriating his thought have proceeded.

The following reviews proceed in a direction intended to move us increasingly closer to the particular concerns of the present study. First, we will examine the work of Thomas F. Torrance as a definitive example of a theological enterprise dedicated to capitalizing on Polanyi's recovery of faith as a legitimate and necessary epistemic category. Second, we will outline Barbara Dee Bennett Baumgarten's description of the practice of visual art as a form of performative theology, grounded in Polanyi's recovery of the association between knowing and acting. Finally, we will pursue a close reading of Joan Crewdson's personalistic theology, a project in many ways more consistent with our own efforts than many other theological efforts that appropriate Polanyi's work but one that nonetheless admits to significant ambiguities and pitfalls.

The Recovery of Faith

Most who have seized upon Polanyi's philosophical program as a resource for theological inquiry have fastened onto the theme that serves to guide Gelwick's early work in *Credere Aude*, namely, Polanyi's legitimization of belief as a valid intellective category or standard. The one who has arguably gone the furthest in attempting to elaborate the similarities between Polanyi's understanding of the structure of knowledge and the task of contemporary theology is Thomas F. Torrance. Torrance merits particular attention at this point because he has not only sought to demonstrate the potential correspondence between Polanyi's philosophy and theological inquiry, but has also sought to extend Polanyi's arguments regarding the relative equivalence between theology and scientific inquiry. Torrance values Polanyi not only for his epistemological insights, but for his analysis of the besetting crisis of the modern mind as well as the opportunities afforded by the emergence of new strains of postcritical thought.[2]

Torrance's appropriation of Polanyi's thought is selective and sometimes critical, but extensive enough that commentators on Torrance's thought have noticed his indebtedness. Both Alister McGrath and John Morrison readily acknowledge Torrance's appreciation of Polanyi,[3] and Colin Weightman has gone so far as to suggest that Torrance owes much of his theological vision to the intellectual perspective afforded by Polanyi.[4] Robert Martin finds in Torrance's theological appropriation of Polanyi's thought a conceptual foundation for Christian education.[5] Roland Spjuth and Elmer Colyer note Torrance's use of Polanyi but do not analyze his appropriation of Polanyi's thought or even expound at length on it.[6]

The three works in which Torrance deals most extensively with what he understands to be the theological implications of Polanyi's thought include *The Christian Frame of Mind, Transformation and Convergence in the Frame of Knowledge*, and "The Framework of Belief," his contribution to a collection of essays dedicated to exploring the ramifications of Polanyi's work for Christian theology.[7] Although Torrance only rarely engages in the focused exposition of Polanyi's thought, it is in these works more than his other major writings that he examines the epistemological issues Polanyi's program brings to the fore relative to all intellective efforts.[8] Otherwise, his appreciation and appropriation of Polanyi's thought is scattered throughout most of his major writings.

Rather than adopting the elements of Polanyi's philosophy uncritically, Torrance seeks at several points to refine them in subtle but, relative to his own intentions, important ways. For example, he recognizes the importance of Polanyi's understanding of the fiduciary character of knowledge[9] and the tacit dimension,[10] and makes use of these principles in his explication of both trinitarian theology[11] and natural theology.[12] However, he also believes that Polanyi's understanding of the intuitive manner in which human beings perceive meaningful forms owes too much to the dynamics of visual perception. Torrance suggests that auditory perception and awareness is actually a better model for understanding the instinctive, pre-critical awareness we have of reality. This is so, Torrance believes, because the image of auditory apprehension both avoids somewhat the more subjective character of visual perception (i.e., relative to the question of meaning, wherein auditory apprehension is understood to be necessarily oriented toward the other) and also evokes more than does visual apprehension the notion of a response.[13]

Torrance also helps elucidate the specific nature of certain elements of Polanyi's thought that might otherwise be open to misinterpretation. For example, he acknowledges, as does Polanyi, that human knowledge manifests a somewhat circular rationality, that is, it unfolds through a process of

mutually reinforcing illuminations rather than through induction from indu-
bitable foundational truths. This is especially true in situations in which "we
are concerned with a conceptual system or a framework of thought which
includes among its constitutive axioms one or more *ultimates*, for which, in
the nature of the case, there is no higher and wider system with reference to
which they can be proved." In light of this inescapable reality, Torrance
advocates a kind of coherence theory of knowledge: "the system stands or
falls with respect to its power as a whole to command our acceptance ...
[and] function as a heuristic instrument in opening up new avenues of
knowledge."[14] This in turn helps clarify Polanyi's understanding of the relationship between knowledge and reality (and thus between epistemology and
ontology): following Polanyi, Torrance asserts that our apprehension of some
entity or event puts us under the "compulsion of its meaning and, as Polanyi
says, we have to affirm it with universal intent."[15] What is important to note
here is that it is not the entity or event *per se* to which we find ourselves
obligated, but the *rationality* manifest in that entity or event.[16] This rationality signifies the participation of the entity in question within a wider horizon
of meaning, and it is in part our subsidiary awareness of this horizon that
enables us to perceive the entity itself. Thus, while we can affirm that there is
a correspondence between our knowledge and reality, it is not a correspondence between a mental "object" present in our mind and a physical "object"
manifest in the world; rather, the correspondence should be understood in
terms of the isomorphic similarity that exists between the structure of our
experience of awareness and the structure of that of which we are aware.

Within the realm of theology, what this means for Torrance is that our
knowledge corresponds to the Word that transcends us and signifies a "Truth
to be acknowledged."[17] The *logos* of the Word, which is itself the *Logos*,
provides the structure according to which we find ourselves obligated to
submit all other claims to knowledge: "It is under the address and claims of
the Word that we have to mint an apposite vocabulary and through thinking
out what the Word communicates to us that we have to reform our conceptual instruments and reconstruct the framework of our knowledge."[18]

By affirming a correspondence between our knowledge and reality,
Torrance evokes Polanyi's idea of a stratified epistemology. This is a theme
Torrance brings to the fore at other points of his exploration of the nature of
Christian truth. He affirms Polanyi's development of the idea of a hierarchy
of knowledge, with its ascending levels of meaningfulness, as well as the
corresponding image of reality that emerges, that is, a hierarchy of being in

which are manifest ascending levels of "intrinsic intelligibility" and "transcendent reality."[19] Torrance sees a fundamental agreement regarding this point between Polanyi's insights and the emergence of postmodern cosmology as pioneered by Albert Einstein.[20] Again, Torrance provides critical insight into the heart of Polanyi's idea: whatever relative objectivity we might claim for our knowledge cannot come from "behind" or "beneath" our knowledge (that is, as "from prescriptions or axioms"), but must be seen as coming from "in front of" or "above" it (that is, from the transcendent forms intended by knowledge as well as from the effectiveness with which our knowledge continues to reveal these forms).[21] In other words, knowledge "gets" its objectivity precisely from its heuristic value, from its ability to carry us from awareness of the entity or event at hand to a horizon of meaning that is at once both wider and deeper than the "level" at which the entity or event is manifest. That there is in this understanding of knowledge a close correlation between the structure of our awareness and that of which we are aware follows for Torrance just as it does for Polanyi.[22]

There is theological merit in this idea when it is correlated with the principle of correspondence between knowledge and reality, for the image that emerges is one that intrinsically describes the theological enterprise. Torrance suggests that the practice of theology requires that a person "make himself dwell in the semantic focus of the many-layered memory or tradition embodied in the New Testament." This results in the apprehension of the unity, the "*integration* of the different strata" of the scriptures "in their bearing upon the objective events and realities they intend," fostering a "structural kinship" between the subject and the object. The events and realities signified by the scriptures are nothing less than the "self-revelation and self-communication of God through Jesus Christ and in the Holy Spirit."[23] It is the integrative character of this stance that impresses Torrance in particular, as contrasted to the disintegrative stance enjoined by exclusively critical inquiry; Torrance recognizes critical inquiry as necessary and helpful, but believes it is completely unable to provide a perspective that enables human beings to see things as wholes and thereby perceive their meaning.[24]

Thus, Torrance's recovery of faith and his affirmation of the necessary function of belief in the practice of theology owes much to Polanyi's understanding of the dynamics of discovery and the structure of objective knowledge. This enables Torrance to characterize the theological task as preeminently "scientific," and makes faith out to be an integral element in the pursuit and exercise of knowledge, rather than a subjective, acritical state. Theological commitment thus goes far beyond assent to propositional statements, and enjoins the search for greater degrees of (inter)personal awareness and intimacy within horizons of increasingly expansive meaning. Furthermore, the fact that we can never exhaust the meaning of reality or attain comprehensive knowledge thereof is grounded theologically in the ineffable mystery of the divine Being.[25]

It is worth briefly noting at this point that Torrance, taking his cue from Polanyi, connects the exercise of faith in the theological enterprise to a distinctly personal understanding of knowledge and being in general. The apprehension of meaningful wholes, the recognition of a transcendent order of meaning, the refinement of subjective awareness into more objective modes of thought and discourse, the exercise of commitment in the direction of a half-glimpsed truth: all are possible only within the context of the experience of the person or, more accurately, of persons.[26] Our awareness of reality and the means whereby we clarify and extend that awareness presuppose "the structure of our active personal inter-relations and takes place within them."[27] Thus, although it may well be that, taken as individuals, persons might best described as "active rational agent[s] in all acts of understanding and knowing" (that is, capable of self-determination), they also necessarily remain all the while "controlled from beyond ... by objective reality and transcendent standards" that helps moderate the subjectivity to which they as individuals are naturally prone.[28] Communion between persons is seen as the inescapable context within which the exercise of faith is manifest.

As noted earlier, Torrance has not been the only one to appropriate Polanyi's thought relative to the question of faith. Martin Moleski, Jerry Gill, Avery Dulles, Lesslie Newbigin, and a number of others have all sought to demonstrate the extent to which Polanyi's elaboration of the fiduciary character of knowledge invests the theological enterprise with renewed vigor.[29] A consistent theme in these studies is the extent to which Polanyi's recovery of faith also entails a recovery of the notion of knowledge as action or performance. It is to a more focused study of this theme that we now turn.

The Recovery of Action

In keeping with the idea that discovery is the highest form of knowing to which human beings can aspire, Barbara Dee Bennett Baumgarten's *Visual Art as Theology* attempts to delineate two related themes.[30] First, Baumgarten critically appropriates Polanyi's observations on the nature of art and artistic production so as to demonstrate the place and function of art relative to other forms of intellective endeavor. Second, Baumgarten intends to demonstrate the similiarities between art and aesthetic appreciation on the one hand and theology and religious awareness on the other; she intends thereby to suggest that artistic creation can and should play an essential role in the formation of spiritual awareness.[31] Throughout her study, she repeatedly affirms the necessarily active character of artistic creation and aesthetic appreciation; furthermore, she also affirms (albeit often only implicitly) that artistic creation and aesthetic appreciation both represent decisively personal actions. Thus, her work stands as a good representative example of someone dedicated to exploring the theological implications of Polanyi's thought within a personalistic horizon.[32]

The thesis and structure of Baumgarten's larger argument is relatively easy to summarize, and it is through the exploration of the implications of her main idea that the body of Baumgarten's work unfolds. Her primary thesis revolves around her appreciation for Polanyi's insights into the heuristic nature of knowledge and the importance of discovery as an epistemological category of the highest order. The triadic structure of knowledge as outlined by Polanyi becomes a pattern according to which aesthetic action (understood primarily in terms of creation, but also including perception) can be understood.[33] Under the general rubric of "discovery," Baumgarten delineates her task by distinguishing between "formalization" and "creation." Both are realized through the process of indwelling, whereby persons, through meaningful actions, pour themselves into a framework of understanding (itself representative of a tradition)[34] that enables them to glimpse hitherto unforeseen aspects of reality.[35] She sees formalization to be representative more of science and creation more of the arts, and thus directs considerably more attention to explicating the creative act.

Both formal (scientific) and creative (artistic) discovery involve the recognition of a problem followed by a more or less successful attempt at imaginatively resolving the problem. Baumgarten sees in the performance of the intuition, by which a problem is recognized and a way forward glimpsed, and the imagination, by which the way forward is clarified and the problem overcome, an example of Polanyi's notion of dual control. "Intuition determines the direction the imagination is to follow, but the imagination is not limited by the integrative workings of the intuition. An area is left open which the imagination summons to achieve an aim that could not be achieved otherwise."[36] Thus the intuition establishes the boundary conditions of the problem, while the imagination exercises marginal control over the possibilities left open in the space delimited by the intuition.

That some problems can be recognized and solved only through creative or artistic means suggests a distinction between the standards of authority that justify discovery. Whereas formal, scientific work seeks "verification," creative or artistic work can only aspire to "validation." The fact that artistic works cannot be verified but only validated in no way minimizes their claims to speak the truth; rather, their truthfulness is understood as existing on a different level or in a different horizon than that of formal, scientific discoveries. "Aesthetic forms must be true in order to be meaningful, and when validated it can be said to be a 'fact' because it is an observable event that bears on reality and its deeper meaning."[37]

Taking her cue from Drusilla Scott, Baumgarten suggests that art is capable of revealing, not supernatural, but "supra-natural" meaning. Whereas the term "supernatural" suggests "a dualistic world in which the world as we know it is broken into by another world that does not obey the laws of nature" and is thus seen as "arbitrary," the term "supra-natural" suggests "a more profound understanding of our world" by not separating itself from the world but maintaining continuity "with nature and its laws." "The supranatural does not render the natural meaningless, but it is a more comprehensive meaningful integration than natural meaning."[38] The artistic task is seen to be the imaginative correlation of elements of the natural order such that a wider, more integral "supra-natural" order may be perceived.[39]

However, there is a significant alteration in Baumgarten's work of the notion of the "supra-natural" relative to the way in which it is understood by Scott, who employs the word in a manner very much in keeping with the distinctions Polanyi made between the levels of meaning manifest in his development of a stratified epistemology. Baumgarten suggests rather that the notion of a "supra-natural" order of meaning should not be taken to imply that this order of meaning is superior or even more meaningful than the less discursive work manifest in formalization (i.e., scientific discovery). "The term 'supra-natural' is not intended to be hierarchical. It signals apprehensions of reality which exist through and beyond normal understandings."[40] By leveling "supra-natural" and natural awareness, Baumgarten intends to demonstrate the complementarity of artistic and scientific awareness; one is not necessarily "better" than the other, they are merely "different." The purpose of artistic creation, while not itself "logical," is to bridge the "logical gaps" evident in formalized knowledge.[41]

This adjustment of understanding relative to the meaning of the term "supra-natural," however, seems to betray latent epistemological prejudices the likes of which Baumgarten would probably argue against were they manifest explicitly. The effect of such leveling is to leave to the creative enterprise only that to which more formal analysis has yet to attend; it creates an "aesthetic of the gaps," and thereby limits what art *can* say only to that which other disciplines *cannot* say. Thus, art risks losing its voice as other disciplines find new ways of talking about aspects of reality previously thought to be the subject of aesthetics.

Baumgarten seems incipiently aware of this problem, as evidenced by her distinction between awareness of the "supra-natural" order of meaning manifest in artistic creation and the "Supra-natural" order of meaning manifest in cosmic or religious awareness. The latter is seen to be more comprehensive (and thus, presumably, more meaningful) than the former.[42] This positing of a "Supra-natural" realm of meaning seems to represent a fall back into the kind of dualistic thinking Baumgarten criticizes in her distinction between "supra-natural" and "supernatural" awareness and the realities to which they correspond. We are left with the vague notion that, although a dualistic perspective is illegitimate in the realm of aesthetics, it is in some way legitimate in the realm of religion.

It is perhaps because her description of aesthetic awareness is limited almost exclusively to visual categories that Baumgarten seems unable to recognize that the different levels of awareness invoked by the distinction between formal and creative discovery (and the different levels of meaning that correspond to such levels) necessitate a more nuanced understanding of knowledge than allowed for by her complementarianism.[43] Although it must be granted that hers is a work directed towards the explication of *visual* art, it must also be acknowledge that visual descriptors, tied as they are to the realm of sensate spatial (and often temporal) awareness, fail almost immediately as adequate descriptors of the more abstracted, conceptual play of the imagination. Baumgarten herself recognizes that visual apprehension alone cannot account for the workings of the intuition in the recognition of a problem nor the workings of the imagination in an effort to overcome that problem.[44] But her overdependence on visual expressions ultimately keeps her from delineating aesthetic comprehension in fully personalistic terms, despite her desire to affirm that the extension of our imagination involves "the act of extending our person into elements that are essential to the achievement of an aim and the appreciation of a comprehensive whole."[45]

Relative to the possibility that we might see creative discovery as a legitimate form of theological inquiry, Baumgarten equivocates a bit. On the one hand, she asserts that art is capable of presenting a more integral vision of religious experience than is theology due to its ability to "present" the elements of religious awareness that "elude verbalization." On the other hand, she recognizes that creative discovery cannot provide lasting structural or systematic integrity to religious experience. Creative discovery "is an unstable coherence that does not rely on observable fact or a factual basis of experience. Instead, it is an imaginative performance visible only to the imagination. Art speaks its own language."[46] In the end, Baumgarten favors theological reflection as a more expansive and integrative form of consciousness than artistic awareness; theology, however, is itself transcended by religious experience, and art is seen as an means of exploring those dynamics of religious experience that elude theological description.

Within the context of the current study, Baumgarten's work might best be described as implicitly personalistic, reaching towards but never quite attaining a view of personhood that is at once both fully embodied and cognizant of some of the more subtle dynamics of Polanyi's epistemology. In other words, her personalism does not seem to extend as far as that of Bruno Manno and David Rutledge, whose work we examined in the previous chapter. Nor, it can be said, is Baumgarten as expansive in her theological vision as have been some others who have sought to employ Polanyian and personalistic categories in an elaboration of an integrative theology. Probably the most notable example to date of someone whose seeks to bring to bear both a fully personalistic as well as a fully Polanyian perspective to the task of theological inquiry has been Joan Crewdson, to whose work we now turn.

A Post-Critical Personalist Theology

Crewdson's *Christian Doctrine in Light of Michael Polanyi's Theory of Personal Knowledge* is the most ambitious theological treatment to date of Polanyi's philosophy from an explicitly personalistic perspective.[47] As such, it is markedly different from those theological appropriations of Polanyi's thought outlined above, and is in many ways closer to our own ambitions than is the work of Torrance, Baumgarten, Manno, Rutledge, or those others mentioned above who have sought to engage theologically Polanyi's work. Because her work is so much more continuous with that of the current project, greater attention will be devoted to the manner in which she theologically appropriates and deploys Polanyi's philosophy than was given to those whose work was outlined in the previous sections.

Crewdson's overarching purpose is to demonstrate that "Polanyi's theory of personal knowledge, which is also a theory of personal being, gives us the kind of personalist metaphysic we need to make a theistic view of reality credible."[48] Implied in this thesis is the notion that theism has, for all intents and purposes, lost its credibility within the Western world and thus needs to be retrieved in a language that will be more accessible to the contemporary mind. Crewdson believes the structure of Polanyi's epistemology provides a means whereby knowledge and reality may be understood without falling into either dualistic or monistic tendencies, both of which she finds problematic (in light of contemporary knowledge about the nature of the world) and which she sees as implied in the traditional Christian worldview.

The first section of Crewdson's work is dedicated to an explication of the details of Polanyi's fiduciary program and the implications of this program for her own constructive theological efforts. She pays particular attention to the referential character of tacit knowledge (that is, its "from-to" structure) and the extent to which such an understanding of knowledge carries with it intriguing suggestions for our understanding of ontology and metaphysics. While her examination of Polanyi's thought could not be described as either comprehensive or systematic, she does a good job of drawing out those elements of Polanyi's thought (tacit knowing, indwelling, a view of knowledge that is simultaneously stratified and unified, etc.) particularly suited to her theological proposals.[49]

Crewdson is particularly impressed with the manner in which Polanyi sought to correlate epistemology and ontology. Working from her reading of Polanyi, she outlines the implications the notion of personal knowledge engenders relative to the question of the mind. Like Polanyi, Crewdson insists on the real and independent existence of the mind, and sees in the existence of the mind and its dialogical relationship with reality the foundation for explicating the nature of reality writ large. She highlights (as we have been) Polanyi's abbreviated but suggestive idea of a stratified universe within which the presence and activity of mind is determinative relative to our understanding of the meaning of life and the world. She insists on the ontological integrity of each level of reality, and begins to explore the implications of this view of the creation relative to our understanding of the possibility of an eternal, divine Creator. This also raises the question of how we should understand the relative freedom of the creation (and that of the Creator, for that matter), and Crewdson affirms that freedom can only be understood relative to the teleological striving that is manifest in the universe and is demonstrated decisively in the intentional acts of personal agents.[50]

Having in this first section established the playing field and outlined the rules of her game, Crewdson then turns in the second section of her work to a consideration of the theological enterprise and the question of theological method. She provides a cursory review of the problem of God in modern thought and, based on her critique of the theological insights of Descartes, Kant, Hegel, Schleiermacher, Feuerbach, and Kierkegaard, finds modern theology incapable of seriously addressing the question of God due to its inability to avoid overemphasizing God's transcendence or immanence (that is, due to its inability to escape from dualistic thinking). She develops instead a dialectical model for theological inquiry, grounded in her understanding of Polanyi's hierarchical epistemology. This dialectical method enables her to explore the question of the existence and nature of God while acknowledging and affirming the reality of both God's transcendence and immanence.[51] She introduces the chief subject of the next section of her work, namely, the doctrine of creation, by providing some organizing theses regarding the nature of the relationship between God and the world.[52]

Crewdson's explication of the doctrine of the creation in the third section of her work represents her first substantive attempt to move beyond methodological issues and demonstrate that Polanyi's philosophy can serve as a template for the development of a constructive theological program. Her intent in this section is to illustrate how Polanyi's epistemology, with its triadic understanding of the subject-object relationship (that is, subject and object bound together by the heuristic passion of the subject, itself evoked by the meaningfulness of the object), can facilitate a view of the God-world relationship in which both the transcendence and the immanence of a personal God are preserved. Crewdson suggests that a fully personalistic view of the Christian worldview is made possible by viewing the creation or the world as the mediating horizon within which the personal being of God meets the personal being of humans existing in the creation. This view not only affirms the simultaneity of God's transcendence and immanence, but also recognizes the reality of personal freedom in the creation even (or, perhaps more accurately, especially) when seen from an evolutionary perspective.[53] This leads to an extended consideration of the nature of God's creative activity as seen from a modern evolutionary perspective. Within this context, the question of the nature of freedom becomes the means by which

Crewdson seeks to resolve the apparent paradox of both human and divine action. The "paradox" of human freedom is manifest most fully in the tension between, on the one hand, the evolutionary history of the species and, on the other, the reality of moral accountability and responsibility. The "paradox" of divine freedom is manifest most fully in the tension between viewing God's creative act as, on the one hand, a (necessary) outpouring of divine generativity and, on the other, as an act of arbitrary will. Crewdson maintains that the paradoxical nature of these tensions for the most part dissipates when seen within a personalistic horizon that characterizes an act, not in terms of the exercise of the will or the manifestation of primordial urges, but as the correlation of two necessary poles in the drive towards personal being actualized in interpersonal relationship.[54]

The doctrine of creation provides the setting for Crewdson's analysis of other fundamental theological themes. The fourth section of her work takes up the problem of the incarnation and christology. Rather than attempt to engage the question of the meaning of the classic "two natures, one person" formula within a personalistic outlook, however, Crewdson opts to put this formula for the most part to one side. Instead, she describes christology as the means whereby the Christian faith sees in the person of Jesus the actualization of the mutual indwelling of God and human nature. Jesus, she suggests, can be seen as the primary locus of interaction between God and humanity, the point of total mutual identification, but should not be thought of as having borne a divine nature or as having "been God." However, the "Christ of faith" and the "Jesus of history" should not be, and cannot be, separated: because in Jesus we see the fullest possible manifestation of mutual indwelling between God and humanity, we can affirm that "Jesus *articulated* the very being of God in finite, historical terms,"[55] and thus affirm (even though we can do this only in "mythic" terms) that the relationship between Jesus and God was unlike any other possible relationship God might share with a specific individual.[56]

Her reflection on the person of Christ takes Crewdson, quite naturally, to a consideration of the nature of redemption. Herein she deploys her understanding of christology as the means whereby she articulates the parameters of the question of atonement, and given her understanding of christology, it is not surprising that the net she casts in this section is rather wide. As in her consideration of christology, Crewdson rejects many traditional notions of atonement as being outdated and "morally unacceptable," opting instead for an understanding of atonement that seeks to express redemption as the means whereby the entire creation will eventually be brought into fulfillment through the cooperation of God and humanity. The perichoretic unity manifest in the life of God is now seen to be the goal towards which the creation is moving. This vision opens up a perspective in which contradiction or paradox is seen as the primary mode in which the Christian experience is lived: particularity and universality, historicity and eternity, individuality and community, life and death, all are affirmed as having a necessary and complementary function in the exercise of faith.[57]

Finally, Crewdson concludes her study with an analysis of what it might mean to pursue the consummation of the "kingdom of God."[58] Many of the ideas Crewdson explores in this section are introduced (or even explored at length) in previous sections, so there is a sense that Crewdson is here attempting to gather together the disparate strands of her observations and demonstrate their mutual coherence. Building on her understanding of the interpersonal mutuality manifest in the relationship between God and the creation, Crewdson emphasizes the importance of human responsibility and stewardship within the created order as a means to fulfilling God's will for the creation. Predictably, she eschews any understanding of the "kingdom of God" that relies extensively on apocalyptic interpretations of the consummation of creation, and favors instead a view that affirms both the transcendence as well as the potential immanence of divine sovereignty.

Despite its scope and the rough correspondence between the philosophical commitments supporting our own efforts and those that undergird Crewdson's, it must be acknowledged at this point that her proposals largely fall short of their ambitions and thus cannot serve as useful examples for our own work. There are two basic reasons at the heart of the shortcomings of Crewdson's study. First, she does not acknowledge some of the more difficult consequences of her line of thinking, and thus her program exhibits rather large logical gaps. Second, she does not sufficiently engage the scriptural or theological heritage of the Christian tradition, and thus misses important alternatives to some of the ideas she introduces.

One of the more noticeable logical gaps in Crewdson's work has to do with her explication of the relationship between God, the world, and humanity. In her consideration of the doctrine of creation, Crewdson suggests that it is necessary to postulate the relationship between God and the creation in much the same way Polanyi conceived of the subject-object relationship. This means that the doctrine of creation ends up affirming a "triadic relation" between "God, the world and emerging centres of personhood" within the world. "Each member of the triad is immanent in, and transcendent of, the other two. Each has a double relationship to each."[59] This represents Crewdson's attempt to follow the logic of Polanyi's notion of dual control to a (theo)logical conclusion.

But there are problems evident in this position, at least from the perspective of traditional affirmations regarding the relationship between God and the world. It is possible to say that God is both immanent in and yet transcends the world; Crewdson affirms this possibility. Likewise, it is possible to affirm that human persons are both immanent in and yet transcend the world; Crewdson also affirms this possibility. Similarly, it is possible to say that the world is immanent within and yet transcends human persons; again, Crewdson acknowledges and affirms this possibility.

However, it is another thing entirely to suggest that the world is both immanent in and yet transcends God, and here Crewdson overlooks some potential problems. She does not seem to recognize that the logic of dual control, applied indiscriminately, results in a finite God, a God subject in some sense to the contingence of the creation.[60] It is particularly surprising that Crewdson fails to recognize this problem in her understanding of the doctrine of creation, given that she earlier characterizes as a categorical error the affirmation of God as "*a* Being with special properties," that is, as one being among other comparable beings all sharing in some common form of being.[61] But because of this limitation, her understanding of the doctrine of creation is ultimately incapable of affirming all that needs to be said about both God and the world.[62] In a similar vein, Crewdson fails to deal with the problems that would result from a view of human nature that is simultaneously immanent within God and also transcends God.[63]

The difficulties evident in Crewdson's understanding of the relationship between God and the creation also serve as an example of her relative lack of engagement with the theological heritage of the church. This is manifest in a number of ways. For example, her perfunctory treatment of the scriptural and the dogmatic heritage of the faith suggests that she approaches the tradition with a hermeneutic of suspicion, one that is not identified or justified throughout her program.[64] Further, she speaks of established formulations of core doctrines with a somewhat dismissive tone, preferring the new wine of theological innovation to the more nuanced palate of traditional doctrines; implied here is an assumption that the exchange between Christian theology and culture is a one-way street (that is, from culture to Christianity and not vice versa).[65] Similarly, she appears somewhat condescending in her attitude towards the historical heritage of philosophical and theological thought.[66] Finally, she affirms a kind of religious relativism that does not seriously address the differences between Christianity and other religious traditions.[67]

All of this raises the question of whether or not Crewdson is being truly faithful to the warp and woof of Polanyi's thought: given Polanyi's insistence on the importance of tradition and the necessary role faithfulness to tradition plays in the renewal of any given community, it would seem that Crewdson would have been better served by being both a bit more thorough and a bit more charitable relative to the dogmatic traditions of the church. Finally, it must be acknowledged that Crewdson is not systematic, and that what it seems we have in her work is a collection of insights that were never explored relative to their relationship to one another, and thus leave large questions unaddressed.[68] In spite of its shortcomings, however, Crewdson's work remains closer in many ways to our own ambitions than are the efforts of many others who have sought to employ Polanyi's philosophy within a theological context.[69]

Summary

Clearly, Polanyi has had a significant influence on some recent theological studies, at least among those with more than a passing familiarity with his work. Given the number of ways in which the notion of personal knowledge and all it entails has been theologically appropriated to date, one might well ask as to the need for yet another attempt in this direction. It is also evident, based on our review of the work of Torrance, Baumgarten, and Crewdson (as well as that of Manno and Rutledge), that there have been relatively few efforts dedicated to the possibility of elaborating Polanyi's thought in a manner that is compatible with the ambitions of the personalistic outlook described in the introduction, while at the same time more responsive to the content of the Christian theological heritage. Each of the scholars whose work is outlined above moves in this direction in their respective ways, but none of them successfully brings Polanyi's philosophical program to completion by elaborating its personalistic tenor while also pursuing its theological fulfillment along lines consistent with traditional Christian doctrine.

Having surveyed these representative examples of those whose efforts to bring Polanyi's thought to bear within the theological enterprise, we can now begin exploring how the parameters of the current project encourage engagement with Polanyi's thought along slightly different lines than those outlined above.

The Possibility of a Scientific Theology

In light of our (admittedly incomplete) review above of the variety of ways Polanyi's thought has been received within the context of contemporary theological studies, it is self-evident to say that there is much to be learned from exploring the potential consilience of these two fields. The question with which we are now faced has less to do with establishing whether or not there is value in bringing Polanyi's philosophy into dialogue with theological studies; that question has already been answered decisively in the affirmative. Rather, the question with which we are now faced has to do with identifying the particular approach to the dialogue between Polanyi studies and theological reflection that best suites our own ambitions.

The possibility of consilience between any two fields of study requires careful attention to the details of their engagement. On the one hand, there is the danger that one field will be swallowed up by the other; in our case, this could involve either trying to "baptize" Polanyi by suggesting that the shape and direction of his thought fully intends a particular theological perspective or (conversely) that the task of theology can be articulated in entirely Polanyian terms. On the other hand, there is the risk that the dialogue between these fields of study will never move beyond superficial exchange; in our case, this could involve noting certain apparent conceptual or methodological elements common to both Polanyi and theological studies and then contenting ourselves that, having identified such "least common denominators," we had done the work of exploring a deeper and more fundamental potential correspondence. None of these options, for a variety of reasons, would be justifiable or ultimately satisfying.

We are thus confronted at this point with a question that takes us beyond the immediate scope of the present study, namely, what we might call the question of truth. The reason this is so follows from the fact that exploring the consilience of multiple fields of study involves (among other things) the tacit deployment of a particular understanding of the nature of knowledge and the relative unity of knowledge. We cannot, of course, give over our attention to a comprehensive consideration of this issue.[70] However, we can find some traction for dealing with this challenge by summarizing the way this problem has been addressed by others invested in the study of the relationship between Polanyi's thought and theological studies.

In his intellectual biography of Thomas Torrance, Alister McGrath examines Torrance's appropriation of various elements of Polanyi's philosophy in support of Torrance's own theological work. McGrath offers a methodological distinction between what he calls the "foundational" use of Polanyi's philosophy as opposed to its "illuminative" use. The former involves a more or less "total commitment to Polanyi's general methods or assumptions," while the latter, being much more circumspect, involves only the exploration of "convergence at points of significance" between Polanyi's work and the theological enterprise. McGrath contends (rightly) that Torrance's appropriation of Polanyi's thought never extended beyond making "illuminative" observations between Polanyi's work and his own.[71]

Our survey earlier in this chapter included examples of efforts that have made (to borrow McGrath's terminology) both "illustrative" and "foundational" use of Polanyi's work; Torrance and Baumgarten clearly lean towards the former, while Crewdson leans toward the latter (Manno and Rutledge, whose work we examined in the previous chapter, are less immediately concerned with the practice of theology *qua* theology than are Torrance, Baumgarten, and Crewdson). However, neither approach has managed to represent the theological potential of Polanyi's work with complete success. Efforts that have relied on a more selective, "illuminative" use of Polanyi have often failed to represent the full scope of his thought, and have often been rather narrow in their application of his thought to the task of theology. Conversely, efforts that have relied on a more ambitious, "foundational" use of Polanyi have often failed to account adequately for the dogmatic content of the theological tradition and the responsibilities that inhere with its reception and perpetuation.

In order to avoid both of these pitfalls, we will pursue neither a strictly "illuminative" nor an entirely "foundational" engagement with Polanyi. Rather, our intent is to initiate a conversation between Polanyi and the theological tradition with the expectation that there is much to be gained on both sides from sustained, meaningful interaction. We anticipate that, as we examine the correspondence between the theological tradition and Polanyi's thought, we will recognize new ways of approaching familiar theological questions while also seeing the extent to which it is only a theological mode of inquiry that can bring to fruition the ambitions of Polanyi's philosophy. At the same time, we must recognize that the parameters of the current project will not allow us to explore in much more than a perfunctory manner many of the specific points of inquiry and controversy within the theological tradition; at best, we can hope only to take some initial tentative steps in the direction of a larger research program.

We can further elucidate our intentions by comparing the two-fold description for interdisciplinary dialogue offered by McGrath with the taxonomy proffered by Richard Allen, who has suggested no fewer than four distinct ways that Polanyi's thought might be brought to bear on theological questions.[72] The first of these involves cultivating what Polanyi believed was an innate but unformed religious sense common to all people, a sense that needs to be exercised in order to come to fruition.[73] The second of these entails applying a spiritual or religious hermeneutic to one's experience, thereby opening up within the mundane context of the world the opportunity for self-transcendence.[74] The third of these involves deploying Polanyi's understanding of commitment in an effort to excavate the character and function of the kinds of foundational beliefs necessary for all knowing and action, including religious faith and practice.[75] The fourth of these involves exploring the consequences of Polanyi's "ontology of comprehensive entities, his cosmology of a stratified universe, and his doctrine of degrees of being" relative to the Christian understanding of God, the world, and the relationship between them.[76] Within the more immediate context of our own efforts, we can see how the first three of these lean more so in the direction of what we have termed an "existential" approach, while the fourth leans more so in the direction of an "emergent" approach. This last way in particular has much to recommend it, and will help organize the direction our efforts will take henceforth.

In many respects, the current study thus serve as a first step in the development of what McGrath has more recently termed a "scientific theology."[77] McGrath suggests that such a theology will strive to offer "a view of the world, including God, which is both internally consistent and which is grounded in the structures of the real world. It aims to achieve extra-systemic correspondence with intra-systemic coherence, regarding both of these criteria as of fundamental importance."[78] There is thus not only a characteristic methodological or, more broadly, epistemological dimension to theology so conceived, but also a particular ontological and a semantic dimension, all of which combine to proffer a critically realist view of reality.[79] By advancing a perspective that is both critical and realist, McGrath intends to move beyond a strictly constructivist or coherentist account of knowledge while also acknowledging the necessarily embedded character of human knowing (i.e., its historical and cultural dimensions).[80] This approach engenders a number of related procedural commitments, including an "a posteriori" approach to the datum at hand, the attempt to elaborate a method of critical inquiry appropriate to the objects under consideration, and a determination to situate one's understanding of particular questions within a more expansive and integrative understanding of reality as a whole.[81] That which distinguishes a scientific theology as *theological* in nature is what may be called its christocentrism: it is precisely in the person and work of Jesus Christ that scientific theological inquiry finds both its proper starting point as well as its proper terminus.[82] Not only is the person of Christ the "historical point of departure for Christianity," it is Christ who is said to be the decisive revelation of God, who brings (indeed, who *is*) the gift of salvation to the world, and who "defines the shape of the redeemed life."[83] This approach, as will be seen in the following section and in the next chapter, offers (perhaps surprisingly) a helpful point of contact between McGrath's description of scientific theology and Polanyi's philosophy.[84]

Truth and Personhood

For Polanyi, it will be recalled, the starting point for all knowing is discovery. The recognition of a hitherto unknown reality signals the beginning of a process that can bring about a complete transformation in one's understanding of the world and oneself. This process can rightly be called one of conversion, a circumstance through which one comes not only to understand better a particular aspect of one's experience but to apprehend a more expansive and meaningful vision of reality as a whole.[85] Any given experience of conversion will generate a heuristic impulse, that is, a dynamic striving aimed at better understanding the event or reality that prompted the conversion in the first place. This impulse unfolds as a search for ever-more meaningful and expansive integrations of the disparate aspects of one's experience. The satisfaction of this impulse (and thus the reality and meaning of the object of the impulse) can be measured in terms of the relative accomplishment or achievement with which one meets by dwelling in the horizon tacitly signified by the discovery.

This generalized, phenomenological account of discovery can be focused in a variety of ways, depending on the specific object(s) of a given heuristic vision. A particular heuristic vision "can live only in the pursuit of its proper enquiry." Within the context of theological studies, this is of course God. This suggests that the especial mode of theological inquiry ultimately involves nothing short of "worship."[86] Polanyi regarded the "Pauline scheme" of "faith, works, and grace" as the "only adequate conception of ... discovery," scientific and otherwise.[87] Indeed, it is perhaps not too much even to say that Polanyi found in the position of one bowed in worship before God the definitive example of the responsible knower seeking elucidation of their knowledge.[88] He even held out the hope that the "progressive enterprise" of the Christian faith, when joined to the "greater precision and more conscious flexibility of modern thought," might yet "engender conceptual reforms which will renew and clarify" humanity's relationship to the divine.[89]

Despite this hope in the constructive capacity of Christian faith, Polanyi ended up with a somewhat truncated view of faith and thus of the theological enterprise. The indwelling of the Christian "within the ritual of divine service differs from any other dwelling within a framework of inherent excellence, by the fact that this indwelling is not enjoyed."[90] The worship of God carries with it obligations that the worshipper knows can never be fulfilled, resulting in a sense of existential tension or "inherent dubiety" that cannot be resolved: the heuristic vision of religious faith can thus never be fulfilled.[91] "Christianity," Polanyi suggested, "sedulously fosters, and in a sense permanently satisfies, man's craving for mental dissatisfaction by offering him the comfort of a crucified God."[92]

Richard Allen has suggested that, by overlooking the Christian hope of eternal life, Polanyi failed to recognize that Christian hope is fulfilled, not in this life, but in the life to come. Drawing on the distinction between "progress *to*" and "progress *in*" the vision of God, Allen suggests that Polanyi's characterization of the life of faith ultimately founders on its conflation of human finitude with "our present existence." By neglecting this distinction, Polanyi ended up with a version of Christianity that was ultimately unachievable, for his measure of the success of the Christian vision did not reach beyond the earthly existence of human beings.[93]

Another way of saying this, and in terms more immediately germane to our own efforts, is to suggest that what Polanyi overlooked is the Christian hope of resurrection. This "hope" need not (indeed, should not) be understood as a non-specific desire for the continuance of individual life after physical death. Rather, the Christian hope of the resurrection is grounded in the reality of the resurrection of Jesus Christ, which signifies the righteousness and the love of God. Following Thomas Torrance, we can say further that the resurrection of Christ signifies a meaningful *gestalt*, a "constitutive axiom" that compels immediate consideration of its truthfulness and reality in terms that admit less to strict logical argumentation and more to wider and more meaningful axiological sensibilities; this need not rule out, however, the possibility of critically analyzing this axiom and its meaningfulness.[94]

Torrance's exposition of the resurrection and its place in the theological enterprise is particularly useful for our purposes owing to his acknowledged indebtedness to Polanyi. Specifically, Torrance posits the early church's witness to the resurrection in its scriptures, in its worship, and in the theological tradition as the subsidiary elements of a unified testimony to the reality of the new life of Christ. By dwelling in the particulars of the apostolic witness, Christians allow their habits of apprehension and reflection to be shaped by the reality to which the whole of the apostolic witness points, namely, the "self-communication of God in Jesus Christ and the Holy Spirit."[95] The experience of the resurrection, as the defining motif of the whole life and ministry of Jesus, can thus be thought of very much as a discovery of a new and hitherto unanticipated reality, one that invites a wholesale reconsideration of not only the person of Jesus himself, but also God, the world, and humanity.[96] The apostolic witness will indeed evince a certain circularity in its rationality, but it is, suggests Torrance, the "proper circularity inherent in any coherent system operating with ultimate axioms or beliefs which cannot be derived or justified from any other ground than that which they themselves constitute."[97] In other words, Torrance describes the testimony to the resurrection of Christ in terms that are (self-consciously) consistent with Polanyi's exposition of the nature and function of any constructive heuristic vision, scientific, theological, or otherwise.

By combining these insights from Allen and Torrance, we can reconsider whether or not Polanyi's suggestion that the "Pauline scheme" of faith, works, and grace might have more to offer than Polanyi himself anticipated. What these insights suggest is that it may be possible to articulate an understanding of truth itself in a way that follows immediately from the church's witness to the person of Jesus Christ. In *Trinity and Truth*, Bruce Marshall has made just such an attempt, one that (as we shall see) is consistent in many ways with the Polanyian tenor of our efforts herein.[98] Marshall's project includes both a negative and a positive component: negatively, he destabilizes both strictly realist and strictly anti-realist characterizations of truth even as, positively, he offers a viable alternative to both that accommodates the best insights of each while avoiding their potential weaknesses.[99] Attending to some of the more salient details of Marshall's study will both help clarify the methodological posture we are pursuing as well as prepare us for the more substantive doctrinal efforts of the following chapter.

The first plank in Marshall's arguments follows from his insistence that, from a theological perspective, "truth is borne, not only or chiefly by sentences and beliefs, but by a person."[100] In particular, truth is born by the person of Jesus Christ, for it is in Christ that the full intention of God for the world has been, is being, and will be realized.[101] This notion follows *a fortiori* from several more fundamental precepts, including traditional Chalcedonian characterizations of Christ's two natures and the participation of all three persons of the trinity in the incarnation (and in the creative, redemptive, and consummative work of God). Marshall suggests that Christians are justified in holding to the "epistemic primacy" of christology (and to the trinitarian ramifications that follow therefrom) because, first, the confession of Jesus as the Christ (and of God as Father, Son, and Holy Spirit) constitutes the *sine qua non* of Christian identity and, second (and more fundamentally), christology (and trinitarian theology) accurately reflects reality.[102]

Our concern at this point has less to do with the means whereby Marshall demonstrates the viability of both of these principles and more to do with the particular epistemological ramifications that follow from them. Marshall does not so much argue for an evidentialist reading of the Christian scriptures and traditions with the intent of irrefutably "proving" the truthfulness of the gospel, but rather seeks to provide a theological account of truth that is consistent with the core confession of the church. In light of the fact that the confession of Jesus as the Christ both includes some understanding of Jesus as *the* truth (cf. Jn 14.6) and also leads more or less directly to the confession of God as Father, Son, and Holy Spirit, Marshall suggests that our understanding of *all* truth (not only theological truth) should at least potentially (and not infrequently directly) be conditioned by these beliefs. Marshall outlines a trinitarian understanding of truth within several distinct but related horizons, namely, relative to the redemptive self-revelation of God in history, relative to the experience of the church, relative to our knowledge of the world, and relative to our understanding of God.

The foundation of our understanding of the trinitarian shape of truth is God's presence and activity in the resurrection of Jesus from the dead. The resurrection of Christ is not strictly the work of any one of the three divine persons, but rather "takes place in the full spontaneity of the being and all the acts of the triune God."[103] It is the Father who guarantees the resurrection of

Christ, who wills it and thereby provides the context within which the work
of the other two persons can be realized. The Son, while he receives the
Spirit of new life from the Father as a gift, is not merely a passive participant
in the resurrection, but actively disposes himself to the fulfillment of the
Father's will; further, the Son takes an active role in making himself accessible to the world following his resurrection, in making it possible for his
disciples to apprehend the truth of his resurrection.[104] While it is the Father
who establishes the conditions for ensuring the reality (i.e., the truthfulness)
of Jesus' resurrection, it is the Son who establishes the conditions whereby
we are enabled to apprehend it truthfulness (i.e., its reality). Further, both the
work of the Father and that of the Son are accomplished in and by the Holy
Spirit. It is the Spirit as given to Jesus by the Father that raises Christ from
the dead.[105] Similarly, it is the Spirit as given to us by the Son that enlivens
our minds to recognize his truthfulness.[106] The coequal participation of the
three divine persons in the resurrection of Christ thus becomes the paradigm
whereby we are enabled to apprehend the truth of all things.

It is not surprising to find that Marshall describes the Christian experience of salvation in similarly trinitarian terms; each of the divine persons
effects a particular aspect of our apprehension of and participation in God's
redemptive action. As in the resurrection of the Son from the dead, the Father
effectively wills the salvation of the creation, having eternally predestined it
for conformity to the image of his Son, thereby establishing the context out
of which the other two divine persons act. The Son accepts his identity as the
image according to which all things are made and by which all things will be
remade, and also accepts his vocation as the one sent into the world to effect
the salvation of creation from within creation itself. The Spirit, "poured out
from the Father by the risen Son and dwelling in us," brings about in us that
process of sanctification whereby we and all the world will be perfected.[107]

The experience and self-understanding of the church as the body of
Christ evinces a trinitarian pattern as well.[108] The baptismal and eucharistic
narratives around which the church orders its life and its witness are given
their veracity (both epistemological and soteriological) in light of the Father's determination that the conditions guaranteeing their truthfulness be
fulfilled. The Son actualizes in himself the conditions whereby the Father's
will for his people and (through their testimony) for the world are realized,
and thereby institutes the actions that open the way for the participation of
the world in the will and life of God. The Spirit, as the gift of both the Father
and the Son to the world, "creates a community—the church—structured by

specific practices, and primarily these practices have to guide any effort to fix the meaning of this community's most central belief," namely, belief in Jesus as the Christ and in God as Father, Son, and Spirit. The work of the Spirit is thus manifest as he enables the church to apprehend "his total mastery of the practical situations in which the community and its members (and indeed all human beings) speak."[109]

Proposing that the epistemic priorities of the church are to be conceived and ordered in trinitarian terms will perhaps not seem radical to many; even those outside the church are likely to be sympathetic to the community's right to order its beliefs and practices in accordance with its core confession. However, Marshall wants more than this; the truth of christology and trinitarian theology should extend beyond the boundaries of the church to all areas of human experience. In order for his theological analysis of truth to itself be true, Marshall suggests, the truth of the gospel must be able in some way to account for all truth, and to do so in trinitarian terms.[110] This is made possible by way of a theological account of God's creative action, including both the creative act whereby God brings the cosmos into existence and the act whereby God sustains its continued existence.[111] Within this context, the Father is seen as the one whose will orders the creation, and especially orders the entities and relations therein to find their ultimate coherence in the Son. The Son brings glory to Father, both by presenting himself to the world as the image of the Father (i.e., as the image of the truth whereby all things are ordered and have their being) and by presenting the redeemed world back to the Father with everything therein conformed to his own image (and thus to the image of the Father).[112] The Spirit likewise brings glory to both the Father and the Son, testifying on the one hand to the truthfulness of both God's creative and redemptive actions and effecting on the other the sanctification of all things and their (re)ordering after the image of the Son according to the will of the Father.[113] His analysis of all truth in terms of conformity to the image of the relations that exist between the three divine persons even allows Marshall to talk about the reality of sin and evil in trinitarian terms, even if in largely negative ones.[114]

It is worth noting that Marshall insists that, while we can say that our knowledge of the divine persons arises out of our awareness of their actions on our behalf, we should not confuse our presumed knowledge of these actions with the comprehensive reality of the persons themselves.[115] In order for us to apprehend the full truth of God's presence and action in the world, it is necessary for us to recognize its gratuitous nature. This suggests that we cannot risk collapsing our understanding of the tripersonal being of God into God's economic activity; Marshall's project, in other words, intends a doctrine of the immanent trinity. There is further evidence of this in his descriptions of the respective roles played by the divine persons in the interpersonal life of the Godhead. The Father is here seen as the "ultimate source of all things in their entirety," the one from whom and by whom all things are ordered, including the trinitarian taxis itself. It is by virtue of his perfect and eternal existence as the icon of the Father that the epistemic (and soteriological) priority of the Son is established. The Son's eternal relation with the Father serves in turn as the ultimate ground for the truth of the faith and practice of the church.[116] At the same time, the action whereby the Holy Spirit draws us into the life of faith (granting us even the capacity to believe) likewise depends on the participation of the Spirit in the relation between the Father and the Son; the Spirit's ability to evoke in us the spirit of love and charity depends on the Spirit's eternal identity as love.[117] It is by virtue of the eternal and self-subsistent being, knowing, and acting of the triune Godhead that all other forms of being, knowing, and acting are made possible and in which they find their coherence.[118]

Having to this point devoted our explication of his study to its decisively theological tenor, it remains for us to examine the extent to which Marshall's proposals bear some resemblance to Polanyi's more philosophical endeavors. As we might expect, such comparative analysis will take us into areas of Marshall's thought not explicitly identified above; given the fact that Polanyi cannot be said to have himself attempted anything like the elaboration of a trinitarian account of truth, it comes as no surprise that we must look beyond the strictly theological aspects of Marshall's arguments in order to find points of contact. However, we can also expect that, once we have outlined the continuity between Polanyi's work and the more general philosophical dimensions of Marshall's efforts, the way will be further opened to realizing the theological direction of the thought of the former.

Both Marshall and Polanyi evince a certain antipathy for strictly foundationalist accounts of truth and knowledge; both are concerned to restore the rightful place of faith in the exercise of reason. At the same time, both are equally anxious to avoid the pitfalls of relativism, and are determined to affirm the congruence between our knowledge of reality and reality itself. Marshall expresses his tendencies in this direction when he identifies our current need to establish a "way of giving reasons for beliefs without creating epistemic subordination and dependence."[119] Similarly, Polanyi describes his own intellectual vocation as a matter of "bringing to light, and affirming as my own, the beliefs implied in such of my thoughts and practices as I believe to be valid."[120] This approach to the intellective enterprise conditions one to the attendant responsibilities of such reflection, and obligates one to discovering precisely what one believes, why one believes it, and how one is to sustain the constructive process of post-critical discovery and verification.

Further, Marshall acknowledges the function and importance of certain epistemic capacities that resemble Polanyi's identification of the tacit dimension. Marshall is not anywhere near as thorough as Polanyi in relation to the latter's analysis of the structure of tacit thought and its prevalence across all forms of human knowing; however, he recognizes that even within the "nexus of belief" that we hold and employ in a more or less self-conscious manner, it is always necessary for a certain range of those beliefs to operate in a more subsidiary manner.[121] More particularly, Marshall suggests that it is particular beliefs about the person of Jesus Christ (and, by implication, about the trinitarian understanding of God signified in and by the incarnation) that must be seen to operate in just such a tacit manner in order for the expansive range of Christian truth to be apprehended.[122] Other epistemic ramifications follow from the priority, tacit though it may be, of the truth of christology and trinitarian theology. Marshall's analysis of the role of attraction and desire in the development of belief resembles Polanyi's analysis of heuristic passion in the unfolding of knowledge. Similarly, both recognize the responsibilities that follow from commitment to belief.[123] In light of the epistemic priority Marshall suggests christology and trinitarian theology have for Christians, it is no surprise to hear him describing their influence in terms that echo Polanyi's description of universal intent.[124]

Marshall and Polanyi also share a number of convictions relative to the reception and creative renewal of tradition and the importance of tradition in all knowing and believing. Marshall suggests that the viability of any given tradition can be measured in terms of its relative powers of inclusion and assimilation.[125] Both of these dynamics have to do with a given tradition's capacity to accommodate "alien beliefs," where these are understood to include not only beliefs that fall entirely outside the epistemic structures of the tradition, but also those beliefs that may fall somewhere within the tradition itself without impinging directly on its core beliefs and practices. Inclusion, then, has to do with a tradition's capacity to accommodate such beliefs when there appear to be good reasons (justified in terms external to the belief structures of the tradition) for holding them. Assimilation has to do with a

tradition's capacity not only to allow for such beliefs but actually to incorporate them into the belief structures of the tradition in such a way as to reconfigure them so that they align with the core beliefs and narratives of the
tradition (while also allowing for the inevitable influence the assimilation of
such beliefs will have on the belief structures of the tradition). Polanyi makes
similar claims about the ability of a given tradition to negotiate the mutual
dependence of its "logical antecedents" and its "logical derivatives," man-
aging the tension of its on-going exploration of reality by constantly adjudi-
cating between the (potentially competing) claims of its core beliefs and its
emerging awareness.[126]

Finally, Marshall and Polanyi describe the contiguity between epistemology and ontology, between knowing and being, in terms that are largely
consistent. Although he often disparages the notion of correspondence as an
adequate means of describing epistemic validity, Marshall is not prepared to
let go of correspondence theories of truth entirely. The notion of correspondence that Marshall largely rejects is that which defines correspondence in
terms of the relative resemblance between ideas or mental states on the one
hand and reality in itself on the other. He is more ready to admit to a notion
of correspondence that sees "truth bearers" or "truth vehicles" in terms of
that which brings about truth (where "truth" is understood as a "relationship
of correspondence").[127] This understanding of correspondence is one that
fosters a particular view of the relation between belief and practice, namely,
one that rules out the possibility of appealing (i.e., in a foundationalist manner) to either in an attempt to justify the other.[128] Marshall uses the term
"habitability" to signify the manner in which believers find themselves occu-
pying the space (both conceptual and literal) their beliefs intend.[129] This
takes him rather close to Polanyi's notion of indwelling, which also admits to
a range of modalities (i.e., conceptual, physical, etc.) and which does not
allow for strictly linear appeals either to belief as a justification for practice
or vice versa but rather recognizes their interdependence. That Marshall
describes the correspondence or habitability of christology and trinitarian
theology in explicitly personalistic terms invites further consideration as to
the theological fulfillment of Polanyi's notion of indwelling.[130]

Our survey of Marshall's trinitarian exposition of truth and its relative
correspondence to aspects of Polanyi's thought has not provided us with a
detailed strategy for engaging specific methodological challenges that attend
the theological enterprise. However, it has yielded some valuable insights
that help us anticipate how a personalistic, Polanyian approach to intellective

inquiry might appear within a theological horizon. Further, it has helped clarify the direction in which we will need to move in order to amplify further the broader vision of our study. In particular, the importance of trinitarian theology, christology, and pneumatology for any personalistic approach to theological inquiry is more apparent now than ever; this observation thus brings us even closer to the work of the following chapter.

Conclusion

Having thus examined several representative studies aimed to varying degrees at employing Polanyi's thought within the ambit of theological inquiry, and having sketched the foundation of a methodological perspective congenial our own ambitions, we are now ready to draw together the various trajectories we have been following throughout this work. More specifically, we are now able to appreciate more fully Richard Allen's proposal, first mentioned towards the end of the second chapter, that the theological fulfillment of Polanyi's thought requires the development of a full-blown theology of divine being and action articulated in terms consistent with the "philosophy of tacit integration."[131] While the following chapter doesn't aim at anything quite so elaborate as a comprehensive doctrine of God, it does draw on the insights and conclusions of this and the previous chapters in its description of how we might understand the personal being of God in terms consistent with Polanyi's thought.

5

The Trinitarian Ground of Personal Being

Introduction

If there is any single field of theological inquiry that evinces an exceptionally polycentric character, it is trinitarian theology; the sheer range of problems that present themselves in this area of study is considerable.[1] Limiting the range of our efforts to the question of divine personhood will ameliorate the difficulty of our task somewhat, but we are still confronted with the challenge of plotting an understanding of trinitarian personhood along a series of coordinates each of which involves a range of issues in themselves. More specifically, we must determine whether or not a Polanyian understanding of personhood is capable of helping us make sense of both unity and plurality relative both to the life God lives in himself (i.e., the immanent trinity) and the life he shares with the creation (i.e., the economic trinity).

In addition to acknowledging the complexities of trinitarian theology, we must also take note of the much-touted renaissance in trinitarian thought that has attended the development of late modern theology in the West. Early modern assessments of the doctrine of the trinity more often tended to disparage its reasonableness and make light of its relevance for the life of faith.[2] More recently, however, trinitarian theology has recovered its place as the *sine qua non* of both faith and practice. Following the path marked by the giants of theological studies in the twentieth century (most notably Karl Barth and Karl Rahner), many have sought to elucidate the trinitarian shape of not only theological reflection, but also of Christian worship, prayer, ethics, evangelism—indeed, it seems every facet of the Christian experience has been explicated in overtly trinitarian terms.[3] It is also worth noting that these efforts have in some cases led to a reconsideration, and not infrequently the outright rejection, of some of the themes traditionally associated with the doctrine of God and with the church's understanding of God's relation with the world. The predominant trend has been away from the consideration of "God-in-Godself" and towards "God-for-us." Again, Barth and Rahner more or less led the way here, the former via his rejection of what Michael Welker has more recently termed "bourgeois theism" and the latter via his well-known assertion that the "*'economic' Trinity is the 'immanent' Trinity and the 'immanent' Trinity is the 'economic' Trinity.*"[4]

With this wider context in mind, we can now turn to our review of the doctrine of the trinity from a Polanyian perspective. This will first involve an exposition of what we might call the "trinitarian problematic," which is a description of those elements of the dogmatic tradition for which we must account in any attempt to provide a fulsome understanding of divine person-hood. Having thus outlined the task before us, we will then turn to a more focused consideration of particular aspects of trinitarian personhood, taking in turn the question of divine plurality and divine unity as they appear in God's redemptive self-revelation (i.e., the economic trinity), the question of divine transcendence, and finally the question of divine plurality and divine unity considered from the perspective of the life God lives in himself (i.e., the immanent trinity). Our primary concern throughout will be elucidating the contribution a Polanyian understanding of personhood has to offer for such questions.

The Trinitarian Problematic

The first step in this endeavor must be an accounting of the specific issues and challenges that confront us at this point. In particular, we need to deline-ate to at least some degree an understanding of the questions that the notion of divine personhood has been intended to address in the theological tradi-tion. Thankfully, we need not attempt anything like a survey, let alone a comprehensive account, of the emergence and development of trinitarian doctrine; rather, we need only highlight those propositions that have largely sustained the development of the Christian doctrine of God.[5]

In its most succinct form, the problem before us can be expressed in the following terms: how are we to understand the personal being of God rela-tive both to God's redemptive self-revelation in space and time as well as to the divine life considered apart from the creation? Both parts of this question push us toward articulating an understanding of God that can help us make sense of both unity and plurality in the divine life. In other words, we must be able to say how divine personhood signifies both divine plurality and divine oneness relative to both the economic trinity as well as the immanent trinity. While it is likely true to say that (on the one hand) the question of divine unity presents itself most forcefully relative to our understanding of the economic trinity and (on the other) the question of divine plurality does so relative to our understanding of the immanent trinity, we must be cautious about overemphasizing this tension; doing so would fail to do justice to a fulsome understanding of divine personhood.

A distinct but related issue implied by these questions has to do with the nature of divine transcendence. As noted above, one of the issues that has attracted a considerable amount of attention in contemporary theology has to do with God's relationship to the world. While we need not engage all of the recent challenges that have been posed to traditional affirmations of God's transcendence, we do need to recognize the potential ramifications of such questions relative to the specific issue of divine personhood.

Another way of approaching this particular issue would be to admit the extent to which our formulation of the trinitarian problematic forces a consideration of the way we are to correlate each of these various perspectives on divine personhood. How, in other words, is divine personhood in its economic configurations related to divine personhood in its immanent configurations (or, in terms consistent with Rahner's *Grundaxiom*, how are we to understand the correspondence between the economic trinity and the immanent trinity)? As we shall see, it is precisely in terms of personal being that this question is best answered.

Faced with the range of challenges outlined above (as well as all of the related questions they imply relative to our understanding of the divine nature, God's presence and activity in the creation, and the experience of salvation in and through Jesus Christ and the Holy Spirit), it is enormously tempting at this point to seek solace in traditional doctrinal formulations. Doing so, however, would ultimately frustrate the wider purpose of this study, for we would then more or less be forced to limit our efforts to finding potential points of contact between the theological tradition and Polanyi's thought. If we are to try and establish the extent to which a Polanyian ontology of personhood provides us with a useful perspective on these questions, then we must allow ourselves to try and articulate our answers to these questions in terms as much beholden to a Polanyian perspective as possible. We cannot, in other words, limit ourselves merely to "baptizing" Polanyi by demonstrating the apparent consistency of his philosophy with, say, Augustine's or Thomas's trinitarian theology. Instead, we must respect the integrity or structure of the church's witness to God as "three persons in one being" while also allowing the purview of Polanyi's thought to lead us towards fresh insights to familiar problems. Rather than trying to subsume one wholly to the other, we are here seeking a measure of rapprochement.

Since it is from within the ambit of the church's attempt to make sense of God's presence and activity in Jesus Christ and the Holy Spirit that the trinitarian problematic first emerged, we will first undertake a consideration of divine personal being relative to the question of plurality and unity in the economic configuration of the trinity. This will push us towards a more formalized consideration of God's existence, thus evoking the question of how we are to understand divine transcendence. We will then have to address once again the question of divine personhood relative to both the plurality and the unity of God, this time relative to the immanent configuration of the trinity. Finally, we will need to demonstrate how it is that personhood provides us with the best means of correlating our understanding of the economic and the immanent trinitarian life of God. It bears repeating that in all of this we will need to limit our efforts to a consideration of divine personhood, and will thus largely have to prescind from a number of related but, for our purposes largely tangential, questions that would require close attention were we trying to elaborate a fulsome doctrine of God.

Economic Divine Personal Being in Polanyian Perspective

There are, arguably, two events that highlight with particular force the question of the nature of divine plurality. The first event is the resurrection of Jesus; the second is the church's reception of the Holy Spirit. Both events are signal moments in the self-revelation of God, and as such move us decisively towards a consideration of economic divine plurality that is grounded in the katabatic redemptive action of God. In other words, the question of economic divine plurality emerges much more forcefully within the context of dogmatic theology than it does within the context of either natural or fundamental theology. We will accordingly delimit our efforts in this section to a consideration of the matter at hand from this particular perspective, while acknowledging that our conclusions may have significant implications for certain questions more closely related to natural or fundamental theology.

The reason that the resurrection of Jesus forces the question of divine plurality is because it obviates the possibility of thinking of the person of Jesus of Nazareth in terms not immediately connected in some way to the divine life of God. Jesus, in other words, can no longer be seen merely as a prophet, a rabbi, or a spiritual master; in light of the resurrection, we must confront the question of what the presence and activity of God evident in the person of Jesus means for our understanding of God himself. This awareness is evident even in the earliest Christian traditions. Writing to the church in Rome, for example, Paul notes that it is by virtue of his having been raised from the dead that Jesus "was declared to be the Son of God with power according to the spirit of holiness" (Rom 1.4, NRSV).

Likewise, the reception of the Holy Spirit similarly pushes against the possibility of understanding divine personhood in terms of undifferentiated unity or singularity. By characterizing their experience of the Spirit in terms that affirmed the distinct identity and action of the Spirit even while affirming the Spirit's unity with both God and Jesus, early Christians ruled out the possibility of what would in the second and third centuries of the Common Era come to be known as Monarchianism or Sabellianism (i.e., "modalism"). This also, of course, eliminated the possibility of understanding divine personhood in similar terms; the personal being of God, of Jesus, and of the Holy Spirit would have to be affirmed in a way that preserved both their distinction and their unity, just as the divinity of God, of Jesus, and of the Holy Spirit would come to be understood in terms that affirmed their plurality even as it acknowledged their unity.

If the resurrection of Christ and the reception of the Holy Spirit both evoke the question of divine economic personhood, then this question is sharpened even further when we note that the person and work of Jesus and that of the Spirit are interdependent. It is the Spirit that empowers Jesus throughout his ministry, and it is the resurrected Jesus who opens the way for the reception of the Spirit by the church. The incarnation of God, in other words, must be understood in fully trinitarian terms, not just as an act of the Son but of all three divine persons: the Father sends the Son, who responds in obedience and love to the Father, and their relationship is sustained by the activity of the Spirit. Thus, alongside Rahner's *Grundaxiom* regarding the identity of the economic trinity and the immanent trinity, Yves Congar's suggestion that there be no christology without pneumatology and no pneumatology without christology is another maxim that signifies in summary form a conviction of late modern theology (further evinced by the development of "Spirit-christology") to which we need be sensitive.[6]

As it happens, this perspective provides an especially useful point of departure for our own examination of the personal being of God relative to the economic trinity. In his examination of the potential ramifications of

Polanyi's thought for dogmatic theology, Robert Palma highlights the need to maintain the unity of christological inquiry. Palma suggests that the unity of formal analysis of the person and work of Christ follows from the unity of the object of inquiry, namely, Christ himself; while we may artificially distinguish questions about Christ's person from questions about his work, or similarly distinguish the question of the divine nature from that of the human nature, we cannot allow ourselves to adopt such a bifurcated view of Christ himself. Thus, Christ can be said from a Polanyian perspective to signify a "divinely constituted historic and coherent gestalt of grace," one that does not admit to arbitrary segmentation.[7] It is never a matter of apprehending the person in order to understand the works (or vice versa), or of apprehending the human in order to understand the divine (or vice versa), or of apprehending a "functional" christology in order to perceiving a more "ontological" one, but rather is a matter of "having both disclosed conjointly through an indwelling of the inclusive reality of Jesus Christ."[8]

Palma's suggestions in this regard can be extended to include our own observation regarding the need to maintain the essential unity of christology and pneumatology; his insistence that it is in his personhood that the unity of christological inquiry also accords well with our own personalistic outlook.[9] In other words, we need to include in our account of the unified "gestalt of grace" signified by the incarnation the essential interdependence of our understanding of Christ and of the Spirit.[10] With this in mind, we can now undertake a Polanyian analysis of the presence and activity of God in the world as manifest in particular in the person of Christ; by so narrowing our efforts, we will be able to engage many of the issues involved in any consideration of the economic trinity without risking a loss of focus. This approach thus more or less assumes that an exposition of the person and work of Christ, conditioned by a tacit awareness of the presence and activity of the Holy Spirit, can provide something of a exemplary pattern after which other instances of divine presence and activity in the world can be modeled.

R.L. Sturch has suggested that a theologically viable doctrine of Christ must include a certain number of elements: first, the full divinity of Christ must be affirmed; second, the full humanity of Christ must also be affirmed; third, the unity of the divinity and humanity of Christ must be grounded in something either common to both or alien to both; fourth, Christ must be said to reveal God; and finally, Christ must be said to provide redemption for humanity.[11] Sturch's criteria provide a concise summary of the principles traditionally associated with orthodox christology, and thus provide something of a benchmark by which we can measure our efforts toward the development of a Polanyian description of the incarnation.

By organizing our efforts according to the five principles that Sturch proposes, we can engage the task before us in a relatively systematic fashion (recognizing that the distinctions made by these principles are only formal and cannot be read back into our understanding of the person of Christ himself). First, then, we need to provide some accounting of how we are to understand the divinity of Christ.[12] Traditionally, of course, this has been articulated in terms of the doctrine of the *homoousious*, that is, in terms of the consubstantiality of Christ's divine nature with that of the Father (as it would also be relative to the Spirit). This insight can aid us in understanding the divinity of Christ, for it offers a perspective on the question of Jesus' divine nature that is amenable to the dynamics of indwelling. In other words, in the relation between Jesus and the Father it is by way of an act of indwelling through the extension of his personal being that the Father translates the transcendent personalizing dynamics of the divine being to the Son in a pattern of integration that bears the Father's image even as it fosters the distinct actualization of the personal being of the Son. The Son thus receives from the Father the gift of the divine being even as he actively integrates and interiorizes this form of personal being as himself.

A brief account of the biblical witness relative to the relationship shared by the Father and the Son will help flesh out this proposal. The above description prompts a renewed appreciation for the testimony provided by the gospel of John to the intimacy Jesus shared with the Father. For example, we find descriptions of Jesus' relationship with the Father that lean, in keeping with the nomenclature we employed in our earlier development of a Polanyian ontology of personhood (in chapter three), in a decidedly existential direction: Jesus repeatedly insists that his vocation is something that he undertakes only under the authority and the power granted to him by the Father (see Jn 5.19-26, 6.37-40, 8.16-29, etc.). We also find descriptions that lean in a more emergent direction: the reciprocity of Jesus and the Father is such that their relationship can be described in terms of mutual indwelling (see Jn 14.8-24, 16.28, 17.5-11, etc.). These provide distinct but complementary points of departure for thinking about the way the Father, via his own personal participation in the divine life, communicates the divine nature to the Son in a manner that upholds the personal being (that is, both their individuality as well as their relationality) of both.

This leads further to a consideration of the presence and activity of the Holy Spirit in this relation. We have already noted the need to provide a pneumatologically rich reading of the person and work of Christ. Within the context of the question before us at present, we need to account for the role of the Spirit in the mutual indwelling of Jesus and the Father.[13] There can be little question regarding the early church's witness to the presence and activity of the Spirit in the life and ministry of Jesus (see, e.g., Lk 1.35, 3.16, 3.21-22, 4.1, 4.14; Jn 20.22; etc.). However, reflection on the precise nature and shape of the Spirit's relation to both the Father and the Son is not nearly as much in evidence in the biblical traditions as it is in the later theological tradition. It would largely fall to the Cappadocian Fathers (Basil of Caesarea, Gregory of Nyssa, and Gregory of Nazianzus) to codify an understanding of the relationship of the Spirit to the Father and the Son in a manner consistent with the established understanding of that between the Father and the Son.[14]

What emerged within the developing theological tradition is a conviction that the Spirit itself signifies the mutuality of the relationship between the Father and the Son. Put in a way more consonant with our own efforts, we can say that the Spirit came to embody the integration and indwelling of a form of personal being grounded in the reciprocity between the other two divine persons. Relative to the life of Jesus the Spirit not only signifies the mutuality of the Father and his anointed one, but is seen as the horizon wherein this mutuality is grounded. The historical experience of the Son in the incarnation, his submission to contingence, embodiment, and death, would call into question the security of his relation to the Father were it not for the presence and activity of the Spirit. Thus, the Spirit serves as the ground of communion between the Father and the incarnate Son as they mutually indwell one another. The distinction between active and passive investment in the act of indwelling again becomes significant at this point: the integration and interiorization of the Father's translation of the personalizing dynamics of the Godhead to Christ is the Spirit's indwelling as an act of interpersonal mutuality. By virtue of his identity in the relation between the Father and Jesus, the Spirit does not abrogate their communion through the insinuation of his own personal being, but rather actively fosters their relation through his acquiescence to their reciprocal indwelling.

Our efforts to this point already invite reflection on the correspondence between the life of God as manifest in the creation and the life of God considered in abstraction from the creation. Before we can take up this issue, however, we must first examine how we might engage the question of the two natures of Christ by way of the notion of indwelling. This requires identifying a means whereby we can affirm the consubstantiality of the human nature of Christ with our own. John McIntyre, building on the work of Gerald O'Collins, offers a helpful summary of the essential elements of a dogmatic understanding of the humanity of Jesus, including "organic, bodily existence, coupled with rationality, free will, affectivity, and memory," all realized within a "dynamic" and "social" context. To these elements, McIntyre adds that we be equally cognizant of the historicity of Jesus, by which he means three things: first, that "Jesus' actual entry into the historical human process was itself part of the Gospel"; second, that historicity includes important subsidiary themes such as "particularity, probability, and so on"; and third, that this same historicity highlights the challenge of finding a way to demonstrate the significance of the life, death, and resurrection of Christ for all people in all times and places.[15]

Having said that, it thus seems that we find ourselves faced here with what is in some ways a more difficult challenge than we did in our earlier effort to make sense of the divinity of Christ (that is, in terms of Jesus' consubstantiality with the Father). More specifically, we find that the personalistic mode of inquiry on which we have depended thus far may be of less assistance to us relative to the question of the humanity of Christ. If we were to explicate an understanding of the humanity of Jesus using the categories and methods we have employed to this point, it is hard to see how we could avoid affirming the independent personhood of Jesus' humanity. In other words, a strictly personalistic, Polanyian account of the humanity of Jesus may afford a perspective on the humanity of Jesus from which it would be all too easy to fall into adoptionism. The dogmatic tradition is clear that in affirming the full humanity of Christ we cannot thereby affirm the independent personhood of Christ's humanity.[16]

This does not mean, however, that we are left without a means of speaking in Polanyian terms about the humanity of Christ. Several elements of Polanyi's thought can help us ascertain in terms consistent with his philosophical vision what it might mean to speak about the character or shape of Christ's human nature. For example, Polanyi's emphasis on the embodied character of human identity and experience (as well as his extension of the notion of embodiment by way of the concept of indwelling) would provide us with a helpful and necessary starting point, and would accord well with McIntyre's emphasis on "organic, bodily existence." Likewise, Polanyi's emphasis on the extent to which one's knowledge and identity is influenced by one's historical and cultural milieu could be put to use explicating what McIntyre describes as the dynamic social and historical context of the incarnation. We might even be able to begin working out an understanding of the problem McIntyre finds in the tension between the particularity of the incarnation and its universal import by employing Polanyi's description of humanity as "life conscious of itself" as a heuristic for reflecting on the place of Jesus in the evolution of consciousness.[17]

For now, however, let us narrow our efforts to a consideration of how Polanyi's thought might help us make sense of the correspondence between the two natures of Christ. Doing so, as we shall see, will not only move us forward in our broader efforts, but will help obviate some of the potential problems we might expect to encounter in articulating an understanding of the humanity of Christ from a Polanyian perspective. We should recall at this point the development in the dogmatic tradition (initially by Leontius of Byzantium and Ephraim of Antioch, but especially by John of Damascus) of the enhypostatic and anhypostatic character of the incarnation.[18] Here we see the value of Polanyi's notion of comprehensive entities subject to dual control as a means of understanding the humanity of Christ. The Polanyian elements of human nature we mentioned above (i.e., embodiment, historical and social situatedness, self-consciousness, etc.) can themselves be said to signify in outline form just such a comprehensive entity: the boundary conditions established by physical embodiment (understood via an expansive description of indwelling) are harnessed by the marginal control afforded by the emergence of reflective consciousness, which in turn establishes the boundary conditions that are then drawn to fulfillment through the marginal control manifest in the deployment of language and conceptual tools, and so on. What this perspective opens to us is the possibility of, first, understanding personhood as the supervenient dynamic of the being of Christ (i.e., that which exerts marginal control over all lower levels), and second, the possibility of affirming in Polanyian terms that the human nature of Christ does not evince an independent personhood, but rather is subject to the marginal control of the personal being of the Son.

Thus, we can affirm that it is at the level of the person that the unity of Christ must be understood, rather than at the level of either of the natures.[19] The humanity of the person of Christ is fully his own, and is complete and integral in its own right in a manner consistent with our own (i.e., Christ is in his humanity consubstantial to us). Further, Polanyi's understanding of dual control and the mutual interpenetration of the levels within a comprehensive entity provides us with a means of working out a fresh understanding of the traditional theological notion of the *communicatio idiomatum*, the *circumin-sessio* of the two natures in their essential personal unity.[20] This also helps guard against both Nestorian tendencies on the one hand and Apollinarian tendencies on the other; the personal being of the Son is not something added extrinsically to the humanity of Christ, but is itself the "organizing principle" (to employ Polanyi's verbiage) of the incarnation. This also fulfills Sturch's requirement that we understand the unity of the two natures in terms consistent with both; personal being is the organizing principle of contingent human existence as well as the eternal existence of the Son (although in saying this we of course acknowledge the qualitative distinction between the personal being of the eternal Son and that of human beings). Finally, it seems a more fulsome reading of the incarnation along these lines would accord well with Maximus the Confessor's account of "theandric" christology.[21]

As we did in our analysis of the relation between Jesus and the Father, so too should we acknowledge here the essentially pneumatological character of the unity of the two natures in Christ. Although it is the personal being of the eternal Son that serves as the organizing principle of two natures of Christ, the indwelling activity of the Holy Spirit is no less necessary in the actualization of the form of personal being signified by the incarnation. Just as the Spirit helps foster the mutual indwelling of the Father and the incarnate Son, so too does the presence and activity of the Spirit in the life of Christ help bring about the union of the two natures. The manner in which this is accomplished is not the same as in the relation between the Father and the Son, for the interpenetration of the two natures cannot be said to recapitulate the mutual indwelling of two persons; were we to affirm this, we would thereby fall into a Nestorian christology.[22] Rather, what must be affirmed is that it is in and through (i.e., via indwelling) the Spirit that the Son effects the integration of the two natures of Christ. In other words, the Spirit can be seen as the horizon within which the Son integrates the boundary conditions of the human nature of Christ and interiorizes them within himself, making them (i.e., his human nature) his own. The indwelling of the Son in the incarnation does not signify the temporary displacement of the eternal Son from the life of God; rather, it signifies the actualization of the form of personal being that is the Son in space and time, which in no way disrupts the eternal communion of the Father and the Son. The Spirit is the one in and through whom this is made possible, for the Spirit guarantees the integrity of the incarnation (that is, of the union of the two natures of Christ) while also preserving the distinction between the life God lives in himself and the relation between God and the creation.[23] This has the further effect of highlighting the gratuitous character of the incarnation and the freedom of God in the act of redemption (and, by implication, in God's creative and consummative acts as well and to the trinitarian shape of these actions).

We have now elucidated in Polanyian terms three of the five criteria proposed by Sturch for any viable understanding of the incarnation; the final two criteria involve the manner in which we understand the person and work of Christ relative to revelation and redemption. To each of these themes we need at this point only give a modicum of attention, because although each one is deserving of lengthy exposition in its own right it is also the case that much of what would be said in any personalistic, Polanyian exposition of the doctrine of revelation or the doctrine of redemption would follow largely from the line of thinking we have outlined above.

The question with which we are faced when we consider the concept of revelation has to do with both what we understand Jesus to have revealed and how we understand him to have revealed it. Based on our efforts throughout this section, we can now propose that a personalistic, Polanyian reading of the incarnation would suggest that what Christ reveals (and how he reveals it) can be understood precisely in terms of interpersonal relation and the actualization of personal being manifest therein. Not only does Christ reveal the relation between himself and the Father, but also invites others into the relational life of God by opening the way through the impartation of the Spirit. This allows for the incorporation of the creation in the life of the Creator while maintaining the distinction and integrity of both. This description of the revelatory import of the incarnation recapitulates a principle described in the theological tradition in terms of the congruity between the *ordo cognoscendi* and the *ordo essendi*.

Similarly, the question with which we are faced when we consider the concept of redemption has to do with what we might call the soteriological achievement of the life, death, and resurrection of Christ. We can readily redraw the answer proposed above to the question of revelation according to a more soteriological pattern: Christ in his person (and in conjunction with the personal presence and activity of the Spirit) actualizes a form of being that overcomes the brokenness and sin of the human condition, and does so in such a manner so as to avail his life to others, thereby bringing them into renewed relation with God.[24] In other words, in and through the incarnation the limitations of the boundary conditions of human existence are subjected to the marginal control of the Holy Spirit, thereby raising them to a new level of achievement without destroying their integrity or freedom. The congruity between the *ordo cognoscendi* and the *ordo essendi* thus signifies correspondence both at the level of being and of knowing; Melancthon's axiom that "to know Christ is to know his benefits" can in one sense be said to anticipate further reflection on developing an understanding of redemption in and through Christ and the Spirit in terms of personal mutual indwelling.

Throughout this section, we have repeatedly been faced with the challenge of articulating an understanding of both unity and plurality as they apply to economic divine personhood. We saw a need to maintain an awareness of the essential unity of Christ himself even as we admitted to the possibility of distinguishing between various aspects of his identity and ministry. We recognized the indissoluble link between our understanding of Christ and that of the Spirit even as we affirmed that they both exist and operate within a single unified field of divine personal action that also includes the active participation of the Father. In all of this, we have repeatedly had recourse to Polanyi's understanding of indwelling and the concomitant principle of dual control as primary means for explicating economic divine personhood. We have also seen on more than one occasion that each of these themes in different ways evoke the question of the transcendent personal being of God. This is, as we noted earlier, an issue that has received a considerable amount of attention in recent theological studies, and so before moving to a more focused consideration of how Polanyi's thought can help us make sense of divine personhood relative to the doctrine of the immanent trinity, we will first explore the possibilities that exist for affirming divine transcendence from a Polanyian perspective.

Divine Transcendence in Polanyian Perspective

At the outset of this chapter, we made note of the revival of interest in the doctrine of the trinity that unfolded throughout much of the last century. Only slightly less obvious has been the extent to which this renaissance has been attended by a determination to revisit the question of divine transcendence; a certain preoccupation with the contingencies of human experience, characteristic of late modern thought in general, has been no less evident in trinitarian theology than in others areas of theological reflection (and, indeed, in most every area of intellective inquiry). One of the consequences this direction in Western thought has had for understanding the doctrine of God is to encourage a reconsideration of whether or not traditional formula-

tions designed to highlight the radical difference between God and the world
remain viable. We cannot hope to provide a comprehensive account of this
development, but will have to content ourselves with a fairly cursory review
of representative attempts to engage the question of divine transcendence.[25]

In her well-known and oft-cited magnum opus, *God For Us*, Catherine
Mowry LaCugna sets out to provide a thorough accounting of what she
describes (following Dorothea Wendebourg) as the "defeat of trinitarian
theology."[26] More specifically, LaCugna intends to show how the elaboration
of the doctrine of the immanent trinity in both Eastern and Western theology
signifies something of a betrayal of the Christian vision of God; rather than
hold to an understanding of the immanent trinity as signifying our understanding of the divine life considered in abstraction from the world, LaCugna
instead subscribes to an understanding of the immanent trinity as signifying
the otherness and mystery of God, an otherness and mystery that is in no way
divorced from God's self-revelation in history (i.e., in the economic trinity).
LaCugna thus leans heavily on Rahner's axiom regarding the identification
of the immanent trinity and the economic trinity.

Rather than provide a detailed summary of LaCugna's arguments, we
need only note some of the more prevalent themes that are repeated throughout her work. First, she is very much concerned with recovering what we
might call a participatory understanding of the doctrine of the trinity. Second,
a relational understanding of personhood serves as a keystone in LaCugna's
thought; she seems more enamored with late modern attempts to recover
personalistic modes of thought in philosophy and theology than with the idea
of persons as subsistent relations as developed in classical trinitarian thought
(although she does acknowledge the contributions of Augustine and Thomas). Third, she relies on the notion of perichoretic mutuality as a foundation
for her understanding of the correspondence between God and the creation
(although she does not go as far as do some others on the question of the
impact of contingence, suffering, and death on the life of God).[27]

LaCugna is not preoccupied with either ethical or pastoral concerns, but
she does devote a significant amount of attention to outlining some of the
more practical consequences of her understanding of the doctrine of the
trinity. In particular, she tries to elucidate the significance of a trinitarian
doctrine of God for Christian worship and for social ethics. Drawing on
liberation theology and feminist thought, she sets forth an egalitarian, communitarian vision of human relations aimed at destabilizing forms of oppres-
sion (i.e., patriarchy, monarchianism, etc.).[28] She is also attracted to

Orthodox theological ethics because of the East's commitment to a personalistic approach to trinitarian theology, but ultimately finds Orthodox thought incapable of affirming both all she wants to say about the relation between God and the world or the perceived need to maintain a preferential option for the poor and marginalized of society.[29]

It would, of course, be unfair to say that LaCugna's work summarizes the entire range of perspectives on contemporary trinitarian theology, or even to think that we have here captured all the nuances of her arguments. Nonetheless, her work is representative of some of the more general trends in recent attempts to reconceive the doctrine of God. In particular, two themes are brought together in her work that have been more fully developed by others, namely, a panentheistic account of divine existence, and the necessary correlation between trinitarian theology and other areas of theological study, notably Christian ethics. Both of these trends can be taken as consequences of the shift in late modern thought, in theology and elsewhere, to the historical and the contingent. Further examination of this shift will be helpful at this point, both as a means whereby we might situate LaCugna's work within its milieu and as a way of identifying how this shift became clearly evident in trinitarian theology.

There have been typically three points at which attempts have been made in recent times to reconceive the relationship between God and the world: the doctrine of creation, the Passion of Christ, and the doctrine of eschatology. We will at this point outline (albeit only briefly) the theological genealogy of each of these tendencies as represented (respectively) in the work of Karl Rahner, Jürgen Moltmann, and Wolfhart Pannenberg. Our purpose here cannot be anything other than a summary description of how the thought of Rahner, Moltmann, and Pannenberg have contributed to what might be called an immanentized or historicized view of God, and thus should not be taken as a description of their respective theological programs *in toto*. Given the influence each of these individuals have exercised, however, we are more than justified in suggesting that their work is representative of many of the trends manifest in late modern theology.

The theology of Karl Rahner can be taken as an extended study in the mediation of divine immanence and divine transcendence.[30] Concerned as he was with demonstrating the continuity between Christian faith and the best of late modern Western thought, Rahner elaborated a theological program in which he sought to harmonize the apparently conflicting demands of human freedom and divine sovereignty. For our purposes, Rahner's work serves as a paradigmatic example of the manner in which the doctrine of creation has been reconfigured in late modern theology in a way that risks subjecting God to finitude and contingence (by "doctrine of creation" we mean here an expansive theological consideration of the nature and structure of the entire created order, including the identity and place of humanity in the world, rather than a more narrowly conceived engagement with questions of cosmogeny). Rahner's transcendental methodology and his emphasis on the innate capacity human beings have to apprehend the mystery of absolute being (by virtue of their constitution as "spirit") required him to offer a nuanced understanding of the relation between the natural and supernatural orders, between nature and grace. By positing the operation in human beings of a "supernatural existential," Rahner sought to mediate between wholly extrinsic and wholly intrinsic views of divine self-revelation and humanity's knowledge of God. However, this notion remains an ambiguous one in Rahner's writings, and is something he used to refer to extrinsic as well as intrinsic examples of religious experience. Further (and of more immediate interest relative to our efforts), his characterization of God as the absolute mystery of transcendent being manifest in human awareness risks minimizing the distinction between God and the world (it is this sense of divine transcendence and the immanent life of God that LaCugna borrows for her own project). Both the transcendence and the mystery of God, considered from a human perspective, are themselves grounded in God (and, indeed, can be said to be God), and thus the correspondence between the immanent life of God and the divine self-revelation manifest in the salvific economy is minimized (hence the famous *Grundaxiom*). In short, Rahner's elaboration of a theology equally informed by divine transcendence and divine immanence (the former understood largely *in terms of* the latter) opens the door to an understanding of the relation between God and the world in which the distinction between the two is blurred.

This same tendency is manifest in a slightly different and perhaps more thorough-going (or at least explicit) manner in the theology of Jürgen Moltmann. Whereas Rahner reconfigures the relation between God and the world within the ambit of the doctrine of creation, Moltmann provides us with an example of a theological system in which the relation between God and the world is reconfigured in light of the cross.[31] For Moltmann, belief in a self-subsistent God existing eternally as three persons in immanent relations would require us to reject the historical and contextual reality of human experience (including that of Jesus). Given the insuperable reality of our historical awareness, Moltmann thus understands trinitarian theology to be nothing other than an abridged description of the Passion of Christ. The incarnation is understood less so as the appearance in time of the eternal Son of God and more so as the context within which the first and second persons of the trinity discover themselves and their identity as Father and Son; Moltmann thus seems to reject the notion of the *logos asarkos*. Further, the resurrection of Christ becomes the ground of Jesus' identity as the Son of God, and also grounds the hope for the consummation of the creation. Moltmann might thus be said to offer a more radicalized version of Rahner's trinitarian axiom, one in which the economic trinity serves as the predicate of the doctrine of the immanent trinity (and indeed of the immanent trinity itself) rather than vice versa. Not surprisingly, this leads to a somewhat tritheistic understanding of the relations or unity between the three divine persons, and thus to a characterization of their perichoretic mutuality in terms of "goal" rather than in terms of eternal, essential unity. Finally, it is worth noting that it seems to be Moltmann's preoccupation with fostering a particular ethical vision, one that eschews all forms of hierarchy in favor of egalitarian interdependence and inclusivity, that has led him to many of his more recent theological conclusions; his view of ethics sometimes drives his understanding of doctrine.

If we have in Rahner an example of one who offers a revised version of the relation between God and the world explicated within the context of the doctrine of creation, and we have in Moltmann one who offers a similar theological effort undertaken relative to the cross of Christ, then we have in Wolfhart Pannenberg an example of one who offers a comparable perspective, this time explicated within the context of the eschatological future of the world.[32] In many ways, Pannenberg can be said to be more responsible (or at least responsive) than Moltmann in his engagement with certain elements of the theological tradition. For example, rather than reject outright the doctrine of the immanent trinity (as Moltmann seems to do), Pannenberg seeks instead to situate our reflection on the immanent life of God in a manner consistent with contemporary thought. Again, like Moltmann he emphasizes the centrality of the economic self-revelation of God in Jesus Christ and the Holy Spirit in our consideration of God, but he does not radicalize (as Moltmann does) Rahner's trinitarian axiom. Pannenberg's thought becomes potentially troubling, though, in his attempt to reconfigure divine transcendence in temporal as opposed to spatial terms. It is not so much his determination to use temporal rather than spatial categories that is the problem; rather, the problem has to do with the question of whether or not Pannenberg has really broken free of the complex of problems that emerge whenever the transcendence of God is understood in contingent, impersonal categories. There is in Pannenberg's thought a creative tension between his explication of pneumatology via field theory and his description of the causal influence of the future on the present and the past. Given the relatively impersonal tenor of the former, it seems legitimate to ask whether or not Pannenberg is capable of upholding the absolute personhood of God. If not, then it would seem that his theology risks collapsing into a form of panentheism that compromises the distinction between God and the world. It may be, however, that this tendency is less representative of Pannenberg himself and is more representative of some who have appropriated his work.

While the combined influence of Rahner, Moltmann, and Pannenberg is considerable, there have been some who have sought to resist the trend towards explicating the existence and life of God in historicized terms. One prominent recent example of just such an effort is Paul Molnar's *Divine Freedom and the Doctrine of the Immanent Trinity*.[33] Molnar forcefully argues that the general direction of contemporary trinitarian theology away from the elaboration of a theology of the immanent life of God and instead towards a preoccupation with the economic trinity more or less represents the abandonment of a Christian view of God. Molnar critiques the theology of LaCugna, Rahner, Moltmann, and Pannenberg, as well as that of Gordon Kaufmann, Sallie McFague, and Elizabeth Johnson; even Colin Gunton doesn't fully escape Molnar's ire. Molnar employs a close reading of Karl Barth (and, less so, Thomas Torrance) in an effort to demonstrate the need for a robust working understanding of the immanent trinity. His primary concern is to reclaim divine freedom, and thereby to reassert the primacy of God's self-revelation in the order of knowledge and the primacy of God's gratuitous grace in the order of salvation. Against the notion that it is primarily in the incarnation that the identity of Jesus as the divine Son of God is grounded, Molnar (re)asserts the doctrine of the *logos asarkos*.[34] Against the notion that the unity of God is best understood in temporal and (more specifically) eschatological terms, he (re)asserts the doctrine of God's eternal self-subsistence in a single, unified, divine essence or nature.[35] Against the notion that the transcendence of God is best understood as the "mystery of the world" or the "unfathomable enigma of being," he (re)asserts the doctrine of the radical distinction between God and the created order and the utter transcendence of the former relative to the latter.[36] Against the tendency to characterize the unity of the divine persons in social or communitarian terms, he (re)asserts the absolute personhood of God and the coequal participation of the three persons in a single divine subjectivity.[37]

Molnar's primary concern is doctrinal and not ethical, but he does take note of the practical and moral consequences of trinitarian theology. He argues that those who abandon the doctrine of the immanent trinity do an injustice to the character of the economic trinity; that is, they ignore the extent to which Christ and the Holy Spirit both signify the need for a reconsideration of unitarian monotheism. In so doing, he further suggests, they demonstrate (albeit implicitly) their proclivity to read the biblical record in light of their own *a priori* ethical convictions; the self-revelation of God, in other words, becomes something of a backdrop against which an arbitrary series of abstracted ideals can be projected. Against this practice Molnar levels Thomas Torrance's critique of theological abstraction, whereby he proposes to reassert the primacy of dogmatics over ethics.[38]

Although his book provides a much-needed reminder of the importance of the doctrine of the immanent trinity, Molnar in the end offers a form of theological reflection that is in some ways less than satisfactory. More specifically, his reflections often seem to devolve into a kind of theological positivism. Molnar is well aware of the challenges Barth's theology has encountered relative to this charge, but (because of his dependence on Barth) seems unable to avoid entirely the charge himself. Granted, his primary purpose has more to do with deploying Barth's thought in an effort to critique contemporary trinitarian theology and less to do with rehabilitating Barth's theology; Molnar takes Barth as he finds him. This handicap in Molnar's work, however, suggests that we should be judicious in developing our own understanding of the shape and function of the doctrine of the immanent trinity so that we do not appear to be arguing in circles.

We have yet to explore the way that Polanyi's thought might be brought to bear in an effort to elucidate the nature of divine transcendence; all we have done to this point is highlight one of the more dynamic lines of tension that runs through contemporary trinitarian theology. However, we must also acknowledge the concerns that have been raised by Richard Allen regarding the potential problems faced by a distinctly Polanyian approach to questions of divine transcendence. Allen has pointed out that Polanyi's notion of the "tacit triad" and his commitment to the ubiquity of the tacit dimension in all forms of knowing invites certain problems when we consider the possibility of aspiring to reliable knowledge of a transcendent God from within space and time.[39] In particular, the "from-to" structure manifest throughout Polanyi's epistemology presents us with certain challenges. Any attempt to work out our knowledge of God strictly based on the "from-to" structure of the tacit dimension risks subsuming God within the natural order (i.e., as an object of focal awareness that we apprehend by way of the tacit integration of finite subsidiary elements).

The essential problem here, it seems, has to do with what precisely we understand to be the kinds of subsidiary elements we expect would admit to the kind of integration and indwelling that would enable us to apprehend God. On the one hand, we may want to elaborate a sophisticated natural theology whereby various aspects of our worldly experience are put forth as particularly suited for facilitating knowledge of the transcendent. Such a natural theology, however, will likely end up with a distorted image of God, one conditioned by anthropomorphic projection.[40] On the other hand, there is also available to us the awareness of God fostered by the redemptive self-revelation of Jesus Christ and the Holy Spirit. This has been our starting point for many of the questions we have explored in this chapter, and is consistent with the approach to theological reflection outlined in the previous chapter as well. Since we have thus already devoted considerable attention to describing the way that Polanyi's thought might inform our understanding of the person and work of Christ (and of the Holy Spirit), we need not revisit this issue at this time.

We can, however, take to heart the cautions Allen offers to those who desire to employ Polanyi's thought within the context of the theological enterprise. He warns, for example, about the extent to which exclusive dependence on the category of revelation can devolve into a kind of theological positivism or unmerited claims of having received private special revelation.[41] Avoiding this pitfall, it seems, is chiefly a matter of articulating a balanced doctrine of Christ, that is, one able to speak adequately about his humanity, his divinity, and their intersection. Further, we must acknowledge that our knowledge of God will always involve a certain provisionality; indeed, any sense we might have about the apparent *non*-provisionality of our knowledge of God should perhaps suggest to us that we have compromised our theological integrity.[42]

It thus remains for us to consider some of the ways that the perspective engendered herein might inform our understanding of divine transcendence. We have already (in chapter two) established the realist tenor of Polanyi's thought. We have also noted the tension that exists in Polanyi's thought relative to existence of God. On the one hand, Polanyi held out hope that the pursuit of shared social and cultural endeavors might eventually "reveal to us God in man and society."[43] This expectation points in the direction of what we might call an "emergent" notion of God (i.e., "God" conceived of as the most expansive and inclusive "comprehensive integration" imaginable). On the other hand, Polanyi also recognized that human beings "need a purpose which bears on eternity," one that, owing to the challenges and crises that typify the human experience, might not be amenable to apprehension "on secular grounds alone."[44] This leaves open the possibility of affirming that religious awareness cannot finally be made to rest on a non-religious foundation. Anabatic human striving must be situated within the wider, more comprehensive horizon of katabatic divine action.

We find further help for our efforts by recalling that, for Polanyi, reliable knowledge always "reveals an aspect of reality, a reality largely hidden to us, and *existing therefore independently of our knowing it.*"[45] This expectation highlights Polanyi's realism, an expectation that applied just as much (and in some ways even more) to metaphysical knowledge as to more mundane forms of knowledge: reliable metaphysical knowledge signifies the existence of entities that can be said to be more real than those more mundane ones signified by empirical and historical forms of knowledge, inasmuch as such entities signify higher and more expansive levels of integration and achievement. Polanyi's ontology is neither a reductionistic empiricism nor an existential idealism, but neither does it require strict dualism; rather, the image that presents itself most readily is one of graduated multi-modalism.

Yet another observation that it will be helpful for us to recall has to do with Polanyi's account of the emergence and development of what he termed the "deductive sciences." Beginning with the "descriptive sciences," we seek to expand our apprehension and understanding of the world, a task that is furthered chiefly through the refinement of our language. The possibilities afforded by the descriptive sciences thus lead to the emergence of the "exact sciences," which in turn (through the further refinement of our language) leads to the possibility of developing purely "deductive sciences."[46] Like theoretical physics, pure mathematics, and abstract art, an objective understanding of divine transcendence, requiring as it does considerable methodological and conceptual clarification, is a visionary intellective effort aimed at elucidating an aspect of reality beyond our immediate purview.

All of this, however, merely acknowledges the possibility of aspiring to reliable knowledge of a transcendent God; it says little to nothing about the actual existence of God or even how we might responsibly go about obtaining such knowledge. One final reminder drawn from our earlier account of the realist character of Polanyi's epistemology will help us make this crucial next step, namely, his insight that the meaningful integrations of our knowledge all to varying degrees recapitulate the integrations of the comprehensive entities represented therein. In other words, the integration and achievement signified by (or as) our knowledge signifies the means whereby our indwelling intersects with the comprehensive entity at hand. Relative to the question of God, what this means is that Polanyi provides us with an alternative way of accounting for an expectation that is well represented in the theological tradition, namely, that our awareness of God follows from our experience or participation in his self-revelation; the *ordo cognoscendi*, as we have already seen, recapitulates the *ordo essendi*.

This, then, provides us with a Polanyian point of entry into an explicit consideration of the transcendence of God. A more comprehensive survey of the ramifications of this approach would proceed with an examination of how our apprehension and understanding of God's transcendence might appear from a variety of perspectives, such as the experience of salvation, the experience of revelation, the experience of mystical union, or the apprehension of God as "uncaused cause" (i.e., natural theology).[47] However, the parameters of the current study help delimit our approach to this question in two ways: first, our examination (in chapter four) of God's self-revelation in Jesus Christ and the Holy Spirit as a starting point for theological inquiry moves us in a particular direction; and second, our preoccupation with personhood further encourages us to limit our approach in ways that will help us address our distinct concerns. Both of these share a preoccupation with the person of Jesus Christ, and thus serve to throw us back on our earlier insights regarding the economic configuration of divine personal being. Having already outlined the parameters of a Polanyian articulation of the doctrine of the economic trinity and having now also charted a Polanyian approach to the question of divine transcendence, we can turn our attention to the challenge of exploring the doctrine of the immanent trinity as seen from a Polanyian perspective.

Immanent Divine Personal Being in Polanyian Perspective

In our review earlier of the "trinitarian problematic," we noted the need to attempt some accounting of the plurality and unity of God within a transcendent horizon. Likewise, both of the previous sections have heightened our sensitivity to the exigency of this task. We thus now turn to an exploration of the value of a Polanyian understanding of personal being, grounded in the concept of indwelling, relative to our understanding of the mutuality of the trinitarian persons and the life they share with one another in distinction from their presence and action in the creation.

In order to test the limits of our working model of personal being, we will depend as much as possible on the nomenclature and logic of indwelling throughout our exploration of relative transcendent divine personhood. This dependence reflects, not so much a desire to destabilize or replace more traditional trinitarian formulations and logic (e.g., descriptions of the Son as eternally begotten of the Father, or of the procession of the Spirit understood in terms of spiration, etc.), but rather a desire to establish the extent to which the vision of personal being promulgated throughout this study can accommodate the task we have set for ourselves. We can organize our efforts around two relatively straightforward questions. First, can a Polanyian notion of personhood help us understand the correspondence between each of the trinitarian persons and the divine nature? And second, how does a Polanyian notion of personhood help us understand the relations between the divine persons themselves? Consideration of the first of these questions will lead us naturally to that of the second.

Our earlier exploration of the relations between the divine persons in the economic configuration of the trinitarian life revolved around a principle drawn from the dogmatic tradition, namely, the consubstantiality of the Son and the Spirit to the Father. There is within the dogmatic tradition no question of our need to affirm the complete identification of each of the divine persons with the divine nature: the Father, the Son, and the Spirit are all fully divine and participate fully in divine knowing, acting, and being. Yet to say no more than this would leave us open to the charge that we are proffering a understanding of trinitarian personhood that suggests the correspondence between each of the divine persons and the divine nature is akin to that between individual subsistents and a common or universal nature, which because of its tritheist overtones is clearly unacceptable. This insight is further confirmed if we consider the question from the perspective afforded by our working model of Polanyian personhood: were we simply to presume a univocal Polanyian understanding of the existence of each of the trinitarian persons and attempt thereby to describe their participation in the divine essence, we would be left with a model of the divine life in which the relations between the persons themselves would be almost entirely accidental. Suggesting that a unadorned Polanyian model of personal indwelling is in itself capable of helping us articulate an understanding of the participation of the divine persons in God's act of being leaves us with three isolated individuals arbitrarily indwelling a distal horizon of shared action. Were we to reverse the direction of divine indwelling and suggest instead simply that the divine being indwells in the same way each of the trinitarian persons, we would be left with three distinct and unrelated instances of divine indwelling more reminiscent of modalism than tritheism.

We find some help in engaging this problem by recalling the logic of the doctrine of the *homoousious*. Our efforts at this point, however, must begin, not with an examination of the consubstantiality of the Father and the Son, but with a consideration of the correlation between the divine nature of God and the person of the Father. This is a theme that has been explored at some length in the theology of Thomas F. Torrance (among others). In particular, Torrance's insistence (on the one hand) that the name "Father" can refer to either the one being of God as well as to the hypostasis of the first person of the trinity and (on the other) that "the eternal Father is the one Principle of the Godhead" provides us with a perspective from which we can begin to work out in Polanyian terms an understanding of the place of the Father in the intratrinitarian relations.[48]

Polanyi described the emergence and development of human personhood (both phylogenetic and ontogenetic) in terms of a process of "anthropogenesis."[49] Polanyi here employed his notion of dual control on a grand scale, describing (in the broad sweep of his argument) the manner in which self-conscious life can be seen as the *"ordering principle"* that exercises marginal control over the boundary conditions supplied and sustained by "fortunate *environmental conditions*."[50] While we of course cannot think of the correspondence between the unity and plurality of God in terms of emergence (i.e., as if the latter signifies an emergent property of the former), this vision provides us with a clue that enables us to propose a means of understanding the correlation between the divine nature and the personhood of the Father. In keeping with our earlier observation that we cannot understand the participation of each of the trinitarian persons in the absolute being of God in an identical manner (i.e., because to do so would be to fall into tritheism or modalism, depending on our understanding of the manner of indwelling formally signified thereby), it now becomes evident that we can propose instead to understand the personalizing dynamics of the divine nature (i.e., both existence and subsistence) as the organizing principle of divine being that serve to ground a distinct personal identity. The (eternal) actualization of this distinct person (i.e., the Father) is thereby seen as the locus in and through which it is possible for the transcendent personalizing dynamics of the divine nature to be (eternally) actualized in particular forms of personal life. This eternal actualization signifies what we can recognize as a form of indwelling in which the transcendent dynamics of God's absolute personal being are integrated and interiorized in (but not as) the person of the Father; the personalizing effluence of divine being is manifest in the form of a person from whom it flows out in the actualization of communion.

From this vantage point, we can move to a consideration of the relations between the trinitarian persons in a manner that will also help us further elaborate our understanding of their consubstantiality (i.e., both their *circumincessio*, their coinherence in one another, as well as their *circuminsessio*, their coequal participation in the divine being); in other words, we come now to an analysis of the relations between the Father, the Son, and the Holy Spirit. Our first question here has to do with establishing whether or not Polanyi's thought has anything to offer relative to the question of the twin processions of the Son and the Spirit. To speak in somewhat general terms, one of the traditional distinctions between Eastern and Western trinitarian theology is the question of the processions and whether or not both the Son and the Spirit should be understood to proceed from the Father (so the East) or whether the Spirit must be understood to proceed from the Father and the Son (so the West). Does the Polanyian understanding of personal being we have been exploring thus far offer any insight into this question?

Addressing this issue involves clarifying how Polanyi's notion of indwelling and our own model of Polanyian personhood can inform our understanding of the generative activity of the Father. Although we affirm that the Father, Son, and Spirit coinhere in an eternal communion of complete interpersonal mutuality, we must also affirm the priority of the Father; to fail to do so would be to move dangerously close to tritheism (at least within a Polanyian milieu). We cannot, therefore, understand the relations between the trinitarian persons simply in terms comparable to Polanyi's elaboration of the mutual indwelling of human persons (intellective or otherwise), for such relations are never more than accidental. In order to understand how indwelling can inform our understanding of the procession of the Son and the Spirit from the Father, it is necessary for us to revisit briefly the details of Polanyi's phenomenology of indwelling.

Polanyi's explication of indwelling included descriptions of the way we both actively and passively participate in the integration and interiorization of the objects of our awareness.[51] The more meaningful and personal the manner of a particular instance of indwelling, the more both these dynamics will be in evidence. For example, Polanyi considered worship, in which the worshiper surrenders to contemplation of the divine by indwelling the "fabric of the religious ritual," to be "potentially the highest form of indwelling that is conceivable," one in which the individual is engaged in the attempt to overcome every obstacle that stands in the way of their complete surrender to God.[52] If we can thus envision indwelling as an activity that simultaneously signifies both active extension of the personal self through the interiorization of subsidiary elements as well as the surrender of oneself to the distinct character of the object(s) of our awareness, we will have a means of understanding the generation of the Son and the spiration of the Spirit in terms consistent with a Polanyian understanding of personal being.[53] For what this two-fold description of the practice of indwelling suggests is that we can see in the manifestation of the interpersonal divine community the fullest actualization of the concurrent striving and surrender of the Father in the exercise of his vocation within the Godhead.

This also gives a clear priority to the generation of the Son understood in terms consistent with the description of the Son as "eternally begotten of the Father" (as the Nicene Creed has it). The Son receives his personal being as a consequence of the simultaneous active and passive indwelling of the Father; this is what renders the Son the very image of the Father. However, the Son receives this form of personal being as the Son and not as a replica of the Father; the Father's act of begetting, following from the action of the transcendent personalizing dynamics within the Godhead, fosters a form of personal being actualized through both differentiation as well as relation in communion. The Father does not translate his own personal being to the Son, but through it translates the effulgence of the personalizing divine being in a pattern of integration and indwelling that evokes a distinct form of personal being that nonetheless bears his image.[54] Thus the Son is "God from God, Light from Light, true God from true God," his coequality within the divine being secured by virtue of his indwelling with the Father.

What thus emerges here is nothing other than a model of divine interpersonal relations. We have seen that according to Polanyi the act of indwelling involves both the integration of subsidiary elements and the interiorization of those elements so integrated within ourselves. We have also noted that indwelling requires both active striving and a more passive surrender, and that these dynamics are equally and simultaneously involved in both the process of integration and that of interiorization. By retracing our understanding of the generation of the Son with an eye to these principles, we can delineate a clearer sense of the notion of relation itself as required by the dynamics of indwelling. First, we noted that the actualization of the personal being of the Father involves both the active integration and interiorization of the personalizing dynamics of the Godhead within himself as well as the Father's acquiescence to the "boundary conditions" of the transcendent divine being. The Father is then seen as translating the personalizing dynamics of the Godhead in a form of active indwelling whereby he generates the Son as a distinct form of personal being after his own likeness.[55] The Son in turn submits himself to receiving from the Father his consubstantiality within the Godhead even as he actively integrates and interiorizes this identity, thereby realizing in himself his identity as the Son, the image of the Father. Thus in the interpersonal relation between the Father and the Son we can (formally) discern two modes of relation, one signifying the active indwelling of the Father in the Son and the other signifying the more passive indwelling of the Son in the extended personal being of the Father.[56] Relation here (i.e., the particular relation of the first two trinitarian persons) is seen as the horizon within which the Father and the Son mutually indwell one another in a manner specific to their respective identities (which are not *a priori* to their relation, but grounded in the relation itself). A Polanyian notion of personal being thus offers a view of divine personhood, not as itself a relation, but as signifying a *mode of relation.*

Understanding the generation of the Son in the terms outlined above highlights the rationale behind the assertion that the generation of the Son must be seen to have (formal) priority over the procession of the Spirit; were the spiration of the Spirit to follow in the same manner (i.e., from the Father), there could not but be two Sons.[57] The question of the procession of the Spirit thus presents itself at this point. If our understanding of the procession of the Spirit cannot be said to follow in an identical manner that of the Son, it can be said to recapitulate the same logic of mutual indwelling.

We have seen that the generation of the Son follows as a consequence of the Father's translation of the personalizing dynamics of existence and subsistence (i.e., relationality and individuality) within the transcendent being of God. The spiration of the Spirit recapitulates this movement, but in a different manner than is manifest in the relation between the Father and the Son.

For here the Father and the Son within their relation of mutual indwelling translate these same personalizing dynamics in the procession of a third distinct person, the Spirit. Because the procession of the third trinitarian person emerges from the relation between the first two, the form of personal being actualized as the Spirit in itself signifies communion (i.e., the mutuality of the Father and Son and their coequal participation in the spiration of the Spirit). Whereas the generation of the Son actualizes a form of personal being grounded in the indwelling of the Father in his self-giving to another, the procession of the Spirit actualizes a form of personal being grounded in the mutuality of participation between the Father and the Son in their shared giving. Thus, whereas the Son evinces a more passive form of indwelling in his integration and interiorization of the indwelling of the Father, his participation in the spiration of the Spirit is more active; he is here no longer simply interiorizing that which he receives, but actively involved in extending the personalizing being of God to the Spirit, thereby participating in the generation of another personal relation marked by mutual indwelling.[58]

It cannot be said that the Father and the Son, through respective forms of independent action, contribute to the procession of the Spirit, nor can it be said that the Son functions as the indwelt self of the Father through which the Father extends the personalizing dynamics of the Godhead in the procession of the Spirit. Rather, the mutuality of the Father and the Son is itself integrated and interiorized in (as) the Spirit. The mutuality of the Father and the Son itself thus signifies a mode of relation, as does the integration and interiorization as the Spirit this mode of mutual indwelling. It is by virtue of the fact that the procession of the Spirit follows from the translation of the personalizing dynamics of the divine being through a mode of relation that signifies communion that there is no fourth divine person; the Spirit is himself the fullness and perfection of the form of personal being that arises from the manner of indwelling grounded in the mutuality of personal relation. Any form of personal being arising out of the mode of interpersonal relation signified by the mutuality of all three divine persons would therefore necessarily be contingent.[59]

We now have before us a tentative outline of the relational personhood of God grounded in a Polanyian understanding of personal being. We have explored the contours of this understanding of the trinitarian relations in relatively abstract terms, relying almost entirely on the language and logic of indwelling to formulate our survey. There is much that would still need to be said for us to presume that we might proffer a thorough accounting of the

trinitarian being of God; in particular, we would need to devote more attention to the question of how the image of the intratrinitarian life of God as
explicated above helps us understand the particular manner in which each of
the divine persons participates in the unified action of God (e.g., in the creation, redemption, and consummation of the cosmos). We cannot at this point
begin to address the range of questions that arise from this multivalent problem. We can, however, offer two suggestions as to how such inquiry might
fruitfully proceed. First, Polanyi's understanding of the acceptance of one's
"calling," understood in terms of the actualization of the responsibilities that
inhere within one's personal milieu, might provide a means whereby the
traditional doctrine of appropriations could be worked out in terms consistent
with the Polanyian tenor of our efforts.[60] Second (and more in keeping with
our analysis in this section), we are now at a place at which we are better
able to approach the question of absolute divine personhood, for what our
examination of transcendent divine relationality has revealed is a way of
understanding the divine nature such that the intratrinitarian relations are
seen as exercising marginal control over the boundary conditions manifest in
the divine being.

We have steadily been moving toward an explicit consideration of the
notion of God conceived of in terms of absolute personal being. Having
begun with an examination of the personal being of God considered from the
perspective of God's redemptive presence and action in Jesus Christ and the
Holy Spirit, we then considered the question of God's transcendence before
turning to the question of the transcendent relational personhood of God. We
have thus now reached that point at which we are prepared to take up the
question of whether or not we must think of the personal being of God in
terms that are restricted to the relations between the three divine persons or if
there might be some other way of conceiving of divine personhood.[61] This
will require that we bring to bear the full weight of the conviction that the
self-revelation of God in the world provides us with a starting point for reflecting on the transcendent life of God. In more Polanyian terms, we can say
that we are leaving behind the more descriptive accounts of Christian experience and are moving into the realm of "increasing formalization and symbolic manipulation," which, even though it means moving into a field of
inquiry characterized by "decreasing contact with experience," will enable us
to establish in more precise terms the focus of our efforts.[62]

We can take our initial lead in these efforts from the long-standing practice in the theological tradition of the development of a theology of perfect

being. The notion of divine perfection and simplicity has long been a staple
of theological inquiry, and is represented paradigmatically by Anselm of
Canterbury's development of the so-called ontological argument (i.e., the
demonstration of the necessary existence of "that than which a greater cannot
be thought").[63] Anselm's arguments explore the nature of divine existence,
power, impassibility, knowledge, compassion, and justice, but give scant
attention to the question of divine personhood, even though he does point out
that the perfect being of God exists as Father, Son, and Holy Spirit.[64] Our
concern at this point is not so much to pick up on the particular arguments
proffered by Anselm and his followers; although the question of God's absolute being continues to generate considerable discussion, it is in itself not
one that we should expect can immediately contribute to our own efforts
(precisely because one does not often find therein focused consideration of
the question of personhood).[65] Rather, our mention of Anselm's argument at
this point provides us with something of a benchmark by which we can
measure our own efforts to elaborate a concept of personal being "than
which a greater cannot be thought."[66]

One of the primary challenges of contemporary trinitarian theology is
explicating transcendent divine personhood in terms that do justice both to its
unitive as well as its relative dimensions.[67] We must therefore find a way of
characterizing each of these in a manner that both accords to some degree
with our mundane and contingent experience of them while also intending a
transcendent reality that exceeds the contingence and immanence of our
experience. It is also necessary within a Christian context (i.e., in light of the
doctrine of creation *ex nihilo*) to explore the possible ways in which we
might understand the dependence of that which we experience and understand as contingent and finite on that which is necessary and eternal, while at
the same time not losing sight of the integrity and freedom of that which is
seen to be contingent.[68]

In the midst of our earlier development of a Polanyian understanding of
personal being (in chapter three), we noted that it would be necessary for us
to supplement the more functional description we arrived at then with insights from the theological tradition in order to provide some ontological
depth to our efforts; our explication of absolute divine personhood represents
a decisive attempt at such integration. Our initial explication of personhood
yielded a tripartite image that closely resembled Polanyi's notion of the "tacit
triad." Following David Kettle's analysis of the mutuality of dual points of
indeterminacy, we posited the simultaneous emergence of three distinct but

interdependent horizons of personhood, namely, the indwelling self, the indwelt or objectified self, and the relational or social matrices wherein personal being arises and is sustained. We also noted that the interaction of these three coordinates could be likened to the kind of "molar achievement" Polanyi associated with comprehensive entities that subsumed various levels of complexity. Our task now is to examine the extent to which we might successfully employ this understanding of personal being in an effort to apprehend the nature of absolute or unitive divine personhood in terms that are also consistent with our exposition of relational divine personhood.

Several problems immediately confront us when we consider the ramifications our working model has for absolute divine personhood. First, the unreservedly relational nature of this model implies that God, like all personal beings, accomplishes the "molar achievement" of the successful integration of his personal being in relation with another; the ghost of Fichte is seen here lurking in the background. Second, the notion that divine being can be characterized as a "comprehensive entity" subsuming levels of varying complexity seems to compromise God's simplicity; if comprehensive entities manifest a certain contingence and are "liable to dissolution" (e.g., the disintegration of a lower level following the loss of marginal control from a higher level), then it would seem we have gone a considerable way towards subjecting God to the vicissitudes of both space and time.[69] We could also restate both of these problems in more Polanyian terms by pointing out the relative incongruity between the idea of absolute divine being and that of indwelling: what possible horizon could we imagine through which God might by indwelling it integrate a range of subsidiary elements in the actualization of his own being?[70]

We find in the traditional scholastic distinction between essence and existence a clue as to how we can overcome such challenges. What the distinction between essence and existence suggests is that it is possible to differentiate various aspects of divine being even if we maintain that we do not expect such distinctions to be anything other than purely formal.[71] In saying this, we need not commit ourselves unreservedly to adopting other elements of scholastic thought; we are, in other words, borrowing a methodological principle without at the same time committing ourselves to the wider conceptual horizon out of which it comes. What remains to be seen is how this move can be usefully employed within our own Polanyian milieu.

In order to maintain our commitment to the elaboration of an understanding of absolute personhood (i.e., a sense of personal being "than which a greater cannot be thought"), it seems we must at least initially maintain a commitment to the notion that the form of being we are seeking here is necessary and thus simple; we must not suppose, in other words, that absolute personal being finds itself dependent in any sense on anything other than itself.[72] Neither, however, does it seem that the notion of necessary simple existence is sufficient as a means of saying all that we might about the character of absolute being. Rather, absolute being must be seen as the source and ground of all forms of being, necessary and otherwise; Pannenberg has made this point in a manner especially relevant for our efforts.[73] We are thus led to the question of which distinctions we might make relative to the concept of absolute personal being.

There is, as we have repeatedly noted, considerable controversy today about whether or not we can continue to affirm that those attributes traditionally associated with the concept of perfect being can be applied to God.[74] However, there can be no question as to whether or not such attributes have been employed in the past as part of efforts aimed at elucidating a Christian understanding of God.[75] Our purpose at this point has less to do with trying to resolve contemporary controversies and more to do with drawing on those aspects of the dogmatic tradition that will help us ascertain the theological viability of a Polanyian notion of personal being. For our purposes, then, the traditional formal distinctions between divine being, divine acting, divine knowing, and the divine attributes will prove especially helpful; even though we would affirm that the notion of absolute being (understood as both necessary and simple) requires us to affirm that there is no real separation between the actualization of these elements, their formal distinction can be helpful as we sort through the challenges associated with elaborating a workable understanding of absolute personhood.

Such differentiations provide us with a way of making sense of how we might talk about God's actualization of absolute being in terms of the kind of "molar achievement" Polanyi associated with comprehensive entities. Formally differentiating between divine being, knowing, acting, and the various divine attributes provides us with a series of horizons that arranged in a certain pattern yield an image of "emergent" absolute personal being. The assertion of simple and necessary existence provides the fundamental boundary conditions within which we find it possible to elaborate the possibility of understanding not only being, but also freedom, benevolence, goodness, justice, power, and other attributes we would expect to accompany the existence of a necessary, simple being. Some consideration of absolute knowledge also needs to be taken into account, the notion of which introduces a higher level of integration than can be had relative to a narrow consideration of bald existence. Similarly, the notion of divine action, like that of divine knowledge, offers yet another level of integration that could be said to exercise a determinative influence (i.e., marginal control) on our understanding of the attributes of divine freedom, benevolence, knowledge, etc.[76] Finally, the notion of absolute divine knowledge and absolute divine action both signify a still-more expansive horizon of absolute being, namely, that of absolute personhood, understood as the "level" of divine being that can be said to exercise marginal control over the other horizons of absolute divine being much the same way the organizational principles of contingent entities harness through marginal control the subsidiary elements of their system(s), thereby actualizing in them patterns of existence that in and of themselves they cannot signify.

This line of thinking is consistent with our working Polanyian model of personal being. We can thus affirm that the dynamics that necessarily attend the emergence and development of contingent personal being can be recognized in a formal sense relative to the question of absolute divine being as well; the fact that the distinctions between being, attributes, knowledge, action, and personhood function in a purely formal manner relative to our understanding of absolute personhood, whereas we would affirm that they function in a real (ontological) manner relative to created persons, serves only to highlight the difference between necessary and contingent being. Thus, the reality and meaning of relational personhood (both human and divine) can be seen to be derivative and dependent on absolute personhood.

The question remains as to whether or not this understanding of absolute personhood allows us to say that God is *a* person in an absolute sense, to which it seems we must respond in the negative. While we were by way of the formal distinctions outlined above able to recognize in the notion of absolute being the tendency towards both subsistent (i.e., individual) and existent (i.e., relational) characteristics of personhood, it would be less accurate to say that these signify the existence of a particular person and more accurate to say that we see in this notion of absolute personhood the operation of personalizing dynamics.[77] Although we have identified the form of transcendent relationality and the form of transcendent individuality in God, we should refrain from thinking that we have thereby identified a form of transcendent personhood in the sense of there being a single divine person. Were we to suggest that we can by way of the method employed here apprehend in God a single absolute person, then we would have to say that the distinctions we made above are not merely formal but real; we would thereby admit no uncertain measure of contingence into our understanding of absolute being (i.e., the threat of the dissolution of the comprehensive entity signified by absolute personhood would present itself quite forcefully).

Given that we have identified in God (conceived in terms of absolute being) the operation of what we have term "personalizing dynamics" (explicated in a manner consistent with a Polanyian notion of personhood), but have determined that these dynamics cannot be understood to signify the existence of a single divine person, can we still hold out the possibility of understanding divine personhood in Polanyian terms? Answering this question involves situating our consideration of absolute personal being within the larger sweep of our efforts in this chapter. In other words, our conclusions at this point help flesh out our earlier description of the "emergence" of the person of the Father relative to the divine nature and his sharing of that nature in the procession of the Son and the Spirit. Whereas we earlier noted that the absolute personal being of God can be (formally) said to exercise marginal control over the boundary conditions established by the divine nature, we see now that what this means is that the transcendent personalizing dynamics of the Godhead are actualized in nothing other than the relations that inhere between the Father, the Son, and the Holy Spirit. In more traditional theological parlance, this means that the unity of the three divine persons is itself the divine being. As in our consideration of relative divine personhood, Polanyi's account of emergence and marginal control provides us with a way of thinking about how the Father, the Son, and the Holy Spirit actualize the superlative essence of God in their mutual relations.

Correlating Economic and Immanent Divine Personal Being

In some respects, the question of how to articulate an understanding of the correlation between the economic trinity and the immanent trinity is one of the more challenging dimensions of trinitarian theology. Basically, what this question presents us with is the need to demonstrate how it is possible that God can be present and active in the world in a way that does not compromise his freedom and existence. We can only ever say that there is one Father, one Son, and one Spirit, and that there are only ever two processions in the generation of the Son and the spiration of the Spirit; this is the point made so forcefully by Rahner's *Grundaxiom*. How, then, are we to understand, for example, the correlation between the birth of Jesus and the eternal generation of the Son? Or again, what is the connection between the Church's reception of the Spirit at Pentecost and the eternal spiration of the Spirit in the relationship between the Father and the Son?

We cannot hope to solve this problem in a satisfactory manner by simply subsuming the doctrine of the economic trinity under that of the immanent trinity, or vice versa. Were we, for example, to collapse the former into the latter, we would end up denying the historicity of the incarnation (and, indeed, of the whole of the creation), and were we to comprehend the latter within the former we would end up denying God's transcendence. The twin doctrines of the economic trinity and of the immanent trinity do not speak univocally at all points and should not be made to do so.

Since our primary concern has been to develop an understanding of divine personhood consistent with Polanyi's thought, we will do well to continue so delimiting our efforts at this point as well. Thus, the question before us becomes one of how to conceive of the personhood of the Father, of the Son, and of the Spirit in a way that does justice to both their respective economic and immanent configurations. This problem first appeared earlier in this chapter when we noted, in the midst of our review of the doctrine of the economic trinity, that the personal indwelling signified by the incarnation in no way means that the eternal Son is for a time displaced from the eternal life of God, but is rather the actualization in space and time of the very form of personal being that is actualized in the immanent trinity as the Son.

As it turns out, it is precisely in terms of the personal being of God that we are best able to make sense of the correlation between God's presence and action in the creation and God's transcendent life. Attempts to work out a satisfactory solution on any other terms are likely to end in frustration, owing to the fact that such efforts will largely devolve into trying to figure out a way to reconcile the transcendent, necessary nature (or substance) of God with the mundane, contingent nature (or substance) of the world. In other words, attempts to work out the correlation between the economic trinity and the immanent trinity in terms of nature rather than in terms of person will fall into dualistic modes of thought that make it near impossible to arrive at a satisfactory resolution to this problem.

When we approach this issue from the perspective of personal being, what we find is that we must make sense of the personhood of the Father, the Son, and the Spirit, as well as the unified personal being of God, in a way that discourages us from thinking that the actualization of divine personhood relative to the creation is not immediately grounded in the eternal actualization of their personhood relative to one another. At the same time, we must also be able to say that the actualization of divine personhood relative to the creation is not a necessary element in the eternal actualization of the personal being of God. In terms of the ontology of mutual indwelling that we have been pursuing herein, what this means is that we must affirm that the indwelling whereby the Father and the Son, for example, achieve the respective integration of their distinct forms of existence is the same in both the incarnation and in the eternal generation of the Son. Likewise, the transcendent procession of the Spirit via the mutual indwelling of the Father and the Son cannot be said to be different or distinct from the gifting of the Spirit to the church and the world by the risen Christ. But in neither case could we say that, for example, that the incarnation is a necessary element in the eternal actualization of the personal being of the Son, or that Pentecost is a necessary episode in the actualization of the Spirit.

What is thus needed is an understanding of indwelling that allows us to affirm distinct modes of personal being for a single person. Here perhaps even more than in our earlier consideration of absolute divine personhood we are stretching Polanyi's categories beyond their original design. But we need not abandon a Polanyian perspective at this point, for what we find is that the concept of mutual indwelling, understood as the reciprocal interiorization and extension of comprehensive entities themselves subject to dual control, provides us with a means of preserving divine transcendence while also affirming the presence and activity of God in the creation.

More specifically, what this perspective affords is a way of describing how God and the world mutually indwell one another. This mutual indwelling is asymmetrical inasmuch as the world depends on God, but God never depends on the world; the world is created and sustained (and will be consummated) in a manner consistent with the pattern of the life of God, but the transcendent life of God is grounded, not in the relationship God shares with the creation, but in the relations between the three divine persons.[78] Relative to the mode of relation that God has to the world, what this means is that in the relations between the Father, the Son, and the Spirit, God extends the offer to participate in the divine life to that which is not God (i.e., the creation) and in so doing interiorizes the object of this action within the divine life. Understood in terms of the dynamics of dual control, what this means is that the act of creation signifies God's exercise of marginal control over the lower-level boundary conditions of contingent being whereby God brings into existence that which is not himself, not by setting the creation at a distance, but within the divine life itself.[79] In other words, this act is carried out in a manner that is precisely in keeping with the dynamics of the relations between the divine persons themselves. Each divine person internalizes the act of creation as part of their personal identity, but none of them depend on their participation in the act of creation for the actualization of their being; the latter is accomplished in their relations with one another.

Relative to the mode of relation that the world has to God, what this means is that God is the one in whom the world lives and moves and has its being (Acts 17.28). The dynamics governing the emergence and development of the cosmos exhibit to varying degrees the dynamics of the life of God. But this also allows for a considerable degree of freedom within the created order, for God's exercise of marginal control leaves open a wide range of possibilities regarding the precise patterns of the boundary conditions of the world. God's presence and action in the world is consistent with the internal dynamics of the creation, rather than being extrinsically imposed.[80] The incarnation of the Son, for example, and the gifting of the Spirit signify the actualization in space and time of the patterns of divine personal life actualized in eternity. The life of the world is thus immanent in the divine life, but cannot be said to transcend it.

Earlier in this chapter we noted that any form of personal being arising out of the mode of interpersonal relation signified by the mutuality of all three divine persons would be contingent. What we see now is that it is precisely in terms of receiving the gift of participation in the divine being that the world can be said to abide within the interpersonal matrix of divine relations that is the life of God. Scilicet, we have here the beginnings of a trinitarian theology of creation delineated in terms of indwelling. Further exposition would require us to explore the ways that each of the divine persons participate in this action in ways appropriate to their distinct respective identities; this, however, would carry us far beyond the parameters of the current study. For now, it is sufficient for us to note that our efforts in this section have led us once again to recognize both the ontological priority of the concept of the person and the value of Polanyi's thought as a resource for articulating the meaning of personal being.

Conclusion

We have now completed our survey of the question of divine personhood as seen from a Polanyian perspective. Having begun with a description of the complex of issues one must engage when attempting to articulate an understanding of God's personal being, we then examined both the unity and the plurality of divine personhood within the context of both God's redemptive self-revelation and the transcendent immanent life of God, and ended by examining the correspondence between these. We have throughout been guided by a Polanyian understanding of personhood, itself grounded in the conjoined concepts of dual control, indwelling, and molar achievement, and have in general found that (first) the theological enterprise is quite responsive to mutual exchange with Polanyi's philosophy and (second) a Polanyian understanding of personhood provides interesting insights into familiar theological formulas and problems.

Perhaps the most obvious conclusion that we can draw at this point has to do with the rather programmatic nature of our efforts: we have gone some distance towards reinterpreting the doctrine of the trinity along Polanyian lines, but have at the same time introduced many new questions. Further clarification would be necessary in order to ascertain the extent to which the paradigm we have outlined in this study would be useful as a guide for further reflection and inquiry. More thorough consideration, for example, of how a Polanyian understanding of trinitarian theology might encourage a reconsideration of the doctrine of appropriations is but one of the questions we would need to ask. Similarly, considerably more work would need to be done unpacking the opportunities a Polanyian reading of the doctrine of the trinity provides for exploring alternative ways of describing the relationship between God and the world relative to God's creative, redemptive, and consummative activity.

In other words, what the current project opens up (and, indeed, almost requires) is nothing less than a fairly unique way of pursuing what Stratford Caldecott has referred to as "the renewal of Christian cosmology."[81] In the midst of his examination of the trinitarian theology of Hans Urs von Balthasar, Caldecott calls for the recovery of theology as a "regenerate science," a mode of inquiry that would not "even do to minerals and vegetables what modern science threatens to do to man himself. When it explained it would not explain away. When it spoke of the parts it would remember the whole. While studying the *It* it would not lose what Martin Buber has called the *Thou*-situation."[82] Caldecott holds out the hope that theology can once again be a discipline open to the reality of the personal without losing any of its aspirations to objectivity, which is of course one of the primary aims of Polanyi's philosophical work.

It is also worth noting that, for Caldecott, it is only a robust doctrine of the trinity that can provide a sure foundation for the development of such a "regenerate science." Caldecott appreciates Balthasar's appropriation of the Thomistic distinction between "essence" and "existence" in all that is not God, as it helps foster an awareness of the extent to which created entities receive everything from God (even their capacity to receive) in a way that fosters their distinction and independent integrity even as it maintains their dependence on God.[83] Additionally, Caldecott picks up on Balthasar's insistence that only the doctrine of the Trinity provides an adequate means of understanding the world as the creative work of God; the unity-in-distinction between the divine persons becomes the foundation for the unity-in-distinction between God and the world (although the correspondence between these two is understood to be analogical).[84] Caldecott's insistence on the centrality of trinitarian theology for theological inquiry encourages further reflection on how a personalistic, Polanyian account of the doctrine of God might afford new perspectives on other theological questions as well.

Several other of the more salient elements of Caldecott's arguments are worth brief mention at this point, given the extent to which they help further elucidate the potential contributions of an expansive Polanyian theology. His analysis of the collapse of cosmological thinking in modern thought, for example, invites comparison with Polanyi's own reading of the intellectual history of modernity.[85] Caldecott identifies a number of stages that mark the development of Western thought, from the prescientific, inductive thought of the classical tradition, through the advent of scientific awareness as a consequence of Christian theism, to the bifurcation of faith and reason in the early modern period and the emergence of secularized, mechanistic thought, to the eventual collapse of confidence altogether in science and reason in the late modern period. The advent of postmodern science has opened the way, Caldecott believes, towards the recovery of more integrative understanding of knowing in which the mutuality of the subject and the object is affirmed and the essential unity of all knowledge is recognized.[86]

Another important aspect of Caldecott's program is his commitment to the inextricability of epistemology and axiology. Human beings are guided in their quest for knowledge by heuristic passions that seek satisfaction in the apprehension of qualitative (as opposed to quantitative) accounts of reality. In a manner very much in keeping with Polanyi's explication of the function of *Gestalten* in human knowing, Caldecott proposes that the quest for beauty and elegance should be understood as a primary impetus within all acts of awareness.[87] Further, the axiological dimension (understood not only in terms of beauty but also of virtue) dimension of knowledge helps account for the integrative nature of knowledge: "Beauty unites not only truth with goodness, but also observer and observed—and knowledge in its full sense is found only in this marriage or compenetration of knower and known. ... But this means that [knowing] is a function of love, a response of love called forth by what is received in the given by one who is disposed to gratitude."[88]

Caldecott even helps clarify the necessarily christological and pneumatological starting point for theological reflection in a way that is largely consistent with our arguments in this and the previous chapter. We have seen that the person of Jesus Christ plays a central (indeed, a determinative) role in both the correlation of faith and reason and the actualization of the kind of transformation necessary for fruitful theological inquiry. Similarly, the integrity of Caldecott's (Balthasar's) vision is grounded in the person of the *Logos*: the life, death, and resurrection of Christ stands as the Archimedean point uniting the created order to the Creator in a pattern reminiscent of the divine life itself. In the person of Christ it becomes possible to recapitulate (relative to both knowing and being) the simultaneous unity and distinction between God and the creation in a pattern grounded in the divine being.[89]

Clearly, what we have accomplished in this study is merely initiate a line of thinking that hints at much larger possibilities; we have before us, to use terms consistent with Polanyi's thought, the intimation of a hidden reality, or at least the intimation of hitherto untapped possibilities for thinking about familiar questions. Pursuance of this vision would require careful and deliberate effort along multiple lines of inquiry. As Avery Dulles once astutely observed, a "thoroughgoing renewal of theology along the lines indicated by Polanyi could profitably engage the joint efforts of many theologians for a considerable span of years."[90] If it can be said that our efforts herein have provided a worthwhile furtherance to such renewal, we will have accomplished our purpose.

Notes

Introduction

1. See <www.trinitywallstreet.org/u/d/news/finfo_35.html>, a page on the Institute's website (downloaded on Nov. 6, 2001); cf. the website for the Episcopal News Service, <www.episcopalchurch.org/ens/2001-132.html> (downloaded on Nov. 6, 2001).

2. See, e.g., Michael Drippe, "The Christian Theological Understanding of the Human Person," in *Epiphany Journal* 14 (1994), 29-43; Jean Galot, "La definition de la personne, relation, et sujet," in *Gregorianum* 75 (1994), 281-299; idem, "'Un seule personne, une seule hypostase': Origine et sens de la formule de Chalcedoine," in *Gregorianum* 70 (1989), 251-276; Laurent Sentis, "Penser la personne," in *Nouvelle Revue Theologique* 116 (1994), 862-873; C. David Grant, "Personal and Impersonal Concepts of God: a Tension Within Contemporary Theology," in *Encounter* 49 (1988), 79-91; C.R. Priebbenow, "The Son and the Spirit as Distinct Persons of the Trinity," in *Lutheran Theological Journal* 20 (1986), 76-80; Adrian Thatcher, "The Personal God and the God Who Is a Person," in *Religious Studies* 21 (1985), 61-75; Andre de Halleux, "'Hypostase' et 'Personne' dans la formation du dogme trinitaire (c. 375-381)," in *Revue d'Histoire Ecclesiastique* 79 (1984), 313-369, 625-670; Lawrence B. Porter, "On Keeping 'Persons' in the Trinity: a Linguistic Approach to Trinitarian Thought," in *Theological Studies* 41 (1980), 530-548; et al.

3. E.g., Han Urs von Balthasar, working in part off of the insights of Jacques Maritain, suggests that "*person* in the sense of a human being, and in contradistinction to mere individuality, receives its special dignity in history when it is illuminated by the unique theological meaning [of the term]. When this is not the case, however, the human person sinks back into the sphere of mere individuality," in his "On the Concept of the Person," trans. P. Verhalen, in *Communio* 13 (1986), 19. Balthasar's characterization of "person" as a distinctly theological category is, to some extent, very much in keeping with the Christian theological tradition, both Western and Eastern. For example, Thomas Aquinassuggested that it would be impossible to recognize the reality of divine personhood apart from revelation; see Thomas Aquinas, *Summa theologiæ*, ed. T. Gilby (New York and London: Blackfriars in conjunction with McGraw-Hill and Eyre & Spottiswoode, 1964), 1a.32.1. Similarly, John of Damascus characterized the Christian elaboration of the doctrine of personhood as a distinct improvement on the Greek philosophical notion of distinction according to subsistence; see John of Damascus, *The Orthodox Faith*, Fathers of the Church 37, ed. J. Deferrari, et al, trans. F.H. Chase (New York: Fathers of the Church, 1958), I.7.

4. Cf. Stephen Hipp's observation that the "quest for personhood is therefore situated within the context of coming to an understanding of the supreme truth constituting the heart of the theologian's speculation, namely the distinction of Persons within the unity of essence, and it is *ex intelligentia mysterii Trinitatis*" that our understanding of not only christological and pneumatological personhood as manifest in the personal self-revelation

of God are also seen to make sense, but even our understanding of ourselves as persons; see Stephen A. Hipp, *"Person" in Christian Tradition and the Conception of St. Albert the Great: a Systematic Study of its Concept as Illuminated by the Mysteries of the Trinity and the Incarnation* (Münster: Druckhaus Aschendorff, 2001), 13. Cf. John S. Grabowski, "Person: Substance and Relation," in *Communio* 22 (1995), 139-140.

5.   This sense of historical distance can also be measured to some extent by the number of contemporary studies that undertake to develop a theological understanding of personhood relative to cognate studies conducted in other areas of formal inquiry (e.g. philosophy, psychology, anthropology, biology, etc.). At this point it is only necessary to note that one of the things such interdisciplinary efforts signify is a distinct lack of consensus with regard to the nature of personal identity; no one discipline seems capable of articulating what it means to be a person. John Teske characterizes the tension manifest in contemporary studies of personhood as the result of seismic shifts in the culture, shifts that have not only undermined confidence in traditional religious teaching and experience, but have also resulted in the demystification of the world and life, an abiding sense of confusion typical of a culture characterized by untrammeled individualism, and a loss of confidence in our ability even to claim reliable self-knowledge. All of these developments, Teske suggests, make the question of personhood *"the* spiritual problem of our time,"* in John A. Teske, "The Social Construction of the Human Spirit," in *The Human Person in Science and Theology*, ed. N.H. Gregersen, W.B. Drees, & U. Görman (Grand Rapids: Wm. B. Eerdman's, 2000), 199. Teske notes that his analysis of modern notions of the self depends to a significant degree on the work of Roy Baumeister; see Baumeister's "How the Self Became a Problem: a Psychological Review of Historical Research," in *Journal of Personality and Social Psychology* 52 (1987), 163-176; idem, *Identity: Cultural Change and the Struggle for Self* (New York: Oxford University, 1986).

6.   Rowan Williams has outlined this tension relative in particular to the question of christological personhood. "Some, indeed," he suggests, "would probably say that the supposed orthodox schema is at least as inconceivable as it is incredible, because it is not possible in the contemporary philosophical climate … to conceive of human nature independently of the historicity, 'internal' and 'external', the contingency, the *Werden*, the 'becomingness', of the human subject. The demise of the idea of a unitary, non-spatial, supra-temporal self renders the Chalcedonian model not only formalist and mythological, but simply nonsensical," in Rowan Williams, "'Person' and 'Personality' in Christology," in *Downside Review* 94 (1976), 254. Cf. Hipp, *"Person" in Christian Tradition*, 15-16.

7.   See, e.g., Egbert Schroten, "What Makes a Person?" in *Theology* 97, no. 776 (1994), 98-105; John F. Crosby, "The Incommunicability of Human Persons," in *The Thomist* 57 (1993), 403-442; Christopher Kiesling, "On Relating to the Persons of the Trinity," in *Theological Studies* 47 (1986), 599-616; Kallistos of Diokleia, "The Human Person as Icon of the Trinity," in *Sobornist* 8 (1986), 6-23; John Drury, "Personal and Impersonal in Theology," in *Theology* 87, no. 720 (1984), 427-431; Kallistos Ware, "The Mystery of the Human Person," in *Sobornist* 3 (1981), 62-69; et al.

8.   See, e.g., Thomas F. Torrance, *Trinitarian Perspectives: Towards Doctrinal Agreement* (Edinburgh: T & T Clark, 1994); idem, *Theology in Reconciliation: Essays Towards Evangelical and Catholic Unity in East and West* (Grand Rapids: Wm. B. Eerdman's, 1975).

9. See, e.g., F. Sontag and M.D. Bryant, eds., *God: the Contemporary Discussion* (Barry-town: Unification Theological Seminary, 1982); Gary Legenhausen, "Is God a Person?" in *Religious Studies* 22 (1986), 307-323; Balthasar, "On the Concept of the Person," 25-26.

10. See, e.g., Daniel J. Price, *Karl Barth's Anthropology in Light of Modern Thought* (Grand Rapids: Wm. B. Eerdman's, 2002); idem, "Discovering a Dynamic Concept of the Person in Both Psychology and Theology," in *Perspectives on Science and Christian Faith* 45 (1993), 170-181; N.H. Gregersen, W.B. Drees, & U. Görman, eds., *The Human Person in Science and Theology* (Grand Rapids: Wm. B. Eerdman's, 2000); Nancey Murphy, "The Human Person: a Nonreductive Physicalist Account," in *Dialog* 38 (1999): 212-220; idem, "Physicalism Without Reductionism: Toward a Scientifically, Philosophically, and Theologically Sound Portrait of Human Nature," in *Zygon* 34 (1999): 551-572; Donald M. MacKay, "Brains and Persons," in *Zygon* 20, no. 4 (1985), 401-412; David Lyon, "Images of the Person in Theology and Sociology," in *Crux* 14, no. 2 (1978), 15-39; et al.

11. E.g., Mark C. Taylor's explication of the "disappearance of the self," a characteristic of postmodern thought he believes to be inextricably bound up with the "death of God," the "end of history," and the "closing of the book." See Taylor's *Erring: a Postmodern A/theology* (Chicago: University of Chicago, 1984), esp. 34-51.

12. Cf. Nancey Murphy's comments (following Jeffrey Stout) with regard to the extent to which the development of a viable theological anthropology would be a necessary first step towards organizing a number of areas of theological inquiry; see Murphy's *Beyond Liberalism and Fundamentalism: How Modern and Postmodern Philosophy Set the Theological Agenda* (Valley Forge: Trinity, 1996), 85, 109. Murphy quotes Stout's *The Flight From Authority: Religion, Morality, and the Quest for Autonomy* (Notre Dame: University of Notre Dame, 1981), 148-149.

13. This somewhat haphazard taxonomy of personalist thought is not intended to suggest that the individuals mentioned here can be taken as representative of distinct "schools," or even that such "schools" can be said to exist in any thoroughgoing sense; our organization of these individuals here intends nothing other than a cursory and convenient way of acknowledging the variety of efforts put forth thus far toward the development of a robust personalist method for theological inquiry. A comprehensive survey of personalist thought has yet to be written, but more circumspect efforts include John F. Crosby, *Personalist Papers* (Washington, D.C.: Catholic University of America, 2004); idem, *The Selfhood of the Human Person* (Washington, D.C.: Catholic University of America, 1996); idem, *The Incommunicability of Human Persons* (Washington, D.C.: Thomist Press, 1993); Rufus Burrow, Jr., *Personalism: a Critical Introduction* (St. Louis: Chalice Press, 1999); A.R.C. Duncan, *On the Nature of Persons* (New York: Peter Lang, 1990); Paul Deats and Carol Robb, eds., *The Boston Personalist Tradition in Philosophy, Social Ethics, and Theology* (Macon: Mercer University, 1986); J.B. Coats, *The Crisis of the Human Person: Some Personalist Interpretations* (London: Longmans, Green, and Co., 1949).

1. The Mind in Action

1. The definitive biographical account of Polanyi's life and work is Walter Taussig Scott and Martin X. Moleski, *Michael Polanyi: Scientist and Philosopher* (Oxford and New York: Oxford University Press, 2005).

2. Richard Gelwick, *The Way of Discovery* (New York: Oxford University, 1977), 31.

3. E.g., Michael Polanyi, "Science: its Reality and Freedom," in *The Nineteenth Century* 135 (1944), 78-83; idem, *The Planning of Science* (Oxford: Society for Freedom in Science, 1946); idem, *The Foundations of Academic Freedom* (Oxford: Society for Freedom in Science, 1947); idem, "The Foundations of Freedom in Science," in *Physical Science and Human Values*, ed. E.P. Wigner (Princeton: Princeton University, 1947); idem, *Pure and Applied Science and Their Appropriate Forms of Organization* (Oxford: Society for Freedom in Science, 1953); etc.

4. Cf. his explication of the dynamics of discovery, with its stages of intuition, research, and tradition, and of the practice of science, with its stages of apprenticeship, discovery, and mastery, in *The Contempt of Freedom* (London: Watts & Co., 1940), 40-43.

5. Gelwick, *Way of Discovery*, 42.

6. In his fifth philosophical monograph, *The Logic of Liberty: Reflections and Rejoinders* (Chicago: University of Chicago, 1951), Polanyi admits to having considered "melting down the material [of the work] and casting it into a mould of a comprehensive system." However, he believed such a move would be "premature," and chose instead to continue elaborating a variety of themes along a "consistent line of thought" with his earlier works. His "comprehensive system" would first emerge in his next major philosophical work, *Personal Knowledge: Towards a Post-Critical Philosophy* (London: Routledge & Kegan Paul, 1958).

7. See, e.g., Stefania Ruzsits Jha, *Reconsidering Michael Polanyi's Philosophy* (Pittsburgh: University of Pittsburgh, 2002); Jerry Gill, *The Tacit Mode: Michael Polanyi's Postmodern Philosophy* (Albany: State University of New York, 2000); Drusilla Scott, *Everyman Revived: the Common Sense Philosophy of Michael Polanyi* (Grand Rapids: Wm. B. Eerdman's, 1995); Richard T. Allen, *Polanyi*, Thinkers of Our Time (London: Routledge, 1990); Andy Sanders, *Michael Polanyi's Post-Critical Epistemology: A Reconstruction of Some Aspects of 'Tacit Knowing'* (Amsterdam: Rodopi, 1988); Harry Prosch, *Michael Polanyi: a Critical Exposition* (Albany: State University of New York, 1986); Gelwick, *Way of Discovery*; etc.

8. See Albert Bagood, *The Role of Belief in Scientific Discovery: Michael Polanyi and Karl Popper* (Ph.D. dissertation: University of Fribourg, 1998) and Jeffrey Kane, *Beyond Empiricism: Michael Polanyi Reconsidered*, American University Series XIV: 6 (New York: Peter Lang, 1984), both of whom compare Polanyi's epistemology with that of Karl Popper and both of whom ultimately affirm Polanyi's thought as being more accurate and useful than Popper's (similarities between the two notwithstanding). See also Terry Hoy, *Praxis, Truth, and Liberation: Essays on Gadamer, Taylor, Polanyi, Habermas, Gutierrez, and Ricoeur* (Lanham: University Press, 1988); Eugene Webb, *Philosophers of Consciousness: Polanyi, Lonergan, Voegelin, Ricoeur, Girard, Kierkegaard* (Seattle: University of Washington, 1988); Iain Paul, *Knowledge of God: Calvin, Einstein, and Polanyi* (Edinburgh: Scottish Academic, 1987). Cf. also Walter Gulick, "An Unlikely Synthesis: What Kant Can Contribute to a Polanyian Theory of Selfhood," in *The Personalist Forum* 9 (1993), 81-107; Bruno Manno "Ways of Viewing Reality: a Proposed Convergence of Polanyi, Lonergan, and Tracy," in *Journal of Christian Education* 81 (1984), 5-10, and "Michael Polanyi and Erik Erikson: Toward a Post-Critical Identity of Human Identity," in *Religious Education* 75 (1980), 205-214; Joseph Kroger, "Theology

and Notions of Reason and Science: a Note on the Point of Comparison Between Lonergan and Polanyi," in *Journal of Religion* 56 (1976), 157-161; etc.

9. E.g., "As much as Copernicus changed the former worldview by making the earth revolve around the sun, Polanyi is changing it by making all knowledge revolve around the responsible person," in Gelwick, *Way of Discovery*, 56; cf. the description of Polanyi's work as a "critical breakthrough" in the "modern understanding of the nature of truth," in John M. Templeton and Robert L. Herrmann, *The God Who Would Be Known: Revelations of the Divine in Contemporary Science* (Radnor: Templeton Foundation Press, 1998), 14, 160.

10. Prosch collated and edited unpublished lectures Polanyi had already delivered between 1968-1970 at both the University of Texas and the University of Chicago; insights from Polanyi's 1970 article "What is a Painting?" were also incorporated in *Meaning*.

11. Torrance, Prosch, and others involved in the study of Polanyi's philosophy for years engaged in something of a running fire fight over the question of Polanyi's understanding of God and the nature of religious knowledge, mostly throughout the pages of the journal of the Polanyi Society (initially entitled *The Polanyi Society*, renamed *Tradition and Discovery* in 1984). As early as the first "Polanyi Consultation," significant differences emerged relative to the interpretation of Polanyi's work (see *The Polanyi Society* 3, no. 1 [1976], 3). The entire "Polanyi Consultation" of 1979, at which Prosch was the guest of honor, was dedicated to exploring Polanyi's understanding of the "objects" of religious awareness (see *The Polanyi Society* 7, no. 2 [1980], 2-6, and *The Polanyi Society* 9, no. 1 [1981], 13-15). Prosch's review (in *Ethics* 89 [1979], 211-216) of Richard Gelwick's *Way of Discovery* delineated the lines of the controversy, putting Gelwick and those who affirmed Polanyi's belief in the independent existence of the objects of religious awareness on one side and Prosch and those who denied that Polanyi affirmed the independent existence of the objects of religious awareness on the other. Gelwick responded to Prosch with an article ("Science, Reality, and Religion: a Reply to Harry Prosch," in *Zygon* 17 [1982], 25-40) that criticized Prosch's misunderstanding of Polanyi's views on religion and God. Prosch rebutted with his "Polanyi's View of Religion in *Personal Knowledge*: a Response to Richard Gelwick" (also in *Zygon* 17 [1982], 41-48). William Scott attempted to bring some clarity to the argument with his own observations based on his relationship with Polanyi and Polanyi's family and friends (in "The Question of a Religious Reality: Commentary on the Polanyi Papers," in *Zygon* 17 [1982], 83-87). Phil Mullins's essay, "Nascent Ritual and the Real" (*The Polanyi Society* 11, no. 2 [1983-1984], 4-9), touched on the issue of Polanyi's understanding of reality, especially as it applies to religious awareness, but did not apply his observations to the controversy. Prosch's attack on Torrance (see Prosch's *Michael Polanyi: a Critical Exposition* [Albany: State University of New York, 1986], esp. 239-257) and his critique of Drusilla Scott's *Everyman Revived* (in *Tradition and Discovery* 13, no. 2 [1985-1986], 20-22) rekindled the controversy. Torrance fired back with a defense of Scott's work (in *Tradition and Discovery* 14, no. 1 [1986-1987], 30), and in turn provoked a rejoinder from Prosch (*Tradition and Discovery* 15, no. 1 [1987-1988], 24-26). John Apczynski, Drusilla Scott, and Joan Crewdson all jumped into the fray as well (Apczynski's "Are Religion and Science Distinct or Dichotomous Realms?", Drusilla Scott's "Quality but Bristling with Difficulties: on Polanyi's View of Reality," and Crewdson's "Nature and the Noosphere: Two Realities or One?" all appeared in *Tradition and Discovery* 15, no. 1 [1987-1988]). Maben W. Poirier sought to draw the various strands of the controversy together ("Harry Prosch's Modernism," in *Tradition and Discovery* 16, no. 2 [1988-1989], 32-39), but

succeeded only in further provoking Prosch ("Those Missing 'Objects'," in *Tradition and Discovery* 17, no. 1-2 [1990-1991], 17-21). There has been some attention given to the question of Polanyi's understanding of religion since the heyday of this controversy; see the conversation between Dale Cannon and Andy Sanders in *Tradition and Discovery* 23, no. 3 (1996-1997), as well as Cannon's later "Some Aspects of Polanyi's Version of Realism," in *Tradition and Discovery* 26, no. 3 (1999-2000), 51-61. Most Polanyians, however, seem content to have let the flames of controversy die down. The notable exception to this irenic spirit is the more recent controversy surrounding Colin Weightman's *Theology in a Polanyian Universe: the Theology of Thomas Torrance*, American University Studies Series VII: Theology and Religion 174 (New York: Peter Lang, 1994), in which Weightman criticizes Torrance for misunderstanding Polanyi on a number of points, including religion. Weightman's work instigated a response from both Apczynski ("Torrance on Polanyi and Polanyi on God: Comments on Weightman's Criticisms," in *Tradition and Discovery* 24, no. 1 [1997-1998], 32-34) and Torrance himself ("Michael Polanyi and the Christian Faith–A Personal Report," in *Tradition and Discovery* 27, no. 2 [2000-2001], 26-32). If the number of published studies espousing (implicitly or otherwise) one view or the other is any indication, then it would be fair to say that Gelwick, Torrance, and those of like mind have carried the day: Polanyi's philosophical work has arguably had greater influence on the study of theology than on any other area, perhaps even epistemology. However, Richard Allen's description of Polanyi's thought seems to attenuate this observation somewhat. Allen has described Polanyi's work as a "curious version of Catholic Modernism: the acceptance of the aesthetic and emotional power of the full and undemythologized dogmas and rites of Christianity coupled with disbelief in their truth except as as [sic] indicating in only a general way that there is some order and meaning in the world," in Allen's *Transcendence and Immanence in the Philosophy of Michael Polanyi and Christian Theism,* Rutherford Studies in Contemporary Theology 5 (Lewiston: Edwin Mellen, 1992), 71.

12.   We do not intend here to conflate these two important and distinct issues, but rather to recognize their frequent association in the literature. The question of Polanyi's understanding of the theological enterprise and the reality of God will be taken up repeatedly throughout the current project.

13.   Cf. the observations of Harold Turner, who noted that *Meaning* is "less representative" of Polanyi's thought than are his earlier, uncontested works, and betrays the heavy editorial hand of Prosch, "a doubtful interpreter of Polanyi," in Turner's "The Theological Significance of Michael Polanyi," in *Stimulus* 5 (1997), 12.

14.   See Gelwick, *Way of Discovery,* 52.

15.   See Gelwick's "Science, Reality, and Religion."

16.   See esp. Michael Polanyi, *Beyond Nihilism* (Cambridge: Cambridge University, 1960). Cf. Helmut Kuhn, "Personal Knowledge and the Crisis of the Philosophical Tradition," in *Intellect and Hope: Essays in the Thought of Michael Polanyi,* ed. T.A. Langford and W.H. Poteat (Durham: Duke University, 1968), 111-135.

17.   See Michael Polanyi, *Personal Knowledge: Towards a Post-Critical Philosophy,* Revised Edition (Chicago: University of Chicago, 1962), 8-9. All references in the current work to *Personal Knowledge* are to the second, corrected edition.

18. Lesslie Newbigin, in his review of Polanyi's interpretation of the Western tradition, suggests that modern Western philosophical skepticism (beginning with Descartes) represents an attempt to follow doubt as a path to certainty; see his *Proper Confidence: Faith, Doubt, and Certainty in Christian Discipleship* (Grand Rapids: Wm. B. Eerdman's, 1994), 16-44. Cf. Polanyi's critique of skepticism, in *Personal Knowledge*, 294-297, and his identification of legitimate and illegitimate forms of doubt (both philosophical and religious), op. cit., 269-286.

19. Polanyi, *Personal Knowledge*, 230-232.

20. See Polanyi, *Personal Knowledge*, 226-237; idem, *The Tacit Dimension* (Chicago: University of Chicago, 1966), 57-58, 86; idem, *Science, Faith, and Society* (Chicago: University of Chicago, 1964), 78; idem, *Scientific Thought and Social Reality*, 40; idem, *Logic of Liberty*, 169; etc.

21. Polanyi, *Science, Faith, and Society*, 77.

22. Polanyi, *Beyond Nihilism*, 1. Cf. "The idea that morality consists in imposing on ourselves the curb of moral commands is so ingrained in us that we simply cannot see that the moral need of our time is, on the contrary, to curb our inordinate moral demands, which precipitate us into moral degradation and threaten us with bodily destruction," in op. cit., 3.

23. Polanyi, *Tacit Dimension*, 4. Cf. idem, *Personal Knowledge*, 87, wherein Polanyi distinguished between three levels or types of tacit knowledge: first, the "ineffable" domain, or that of which we find it difficult if not impossible to speak; second, the "co-extensive" domain, or that which attends our explicit awareness of the meaning of our articulations; and third, the "domain of sophistication," in which articulation either encumbers thought or outstrips thought and thus evokes discovery.

24. Polanyi identified five ways in which our knowledge transcends our ability to explicitly describe it. First, there is the indeterminacy involved in the relationship between our knowledge and the reality to which it refers. Second, there is the unspecifiability involved in establishing standards according to which accurate perceptions can be recognized. Third, there is the unspecifiability involved in establishing standards according to which true knowledge can be distinguished from mistakes or delusion. Fourth, there is the inarticulate process whereby we integrate the various subsidiary elements that contribute to our awareness of wholes. Fifth, there are the unspoken and sometimes unrecognized shifts in the fundamental beliefs and commitments we hold. For further elaboration of these, see Polanyi's "Logic and Psychology," in *American Psychologist* 23 (1968), 27-43; idem, "The Unaccountable Element in Science," in *Philosophy* 37 (1962), 1-14, republished in *Knowing and Being: Essays by Michael Polanyi*, ed. Marjorie Grene (London and Chicago: Routledge & Kegan Paul and University of Chicago, 1969), 104-120. Cf. also idem, *The Study of Man* (Chicago: University of Chicago, 1959), 11-12, where Polanyi demonstrates that a comprehensive knowledge of humanity is impossible because whenever we acquire knowledge we enlarge our understanding of the world, and thus we enlarge the world, and the process by which we come to new knowledge must always remain prior to our awareness of this process as an object of knowledge itself.

25. Cf. Polanyi, *Personal Knowledge*, 5.

26. E.g., the "intellectual tastes of the animal prefigure, no doubt, the joys of discovery which our articulate powers can attain for man, but in the animal they do not remotely approach these joys in scope and elevation. As language enlarges the range of our thought, the ape's pleasure in playing with a stick is expanded to a complex system of emotional responses by which scientific value and ingenuity of many kinds are appreciated throughout natural science, technology and mathematics," Polanyi, *Personal Knowledge*, 133.

27. Polanyi, *Personal Knowledge*, 337.

28. Polanyi, *Personal Knowledge*, 70; cf. 82.

29. In the case of both (that is, continuity between knowledge as possessed by humans and knowledge as possessed by animals on the one hand, and, on the other hand, informal and formal knowledge), Polanyi was motivated by a concern to make sense of human knowledge within a scientific context, one informed by the evolutionary history of the human species; see, e.g., Polanyi, *Personal Knowledge*, 327-328, 335-340, etc.

30. See, e.g., Polanyi, *Personal Knowledge*, 95-100. It is worth noting that both perception and drive satisfaction are, quite obviously, tied to the human experience of embodiment, of which Polanyi would make much in his philosophical work; cf. "The tracing of personal knowledge to its roots in the subsidiary awareness of our body as merged in our focal awareness of external objects, reveals not only the logical structure of personal knowledge but also its dynamic sources," in op. cit., 60. The importance of embodiment on his epistemology will be further explored later in this chapter.

31. Polanyi, *Science, Faith, and Society*, 24; cf. op. cit., 33.

32. Polanyi, *Tacit Dimension*, 6.

33. Michael Polanyi, "Science and Religion: Separate Dimensions or Common Ground?", in *Philosophy Today* 7 (1963), 5.

34. Polanyi, *Tacit Dimension*, 7; between the "high" levels of awareness signified by scientific and artistic achievement and the "low" levels of awareness signified by sensation and perception, Polanyi situated diagnostic, technical, and kinesthetic skills.

35. It is worth noting at this point that Polanyi believed that there are at least four different kinds or degrees of form that we are inclined to recognize. These possibilities include: first, inanimate or abstract structures; second, organic or living beings; third, conscious or active (intentional) beings; and fourth, self-conscious or reflective beings. See Polanyi, *Personal Knowledge*, 343-346; cf. idem, *The Study of Man*, 39-41, 50-53.

36. Cf. Polanyi, *Personal Knowledge*, 104.

37. There is evidence of thinking consistent with the distinction between subsidiary and focal awareness in some of Polanyi's earliest philosophical work; e.g., his explication of the differences between pure and applied science in *Contempt of Freedom*, 8-10, and his explication of polycentric tasks in *Logic of Liberty*, 171-181. However, he did not formally introduce the distinction as a pervasive working principle in his thought until his Gifford lectures; see Polanyi, *Personal Knowledge*, 55-58.

38. Polanyi, *Personal Knowledge*, 55-56; cf. 331, where Polanyi describes the asymmetrical character of subsidiary and tacit awareness, i.e., inasmuch as we are aware of the particular elements of any complex system, we are to that degree unaware of the meaning intended by or in the totality of the system. This insight needs to be set off against Polanyi's comments elsewhere regarding the dynamic "give and take" of knowledge, exemplified especially in the reciprocal differentiation and integration by which formal inquiry proceeds.

39. Cf. Polanyi, *Tacit Dimension*, 10-12.

40. Cf. Polanyi, *Tacit Dimension*, 95-96.

41. Joan Crewdson, *Christian Doctrine in the Light of Michael Polanyi's Theory of Personal Knowledge: a Personalist Theology* (Lewiston: Edwin Mellen, 1994), 47; cf. Polanyi, "Sense Giving and Sense Reading," in *Knowing and Being*, 182.

42. E.g., Polanyi, *Scientific Thought and Social Reality*, 141-142.

43. See Polanyi, *Personal Knowledge*, 58-59. A subtle but important distinction can be made here regarding the proper object of our focal awareness; Polanyi would insist that the proper object of our focal awareness is the act of driving the nail, rather than the nail itself. Thus there is an operational principle at work behind both our awareness of the hammer, our awareness of the nail, and our awareness of the board, and it is this almost wholly conceptual principle or image on which our attention is focused. If we at any point shift our attention to the subsidiary elements of our awareness and thereby becoming focally aware of the hammer, the nail, or the board, we will fail in the task of driving the nail.

44. Michael Polanyi, "Knowing and Being," in *Knowing and Being*, 128. It is also worth noting that Polanyi did not designate subsidiary and focal awareness as two "degrees" of attention (e.g., unconscious and conscious), but as "*two kinds* of attention given to the *same* particulars," ibid.

45. See Polanyi, *Tacit Dimension*, 10-13; Polanyi and Prosch, *Meaning*, 33-36.

46. Polanyi, *Tacit Dimension*, 34.

47. Polanyi, *Tacit Dimension*, 36.

48. Polanyi, *Personal Knowledge*, 382; cf. idem, *Scientific Thought and Social Reality*, 128. Bernd-Olaf Küppers identifies Polanyi as the first to recognize the importance of boundary conditions for understanding complex phenomena and systems (even though he mistakes Polanyi's vocation as that of a physicist and not a chemist); see Küppers's "Understanding Complexity," in *Emergence or Reduction? Essays on the Prospects of Nonreductive Physicalism*, ed. A. Beckerman, H. Flohr, and J. Kim (Berlin: Walter de Gruyter, 1992), 248-250. Cf. also Struan Jacobs, "Michael Polanyi and Spontaneous Order, 1941-1951," in *Tradition and Discovery* 24, no. 2 (1997-1998), 14-28, in which Jacobs compares Polanyi's earlier philosophical work on social theory with that of F.A. Hayek relative to the idea of spontaneous order.

49. Polanyi, *Tacit Dimension*, 88.

50. Polanyi, *Tacit Dimension*, 41.

51. Polanyi, *Tacit Dimension*, 45; cf. Polanyi and Prosch, *Meaning*, 49-50, which provides an illustration of the interaction between boundary conditions and marginal control through an explication of language and the act of speech.

52. Polanyi's understanding of operational principles can be found in his review of commitment in *Personal Knowledge*, 59-61. An operational principle may be understood as any purposeful effort which evidences a commitment to a specific means in order to achieve a particular desired outcome or, put another way, the coordination and synthesis of various forms (physical or otherwise) within a teleological framework.

53. See Polanyi, *Personal Knowledge*, 327-330. Cf. also the characterization and critique of dualism as a philosophical perspective that emerges "when one shifts one's attention from the direction on which the subsidiaries bear and focuses instead on the subsidiaries themselves," in Polanyi and Prosch, *Meaning*, 49.

54. Polanyi, *Tacit Dimension*, 33; cf. op. cit., 13, at which point Polanyi suggests that such knowledge always signifies a particular view of reality itself.

55. Cf. "the study of life must ultimately reveal some principles additional to those manifested by inanimate matter, and to prefigure the general outline of one such, yet unknown, principle," Polanyi, *Tacit Dimension*, 38.

56. Recent efforts aimed at demonstrating the interface of the physical sciences and theological inquiry along the lines of the study of nonlinear dynamics (e.g., emergence, autopoiesis, decoupling, supervenience, and downward causation) often do not account for the potential value of Polanyi's understanding of dual control as a means of overcoming many of the problems encountered in such studies. See, e.g., Robert John Russell, Nancey Murphy, and Arthur R. Peacocke, eds., *Chaos and Complexity: Scientific Perspectives on Divine Action* (Vatican City State: Vatican Observatory Publications, 1997); Niels Henrik Gregersen, "Autopoiesis: Less Than Self-Constitution, More Than Self-Organization," in *Zygon* 34 (1999), 117-138; idem, "The Idea of Creation and the Theory of Autopoietic Processes," in *Zygon* 33 (1998), 333-367; Dennis Bielfeldt,"Can Western Monotheism Avoid Substance Dualism?" in *Zygon* 36 (2001), 153-177; idem, "Supervenience as a Strategy for Relating Physical and Theological Properties," in *The Interplay Between Scientific and Theological Worldviews*, ed. N.H. Gregersen, W. Drees, U. Görman, and C. Wasserman (Geneva: Labor et Fides, 1999); idem, "God, Physicalism, and Supervenience," in *Center for Theology and Natural Science Bulletin* 15 (1995), 1-12; etc.

57. Polanyi, *Personal Knowledge*, 171-174; cf. idem, *Science, Faith, and Society*, 66.

58. Cf. "A problem is an intellectual desire ... and like every desire it postulates the existence of something that can satisfy it. ... How can we concentrate our attention on something we don't know? Yet this is precisely what we are told to do: 'Look at the unknown!'—says Polya—'Look at the end. Remember your aim. Do not lose sight of what is required. Keep in mind what you are working for. *Look at the unknown. Look at the conclusion.*' No advice could be more emphatic," in Polanyi, *Personal Knowledge*, 127 (emphasis in the original).

59. Polanyi, *Personal Knowledge*, 134-162.

60. E.g., "We must commit each moment of our lives irrevocably on grounds which, if time could be suspended, would invariably prove inadequate; but our total responsibility for disposing of ourselves makes these objectively inadequate grounds compelling," in Polanyi, *Personal Knowledge*, 320; cf. 314.

61. E.g., "All our highest endeavours must work through our lower nature and are necessarily exposed thereby to corruption. You may recognize here to cosmic roots of tragedy and of man's fallen condition," in Polanyi, "Science and Religion," 13. Cf. Polanyi's observations regarding the "surprising affinity" between his understanding of personhood and the Christian doctrine of original sin, in *Scientific Thought and Social Reality*, 128-129. Cf. also Polanyi's observation regarding the fragility of human relations and communities that, despite whatever commitments and beliefs we may have about truth and the fundamental disposition of all humans to truth, it is nonetheless surprising that communities should exist at all, given our own inability to resist "temptations to untruthfulness" and the imperfection of our own love of truth, in idem, *Science, Faith, and Society*, 71.

62. Polanyi believed that his notion of tacit knowledge corresponded to "Sartre's vision of man acquiring existence *en soi* by invading the world with his projects," but found much of Sartre's resolution of the challenges manifest in the human experience wanting; see Polanyi, "Science and Religion," 8-14.

63. See Polanyi, *Personal Knowledge*, 203-214.

64. Polanyi believed that positivists and utilitarians would deprecate convivial relationships because they could see no real value in the traditions and rituals that support such communities, and that romanticists would decry convivial relationships because they believed such commitments could only suppress the freedom of the individual; see Polanyi, *Personal Knowledge*, 211.

65. Polanyi, *Personal Knowledge*, 160-170.

66. Polanyi, *Science, Faith, and Society*, 16-17; cf. 49.

67. Polanyi, *Tacit Dimension*, 72 (emphasis in the original).

68. Polanyi, *Personal Knowledge*, 53. Polanyi held this to be true both for specialized cultures dedicated to formal inquiry (e.g., the scientific community) as well as for more expansive cultures dedicated to pursuing more general political, juridical, or social aims. He used the emergence and development of Protestantism as a representative example of how a culture dedicated to broader and more elusive goals both differs from and is similar to a specialized society dedicated to formal inquiry; see idem, *Science, Faith, and Society*, 56.

69. Cf. "Originality is commanded at every stage by a sense of responsibility for advancing the growth of truth in men's minds. Its freedom is perfect service," in Polanyi, *Tacit Dimension*, 77.

70. The rules for shaping and engaging the process of inquiry are "rules of art" and as such cannot be precisely or exhaustively delineated and are usually passed on via the interpersonal relationship of mentor to student. See Polanyi, *Science, Faith, and Society*, 14; idem, *Personal Knowledge*, 30-31.

71. Polanyi, *Science, Faith, and Society*, 45.

72. Polanyi, *Science, Faith, and Society*, 54.

73. Polanyi, *Science, Faith, and Society*, 52.

74. Cf. "Traditions are transmitted to us from the past, but they are our own interpretations of the past, at which we have arrived within the context of our own immediate problems," in Polanyi, *Personal Knowledge*, 160.

75. Cf. Polanyi, *Tacit Dimension*, 74.

76. Polanyi, *Science, Faith, and Society*, 56-57.

77. Polanyi suggests that such basic expectations include: a) "listening to one another's views and occasionally even those of the wider public"; b) "recall the lessons of the past"; c) those in "one area will try to learn from others elsewhere"; and d) weighing their decisions "in regard for their future consequences," in Polanyi, *Science, Faith, and Society*, 60. It could, of course, be argued that these expectations themselves reflect the standards of a particular culture and thus are open to revision and renewal.

78. Cf. "Throughout [Polanyi's] work, the theme of finding, discovering, growing, expanding, enriching is constant. It is present in his view of science and all the arts. It is present in his conception of reality. ... Viewed in its totality, Polanyi's philosophy is one that is aimed primarily at the equipping and encouraging of humans in the ending task of pursuing meaning and truth" in Gelwick, *Way of Discovery*, 84; cf. xvi.

79. Polanyi, *Science, Faith, and Society*, 32.

80. Polanyi, *Science, Faith, and Society*, 33.

81. Polanyi, *Science, Faith, and Society*, 35.

82. Polanyi, *Tacit Dimension*, 24-25. Cf. Polanyi's examination of the extent to which developments in relativity theory (tensor calculus, matrix calculus, quantum mechanics, etc.) demonstrate the human capacity to "discover and exhibit a rationality which governs nature, before ever approaching the field of experience in which previously discovered mathematical harmonies were to be revealed as empirical facts" in idem, *Personal Knowledge*, 14-15. Similarly, our acceptance of contemporary theories of objectivity in the name of "simplicity" or "economy" or "efficiency" merely disguises our passion for the intellectual fulfillment and satisfaction we feel at realizing the discovery of the natural order; see op. cit., 15-17.

83. Polanyi, *Personal Knowledge*, 50-52.

84. Polanyi disregards attempts to explain problem solving in terms of chance and accident and instead prefers (following Köhler, Wallas, and Poincarè) the four-stage model of "preparation," "incubation," "illumination," and "verification." Something can only be a discovery if it is first recognized as a problem; discovery is not reversible, that is, it cannot be traced back across a series of predetermined, precise steps, but depends on crossing a "logical gap," an act which involves departing from the "commonly accepted process of reasoning," in Polanyi, *Personal Knowledge*, 120-124.

85. Gelwick, *Way of Discovery*, 70; cf. Allen, *Polanyi*, 37.

86. In the third of his McInerny lectures, Polanyi acknowledged his indebtedness to Samuel Butler's notion of "assimilation" for influencing his understanding of indwelling; see *The Realm of the Unspoken* (Los Angeles: Pacifica Tape Library, 1962).

87. Polanyi recognized a distinction between the character of our indwelling of physical objects as compared to that of skills and of concepts. He referred to the imagery of "*Einfühlung*" as it had been explicated by Dilthey and Lipps as a means of understanding intellective indwelling; see his "Science and Religion," 8.

88. Polanyi, *Personal Knowledge*, 59-60; see also op. cit., 49-50, for a detailed explication of Polanyi's understanding of skills and the extent to which our practice of sophisticated procedures is representative of indwelling. Cf. idem, *The Study of Man*, 31, 94; idem, "Science and Religion," 7.

89. Cf. Polanyi, "Science and Religion," 6. Cf. "We can either think of the self as dwelling within a framework of truths believed, or as expanded consciousness, which has assimilated these beliefs, allowing them to function instrumentally as an extension of the body. Polanyi uses both forms of the metaphor of indwelling and both tell us something about the self-world relation. For example, I can view myself as part of nature, so that it becomes an extension of my body, in which case I am *subsidiarily* aware of it as a set of beliefs, in which I am at home. Alternately, I can view the world as outside myself, something with an independent existence to which I relate as other and on which I fix *focal* attention as I explore its reality and meaning," in Crewdson, *Christian Doctrine*, 24 (emphasis in the original).

90. Cf. Polanyi's assessment that an object is "transformed into a tool by a purposive effort envisaging an operational field in respect of which the object guided by our efforts shall function as an extension of our body. ... Like the tool, the sign or the symbol can be conceived as such only in the eyes of a person who relies on them to achieve or to signify something. *This reliance is a personal commitment which is involved in all acts of intelligence by which we integrate some things subsidiarily to the center of our focal attention*," in *Personal Knowledge*, 60-61 (emphasis in the original). Cf. "Intelligent contemplation demands indwelling, because every conceptual frame has its own logic and amounts to a paradigm, or way of reasoning," in Crewdson, *Christian Doctrine*, 23.

91. Polanyi, "The Logic of Tacit Inference," in *Knowing and Being*, 147-148.

92. Polanyi, *Tacit Dimension*, 16.

93. See Polanyi, *Personal Knowledge*, 339.

94. Polanyi, *Personal Knowledge*, 263; cf. idem, "The Body-Mind Relation," in *Man and the Science of Man*, ed. W.R. Coulson and C.R. Rogers (Columbus: Charles E. Merrill, 1968). It is worth noting that Polanyi acknowledged that any "theory of knowledge" implies "an ontology of the mind," and thus the study of knowledge leads, for Polanyi, immediately to a consideration of the question of reality. Cf. also Polanyi's explications of the social ramifications of epistemology, in *Personal Knowledge*, 264.

95. Polanyi, *Personal Knowledge*, 372-373.

96. Polanyi, *Tacit Dimension*, 17.

97. Polanyi, *Personal Knowledge*, 312.

98. Polanyi, *Personal Knowledge*, 82-87. Cf. the observation made by J.M. Templeton and R.L. Herrmann regarding the awakening of such intellective powers in humanity and the development of those powers within an evolutionary and historical context, in Templeton and Herrmann, *The God Who Would Be Known*, 211.

99. See Polanyi, *Personal Knowledge*, 195-202. Polanyi here further applied the insights he developed in his analysis of the crisis of the modern mind, noting that the opposite of the ecstatic cosmic vision is one in which despair takes the place of contemplative satisfaction because events are seen as unrelated particulars with no signifying association between them. This nihilistic perspective is the "logical outcome of distrusting our participation in holding our beliefs. Left strictly to itself, this is what the world is like," in ibid., 199.

100. In addition to the critical appraisals of Polanyi's thought noted above (see above, notes 7 and 8), there have been a number of efforts aimed at examining the implications of Polanyi's philosophy within the context of particular fields of study, including (among others) education (e.g., J.E. Tiles, "On Deafness in the Mind's Ear: John Dewey and Michael Polanyi," in *Tradition and Discovery* 18, no. 3 [1992], 9-16; R.T. Allen, "The Philosophy of Michael Polanyi and its Significance for Education," in *Journal of the Philosophy of Education* 12 [1978], 167-177; J.W. Wagener, "Toward a Heuristic Theory of Instruction: Notes on the Thought of Michael Polanyi," in *Educational Theory* 20 [1970], 46-53; etc.), social and political theory (e.g., P.C. Roberts and N. Van Cott, "Polanyi's Economics," in *Tradition and Discovery* 25, no. 3 [1999], 26-30; P. Nagy, "Philosophy in a Different Voice: Michael Polanyi on Liberty and Liberalism" in *Tradition and Discovery* 22, no 3 [1996], 17-27; T. Hoy, "Michael Polanyi: Moral Imperatives of a Free Society," in *Thought* 58 [1983], 393-405; R.J. Brownhill, "Freedom and Authority: the Political Philosophy of Michael Polanyi," in *Journal of the British Society for Phenomenology* 8 [1977], 153-163; etc.), and literary analysis (e.g., E. Hocks, "Dialectic and the 'Two Forces of One Power': Reading Coleridge, Polanyi, and Bakhtin in a New Key," in *Tradition and Discovery* 23, no. 2 [1997], 4-16; etc.). Furthermore, this does not account for the numerous appropriations that have been made of Polanyi's thought by Christian theologians, representative examples of which will be examined more thoroughly in the fourth chapter.

101. Polanyi, *Personal Knowledge*, 347.

102. Contained in this notion is the assumption that our experience of personhood is more fundamental even than our experience of subjectivity. This assumption bears extended

consideration, but we do not have the space to address it at this point. Suffice it to say for now that our experience as a subject represents in part an objectification of our experience as a person, and thus our experience as a person (which we may distinguish here from our awareness) is anterior to our awareness of ourselves as a subject. This suggestion is very much in keeping with the tenor of Polanyi's thought; cf. David Rutledge's analysis of the observability and accessibility of the self as understood by Polanyi, in Rutledge's *The Recovery of the Person in the Post-Critical Thought of Michael Polanyi* (Ph.D. dissertation: Rice University, 1979), 276-281.

103. Polanyi, *Personal Knowledge*, 265.

104. Polanyi, *Personal Knowledge*, 267.

105. Cf. "It is the height of intellectual perversion to renounce, in the name of scientific objectivity, our position as the highest form of life on earth, *and our own advent by a process of evolution as the most important problem of evolution. ...* A preoccupation with the way populations of a new kind come into existence has made us lose sight of the more fundamental question: how any single individual of a higher species ever came into existence," in Polanyi, *Tacit Dimension*, 47 (emphasis added).

106. Polanyi, *Science, Faith, and Society*, 76.

107. E.g., Polanyi, *Tacit Dimension*, 35.

108. Polanyi, *Tacit Dimension*, 39.

109. Polanyi acknowledged that Dilthey and Lipps were responsible for laying the foundation for his own understanding of thinking as indwelling. Polanyi agreed with their assessment of the importance of indwelling as a foundation for knowledge, and with their claim that indwelling is achieved through recapitulation, but disagreed that this form of knowing (which they suggested is proper to the humanities) is restricted to the humanities and has no place in empirical science; Polanyi, *Tacit Dimension*, 16-17.

110. Polanyi, *Personal Knowledge*, 82-87.

111. Cf. "Our vision of reality–our ultimate interpretive framework–is something larger and less detailed than the theories developed to express it, but without the perceptions and the passions generated by it, we would not know how to go about setting up smaller and more manageable instruments of investigation," in Martin X. Moleski, *Personal Catholicism: the Theological Epistemologies of John Henry Newman and Michael Polanyi* (Washington, D.C.: Catholic University Press, 2000), 80. Cf. also Polanyi's development earlier in his philosophical career of the "relaxation method," which he identified as a means of dealing with "polycentric" tasks the likes of which required *"dealing with one centre at a time while supposing the others to be fixed in relation to the rest, for that time,"* and then moving on to another center; see Polanyi, *Logic of Liberty*, 170-180 (emphasis in the original).

112. It is perhaps worth noting that Polanyi's understanding of emergence and dual control as manifest in complex, stratified entities has been subjected to critique. Olding contends that Polanyi, in his elaboration of the idea of hierarchically arranged levels of knowledge and existence, confuses methodology and ontology, mistaking heuristic or purely con-

ceptual devices for real entities. Olding also criticizes Polanyi for allowing a place for personal "interests" in his work. In the final analysis, however, Olding's critique amounts to little more than a casual bit of logic-chopping, and his repudiation of the role of personal interest in knowledge and existence entirely misses the essential point of Polanyi's program. See A. Olding, "Polanyi's Notion of Hierarchy," in *Religious Studies* 16 (1980), 97-102. Cf. Stefania Jha's analysis of Adolf Grünbaum's positivist critique of Polanyi, in Jha's *Reconsidering Michael Polanyi's Philosophy*, 133-148.

113. Polanyi, *Personal Knowledge*, 280.

114. Cf. "Theology as a whole is an intricate study of momentous problems. It is a theory of religious knowledge and a corresponding ontology of the things thus known. As such, theology reveals, or tries to reveal, the implications of religious worship, and it can be true or false, but only as regards its adequacy in formulating and purifying a pre-existing religious faith," in Polanyi, *Personal Knowledge*, 281.

115. Cf. "Modern man's critical incisiveness must be reconciled with his unlimited moral demands, first of all, on secular grounds. The enfeebled authority of revealed religion cannot achieve this reconciliation; it may rather hope to be revived by its achievement," in Polanyi, *Tacit Dimension*, 62. It is worth noting that Polanyi later observes that humanity requires "a purpose which bears on eternity," and admits that it may not be possible to reconcile our "critical incisiveness" an "moral demands" strictly "on secular grounds alone." The fact that late modern religious devotion is constrained by "an absurd view of the universe" serves to limit its immediate relevance, but Polanyi expected that once contemporary religious faith had overcome its "absurd view of the universe" (and he is not forthcoming about what in particular he has in mind here), religion would be able to make a decisive contribution to the human enterprise; cf. op. cit., 92.

116. Cf. "The power of a framework composed of words and gestures to elicit its own religious comprehension in a receptive person will depend partly on the non-religious significance of its elements. The framework must impress a child or an unbeliever in the first place by the appeal made by its dogma, its narratives, its morality and its ritual exercise, before these have been religiously comprehended by him," in Polanyi, *Personal Knowledge*, 282.

117. Cf. Polanyi's comments on the emergence of idolatry in theology, in Polanyi, *Personal Knowledge*, 284.

118. See Richard Gelwick, "Discovery and Theology," in *Scottish Journal of Theology* 28 (1975), 301-322.

119. Arguing against Tillich's distinction between scientific knowledge and theological knowledge, Polanyi suggests that, within a stratified epistemology, science and theology should be mutually reinforcing and correcting; see Polanyi, "Science and Religion," 4-14. Cf. *Tradition and Discovery* 22, no. 1 (1995-1996), which includes essays dedicated to exploring Polanyi's relationship with Tillich, including Charles T. McCoy's "The Postcritical and Fiduciary Dimension in Polanyi and Tillich," Richard Gelwick's "The Polanyi-Tillich Dialogue of 1963: Polanyi's Search for a Post-Critical Logic in Science and in Theology," and Donald W. Musser's "Polanyi and Tillich on History."

120. It is worth noting that several others, however, have gone on to apply elements of Polanyi's thought to the question of personhood. See, e.g., Larry Cochran, *Position and the Nature of Personhood: an Approach to the Understanding of Persons* (Westport: Greenwood Press, 1985). Cf. also the work of Bruno Manno and David Rutledge, which will be reviewed more thoroughly in chapter three.

121. See Rutledge, *Recovery of the Person*, 9-20.

2. Contact with Reality

1. See, e.g., Polanyi's comparative analysis of the emergence and development of powers of articulation in human children and in apes, in his *Personal Knowledge: Towards a Post-Critical Philosophy*, Revised Edition (Chicago: University of Chicago, 1962), 69-71.

2. The "tacit judgments involved in the process of denotation do tend to coincide between different people and ... different people also tend to find the same set of symbols manageable for the purpose of skillfully reorganizing their knowledge." Thus, even though effort to say something intelligible is also a tacit acknowledgement of our "incapacity to do better," it must also be a tacit affirmation of our capacity to effectively communicate to some degree apart from which we would never be able to say anything; see Polanyi, *Personal Knowledge*, 204-206.

3. Even early in his philosophical career, Polanyi expected that there existed a correlation between modes of knowing and modes of existence or being; see, e.g., Michael Polanyi, *The Logic of Liberty: Reflections and Rejoinders* (Chicago: University of Chicago, 1951), 23-24.

4. I.e., commitment is seen as the necessary impetus behind language in part because of the inevitable indeterminacies of language, including the asymmetry between our meaning and our verbiage, the impossibility of completely impersonal expression, the inexhaustible depth of meaning a given expression may have, the unspecifiability of the laws of usage, and the heuristic or interpretive intent of every expression. Cf. the epistemological indeterminacies mentioned above (page 173, note 24). See also David W. Rutledge, *The Recovery of the Person in the Post-Critical Thought of Michael Polanyi* (Ph.D. dissertation: Rice University, 1979), 165-167.

5. It was in part against what he saw as the inevitable erosion, following from the objectivist mindset, of the human capacity for sustained commitment to transcendent principles and realities that Polanyi addressed his critique of the modern mind. Polanyi saw the greatest damage being done by modern forms of skepticism, and thus forms of "religious doubt" constitute the "main subject" of his critique of doubt; see Polanyi, *Personal Knowledge*, 279-285, 303, 324. Cf. "A living, changing, self-transcending world cannot be known by the intellect alone, working according to the laws of formal inference. It has to be discerned by an imaginative grasp of relations and coherences. In the end, all cognition takes place within a framework of personal commitment," in Joan Crewdson's *Christian Doctrine in the Light of Michael Polanyi's Theory of Personal Knowledge: a Personalist Theology* (Lewiston: Edwin Mellen, 1994), 11.

6. Polanyi, *Personal Knowledge*, 305 (emphasis in original).

7. Polanyi, *Personal Knowledge*, 288-291; cf. 292-294.

8.   Polanyi believed that the differentiation of ourselves from reality both was the necessary first step for aspiring to reliable knowledge and evoked the "fiduciary hazards" that made commitment necessary. Without such differentiation, we remain trapped in egocentric or autistic delusions. Thus the goal of connection with the world, with the real, cannot be understood to mean a kind of reabsorption; rather, the emergence and perpetuation of distinct, responsible identities in communion with one another seems to be implied in the direction of evolution itself. See Polanyi, *Personal Knowledge*, 313.

9.   See Polanyi, *Personal Knowledge*, 22-29; cf. *"The fiduciary passions which induce a confident utterance about the facts are* **personal***, because they submit to the facts as universally valid, but when we reflect on this act non-committally its passion is reduced to* **subjectivity***,"* op. cit., 303 (emphasis and double emphasis in the original). See also Richard Gelwick, *The Way of Discovery* (New York: Oxford University, 1977), 76.

10. Polanyi, *Personal Knowledge*, 308. It is also worth noting that Polanyi suggested that this movement is representative of a larger movement the likes of which is best exemplified by the "Christian scheme of Fall and Redemption," in which we are "saved" from the limitations of our historicity and subjectivity by the "grace" of "powers for which we cannot account in terms of our specific capabilities," op. cit., 324. Cf. idem, *Science, Faith, and Society* (Chicago: University of Chicago, 1964), 73.

11. Polanyi, *Personal Knowledge*, 320-321.

12. Polanyi, *Personal Knowledge*, 346.

13. Polanyi, *Personal Knowledge*, 334.

14. Polanyi, *Personal Knowledge*, 380.

15. Polanyi, *Personal Knowledge*, 252-255, 311. Earlier in his philosophical career (prior to his explication of the structure of the tacit dimension), Polanyi found himself more insistent on the need for commitment for understanding knowledge, so much so that he worried he would be perceived as a philosophical relativist. He had at one point gone so far as to say that he could give no compelling reasons as to why a given community or tradition should be allowed to perpetuate itself, just as he could find no compelling reason as to why he himself should live. What he then believed was necessary was not arguing against others who held competing beliefs, but rather bringing them to a point of total conversion. Polanyi was anxious to avoid relativism because of its indefensibility, but at the time he was only able to say that his position as a realist and non-relativist were themselves matters of commitment on his part. Even though truth is not "demonstrable," it is "knowable," but this itself is part of his commitment; see Polanyi, *Science, Faith, and Society*, 81-82. His explication of the dynamics of discovery and the tacit dimension, with its situation of knowledge between both a subjective *and* an objective pole, enabled him to move away from the incipient relativism of his earlier thought.

16. Polanyi, *Personal Knowledge*, 104.

17. Polanyi, *Personal Knowledge*, 80.

18. Michael Polanyi, *The Tacit Dimension* (Chicago: University of Chicago, 1966), 83 (emphasis in the original).

19. Polanyi, *Personal Knowledge*, 58.

20. Polanyi, *Personal Knowledge*, 104-112.

21. Cf. also Polanyi's distinction between "physiognostic" and "telegnostic" meaning. The first refers to those instances in which the "isolated particulars" (i.e., subsidiary elements) and "what they jointly mean, are not clearly separated in space." The second refers to those instances in which the "uncomprehended particulars [i.e., subsidiary elements] are inside our body or at its surface, and what they mean extends into space outside," in Michael Polanyi, "Knowing and Being," in *Knowing and Being: Essays by Michael Polanyi*, ed. Marjorie Grene (London and Chicago: Routledge & Kegan Paul and University of Chicago, 1969), 128-129. Cf. Gelwick, *Way of Discovery*, 71-76.

22. It is worth noting here that this taxonomy, described here as representative of Polanyi's later thought, is found in *Meaning*, the contested work in Polanyi's canon. It is largely because *Meaning* is the only work bearing Polanyi's name within which we find an extended and focused consideration of the nature of language that *Meaning* can and should be read as part of Polanyi's corpus, even if the ideas expressed therein often need to be situated within the broader horizon of the rest of Polanyi's work. His earlier efforts at describing the nature of expression and interpretation are for the most part found in *Personal Knowledge*, esp. 69-131; cf. 190-202, wherein Polanyi describes the continuity that exists between various abstract forms of articulation and interpretation.

23. Michael Polanyi and Harry Prosch, *Meaning* (Chicago: University of Chicago, 1975), 69-71.

24. Polanyi and Prosch, *Meaning*, 73; cf. 71-75.

25. Polanyi and Prosch, *Meaning*, 78.

26. Polanyi and Prosch, *Meaning*, 79-80.

27. Polanyi and Prosch, *Meaning*, 82-94.

28. See esp. Polanyi and Prosch, *Meaning*, 84-86, 90-91.

29. Polanyi and Prosch, *Meaning*, 95-107.

30. Polanyi and Prosch, *Meaning*, 108-119.

31. Polanyi and Prosch, *Meaning*, 88.

32. Polanyi and Prosch, *Meaning*, 121.

33. See Eliade's *Myth and Reality*, trans. W.R. Trask (New York: Harper & Row, 1963), 21-38. Polanyi acknowledges not only his indebtedness to Eliade for his understanding of myth, but also to the work of Ernst Cassirer and Lucien Lévy-Bruhl. See Ernst Cassirer, *Philosophy of Symbolic Forms*, 3 vols., trans. R. Manheim (New Haven: Yale, 1953-1957); Lucien Lévy-Bruhl, *Les fonctions mentale dans les sociétés inférieures* (Paris: Presses Universitaires de France, 1951).

34. Polanyi and Prosch, *Meaning*, 132-133; cf. 140-144. Polanyi applies this observation to the question of the truthfulness of myths and concludes that in some ways the mythic or "archaic" mind is in some ways more sophisticated than the modern "scientific" mind (as evidenced, for example, in the mythic mind's ability to recognize, albeit not in such terms, that knowing consists in part of the integration of subsidiaries within a meaningful focal whole, and in the readiness with which the mythic mind is able to accommodate itself to the notion of indwelling as a means of knowledge). Because of their power to "evoke in us an experience which we hold to be genuine," myths can be said to be truthful in spite of whatever errors they might be said to contain; see op. cit., 145-148.

35. Polanyi comes very close at one point to saying that the mythic imagination necessarily reaches out in the direction of what might called a personalistic vision: "The archaic mind seems sharply impressed by the sensory qualities of meaningful relations, and its imagination greatly exaggerates the interaction between subsidiaries and their focus. We meet with no evidence of this exaggeration in the from-to relation between the names of inanimate things ... It is only when the focus of the semantic relation is a living being, and particularly when it is a human person, that the imagination seems to enlarge so greatly on the dynamic forces involved in the subsidiary-focal structure of integrations. Of course, the vastly indeterminate manifestations of a human being may well lend to him a mysterious quality which often stimulates the imagination far beyond the range of experience. It is most interesting to note at this point that the modern mind errs in the opposite direction," in Polanyi and Prosch, *Meaning*, 137-138.

36. Polanyi and Prosch, *Meaning*, 125. Cf. "According to Eliade the union of incompatibles was first elevated to a general theological principle by Nicholas of Cusa under the influence of the via negativa of Pseudo-Dionysius. He called it the *coincidentia oppositorum* and argued that such a *coincidentia oppositorum* was the least imperfect definition of God," in op. cit., 129.

37. Polanyi and Prosch, *Meaning*, 128.

38. Polanyi and Prosch, *Meaning*, 126.

39. Polanyi and Prosch, *Meaning*, 123-125.

40. Polanyi and Prosch, *Meaning*, 152.

41. Polanyi and Prosch, *Meaning*, 153.

42. E.g., the question of how it is possible that the "infinite God of all Gods [sic]" can be honored by the worship of "a few anthropoidal creatures, only recently descended from the trees, performing rituals in certain finite places, thought by them to be hallowed, and at certain finite times, thought by them to be holy days," or the question of how a "precatory prayer" could be offered to a God "whose very essence is thought to be always to do what is best for all," in Polanyi and Prosch, *Meaning*, 154-155. The rather dismissive and condescending tone of this passage does not seem consistent with Polanyi's other writings, and may be indicative of Prosch's editorial influence.

43. Polanyi and Prosch, *Meaning*, 156. The paradigm of "Pauline Christianity" in particular demonstrates the tensions of religious belief, emphasizing as it does our dependence upon God "for the ultimate victory through Christ" over both our abiding sense of sinful-

ness as well as the distance by which we are separated from God; op. cit., 157. Cf. "The indwelling of the Christian worshipper is therefore a continued attempt at breaking out, at casting off the condition of man, even while humbly acknowledging its inescapability. ... Christianity sedulously fosters, and in a sense permanently satisfies, man's craving for mental dissatisfaction by offering him the comfort of a crucified God," in Polanyi, *Personal Knowledge*, 198-199.

44. Polanyi and Prosch, *Meaning*, 159.

45. It is probably the chapter in which Polanyi (and Prosch) deals with the question of the nature of religious belief more than any other section of *Meaning* that has given this work its dubious status in the Polanyi canon. It would take us far beyond our immediate concerns to demonstrate the ways in which this particular section of *Meaning* both does and does not seem to conform to other areas of Polanyi's thought. However, it can at least be said that what seems most problematic about this section is not so much its characterization of religious awareness or its relative conflation of the mythic and the religious mindset, but the dismissive stance evident therein towards even the possibility that mythic and religious truth might manifest a form(s) of rationality consistent with more naturalistic forms of rationality; see Polanyi and Prosch, *Meaning*, 154-160.

46. Martin X. Moleski, *Personal Catholicism: the Theological Epistemologies of John Henry Newman and Michael Polanyi* (Washington, D.C.: Catholic University Press, 2000), 73; Moleski refers to Polanyi's description of language as including "writing, mathematics, graphs and maps, diagrams and pictures; in short, all forms of symbolic representation which are used as language in the sense defined by the subsequent description of the linguistic process," in Polanyi, *Personal Knowledge*, 78.

47. Polanyi makes a similar observation when he notes that our "perceptions and bodily motions have ... the same structure that we have ascribed generally to meaningful relations," in Polanyi and Prosch, *Meaning*, 138.

48. See Polanyi and Prosch, *Meaning*, 74.

49. See Polanyi, *Personal Knowledge*, 77-82.

50. Polanyi, *Personal Knowledge*, 381.

51. Cf. Edward Pols, "Polanyi and the Problem of Metaphysical Knowledge," in *Intellect and Hope: Essays in the Thought of Michael Polanyi*, ed. T.A. Langford and W.H. Poteat (Durham: Duke University, 1968), 58-90.

52. Cf. Polanyi's observation that we should assume a *"correspondence between the structure of comprehension and the structure of the comprehensive entity which is its object,"* in *Tacit Dimension*, 33-34 (emphasis in original).

53. Polanyi, *Tacit Dimension*, 35.

54. Cf. John M. Templeton and Robert L. Herrmann, *The God Who Would Be Known* (Radnor: Templeton Foundation Press, 1998), 219-224.

55. Polanyi, *Science, Faith, and Society*, 37.

56. Cf. Polanyi, *Tacit Dimension*, 5-6.

57. Polanyi, *Personal Knowledge*, 311. Polanyi tied this observation to the logic of commitment: "By trying to say something that is true about a reality believed to be existing independently of our knowing it, all assertions of fact necessarily carry universal intent. *Our claim to speak of reality serves thus as the external anchoring of our commitment in making a factual statement,*" ibid. (emphasis in original).

58. Cf. "The act of personal knowing can sustain these relations only because the acting person believes that they are apposite: that he has not *made them* but *discovered them.* The effort of knowing is thus guided by a sense of obligation towards the truth: by an effort to submit to reality," in Polanyi, *Personal Knowledge*, 63 (emphasis in original).

59. Cf. Polanyi's expectation that a heuristic field represents "*an access to an opportunity*" as well as "*the obligation and the resolve to make good this opportunity, in spite of its inherent uncertainties,*" in Polanyi, *Personal Knowledge*, 403 (emphasis in original).

60. Cf. Michael Polanyi, "On Body and Mind," in *The New Scholasticism* 43 (1969), 195-204; idem, "The Body-Mind Relation," in *Man and the Science of Man*, ed. W.R. Coulson and C.R. Rogers (Columbus: Charles E. Merrill, 1968).

61. See, e.g., Polanyi, *Personal Knowledge*, 145-150.

62. E.g., "Our conceptual imagination, like its artistic counterpart, draws inspiration from contacts with experience. And like the works of imaginative art, the constructions of mathematics will tend therefore to disclose the hidden principles of the experienced world of which some scattered traces had first stimulated the imaginative process by which these constructions were conceived," in Polanyi, *Personal Knowledge*, 46.

63. Polanyi, *Personal Knowledge*, 104.

64. Polanyi, *Personal Knowledge*, 114; cf. 16-17, 169-170, etc.

65. Polanyi, *Personal Knowledge*, 113.

66. Polanyi, *Personal Knowledge*, 114-117, 54-55, 132-202.

67. Polanyi, *Personal Knowledge*, 114.

68. Polanyi, *Personal Knowledge*, 356-359; cf. 387.

69. Polanyi, *Personal Knowledge*, 359-361; cf. 387-388.

70. Polanyi, *Personal Knowledge*, 363-364; cf. 388-389.

71. Polanyi, *Personal Knowledge*, 364-368; cf. 388.

72. Polanyi, *Personal Knowledge*, 382-390; Polanyi acknowledged his indebtedness to Teilhard de Chardin for his characterization of the "noösphere," ibid., 388.

73. Polanyi, *Personal Knowledge*, 373-374. Joan Crewdson characterized Polanyi's view of the evolutionary history of the world as a series of "'steps on the road to personhood,' and personhood as the product of an environment which both challenges and rewards life's adventures," in Crewdson, *Christian Doctrine*, 206.

74. Polanyi, *Personal Knowledge*, 374-378.

75. Polanyi, *Personal Knowledge*, 389-390; cf. 402-405.

76. Polanyi, *Personal Knowledge*, 405.

77. See Crewdson, *Christian Doctrine*, 16-19, 70-106.

78. See, e.g., Michael Polanyi, "Science and Religion: Separate Dimensions or Common Ground?" in *Philosophy Today* 7 (1963), 12. Cf. "Evolution gave rise to persons, who witness to the union of thought and being. Polanyi finds in this unity the key to a valid epistemology and to a unitary metaphysic that allows mind to participate in what it knows, because it already dwells in, and is a part of, it," in Crewdson, *Christian Doctrine*, 20.

79. Crewdson, *Christian Doctrine*, 19.

80. There is some indication that Polanyi himself, acknowledging the direction of his epistemology, intended to address the theological significance of his work. Joan Crewdson reported, based on her personal interactions with Polanyi, that it was only age and illness that prevented Polanyi from pursuing this goal; see Crewdson's *Christian Doctrine*, ix-x.

81. Polanyi, *Science, Faith, and Society*, 84.

82. Polanyi, *Tacit Dimension*, 92.

83. Polanyi, *Personal Knowledge*, 284.

84. See Polanyi, *Personal Knowledge*, 311, 379-380, 392, 405, etc. See also Polanyi's description of the manner in which human beings advance in their understanding of the world by moving "up" through stratified levels of meaning, acknowledging the obligations and responsibilities inherent in each, to a comprehensive view of the universe. Polanyi compared this movement to the "Christian scheme of Fall and Redemption," in which we are "saved" from the limitations of our historicity and subjectivity by the "grace" of "powers for which we cannot account in terms of our specific capabilities," op. cit., 324.

85. The manner in which the argument has unfolded throughout this section is slightly different from other ways in which the theological direction of Polanyi's thought has been argued, but the conclusions are largely the same. Cf. the observations of Joan Crewdson, who, based on her interactions with Polanyi, "supports the view that Polanyi's religious faith is deep and real and that, indeed, his theory of knowledge has a profoundly religious foundation," in Crewdson, *Christian Doctrine*, 332-333; cf. also John Apczynski's assessment that the "intrinsic logic" of Polanyi's philosophy leads to questions of religious commitment and knowledge, in his *Doers of the Word: Toward a Foundational Theology Based on the Thought of Michael Polanyi* (Missoula: Scholar's Press, 1977), v.

86. See esp. above, page 171-172, note 11. Interestingly, Marjorie Grene, who spent a great deal of time collaborating with Polanyi and assisting him in his philosophical work, takes the religious tenor of Polanyi's work seriously enough to criticize it from her own self-described "agnostic if not atheistic" perspective; see Grene's "The Personal and the Subjective," in *Tradition and Discovery* 22, no. 3 (1995-1996), 14-15.

87. I am indebted to Colin Grant's article, "Identifying the Theological Enemy: Polanyi's Near Miss," in *Modern Theology* 3, no. 3 (1987), 255-268, for the title of this section. However, I should point out that the "near miss" identified herein is of a slightly different nature than that explicated by Grant. Grant sought to demonstrate that Polanyi mistakenly confused elements of positivism and elements of objectivism relative to the question of self-consciousness, and thereby fell in his arguments against objectivism into a perspective resembling the positivism against which he also intended to argue. My concern at this point has more to do with simply illustrating the extent to which Polanyi failed to engage the theological implications of his own work, and will forego any analysis of the structure of Polanyi's philosophy (or psychology) in an effort to explain this lacuna.

88. Moleski, *Personal Catholicism*, 53. Moleski refers to Polanyi's comments in the second edition of *Science, Faith, and Society*, 17.

89. William T. Scott, "The Question of Religious Reality: Commentary on the Polanyi Papers," in *Zygon* 17 (1982), 85-86.

90. Polanyi's lack of formal training in philosophy is sometimes leveled against him by critics; his own acknowledgement of the enormous help given to him by Marjorie Grene as he struggled both to make sense of his own ideas as well as to situate them within the intellectual milieu of his time also indicates that he may have felt at times that he ultimately fell short of his own ambitions.

91. E.g., while presenting "A Society of Explorers," the last of the four McInerny Lectures he presented at the University of California-Berkeley in 1962 under the series title "History and Hope," Polanyi acknowledged that his understanding of tacit thought and indwelling suggested intriguing and important consequences for religious faith (and, significantly, that it also strengthened his own religious beliefs). But he immediately indicated that he believed that "our ideals of critically established truth and unlimited social improvement must be reconciled primarily on secular grounds." Such grounds, when actualized, would, Polanyi felt, provide a more stable base for the renewal of belief in revealed religion than could the invocation of the authority of revealed religion serve as a foundation for such efforts. See Michael Polanyi, *A Society of Explorers* (Los Angeles: Pacifica Tape Library, 1962); cf. idem, *Science, Faith, and Society*, 84.

92. Cf. Colin Grant on Polanyi's inability to acknowledge all the implications of his own philosophy: "It may well be that it is a mark of true genius to propound a vision which exceeds its originator's own articulation," in Grant's "Identifying the Theological Enemy," 267.

93. Cf. Avery Dulles's suggestion that the theological value of Polanyi's thought has more to do with the "transfer value" of his observations regarding the nature of knowledge than to do with his observations about religion and theology, in Dulles's "Faith, Church, and God: Insights from Michael Polanyi," in *Theological Studies* 45 (1984), 537-550.

94. Thomas F. Torrance, *Transformation and Convergence in the Frame of Knowledge: Explorations in the Interrelations of Scientific and Theological Enterprise* (Grand Rapids: Wm. B. Eerdman's, 1984), 107.

95. See Richard T. Allen, *Transcendence and Immanence in the Philosophy of Michael Polanyi and Christian Theism*, Rutherford Studies in Contemporary Theology 5 (Lewiston: Edwin Mellen, 1992), 99.

3. Post-Critical Personhood

1. David Whitt Rutledge, *The Recovery of the Person in the Post-Critical Thought of Michael Polanyi* (Rice University: Ph.D. dissertation, 1979), 3.

2. It seems likely that Polanyi did indeed seek to engage the existentialist tradition on this point, but in a way that highlighted the way in which classic existentialism had produced a malformed understanding of existential anxiety; see Michael Polanyi, *Personal Knowledge: Towards a Post-Critical Philosophy*, Revised Edition (Chicago: University of Chicago, 1962), 236-237.

3. Polanyi, *Personal Knowledge*, 213.

4. Polanyi, *Personal Knowledge*, 214.

5. Polanyi, *Personal Knowledge*, 320.

6. Polanyi, *Personal Knowledge*, 300.

7. Cf. Michael Polanyi and Harry Prosch, *Meaning* (Chicago: University of Chicago, 1975), 5-9.

8. Polanyi, *Personal Knowledge*, 237.

9. Cf. Polanyi, *Personal Knowledge*, 195-202.

10. See Michael Polanyi, *Tacit Dimension* (Chicago: University of Chicago, 1966), 83-85; cf. idem, *Science, Faith, and Society*, 2nd Ed. (Chicago: University of Chicago, 1963), 53-59.

11. Cf. Polanyi's assessment of the reciprocity of our knowledge of ourselves and of others, in Polanyi, *Personal Knowledge*, 327-328, 373; Polanyi and Prosch, *Meaning*, 48.

12. H. Richard Niebuhr, *The Responsible Self: an Essay in Christian Moral Philosophy* (New York: Harper & Row, 1963), 73.

13. Polanyi, *Personal Knowledge*, 309.

14. Polanyi, *Personal Knowledge*, 380.

15. Joan Crewdson, *Christian Doctrine in Light of Michael Polanyi's Theory of Personal Knowledge: a Personalist Theology*, Toronto Studies in Theology 66 (Lewiston: Edwin Mellen, 1994), 19.

16. See Polanyi, *Personal Knowledge*, 387-388.

17. Polanyi distinguished between language and articulation, the latter being both more fundamental and more expansive than the former (and thus harder to identify precisely). Language is necessarily a more formal, abstract, and restricted enterprise, whereas articulation signifies a pre-linguistic mode of awareness that itself depends on the even more primitive inarticulate capacities humans share with other animals. See Polanyi, *Personal Knowledge*, 69-87.

18. Cf. Michael Polanyi, *Scientific Thought and Social Reality*, F. Schwarz, ed. (New York: International Universities, 1974), 127, 143; idem, "On Body and Mind," in *The New Scholasticism* 43, no. 2 (1969), 195-204.

19. Polanyi insisted that "we must recognise belief or intuitive apprehension once more as the source of knowledge from which our acts of discovery take their rise, for it is in belief that our minds are in direct touch with reality, in belief that our thought is open to the invisible realm of intelligibility independent of ourselves, and through belief that we entrust our reason to the rational order and reliability of the contingent universe. Behind and permeating all our scientific activity, whether in critical analysis or discovery, there is an elemental, overwhelming faith in the rational constitution of things, but faith also in the possibility of grasping the real world with our concepts, and above all faith in the truth over which we have no control but in the service of which our human rationality stands or falls. Faith and intrinsic rationality are interlocked with one another," in Thomas F. Torrance, *Christian Theology and Scientific Culture* (Oxford and New York: Oxford University, 1981), 63-64.

20. It is perhaps not too much even to say that embodiment in all of its forms involves nothing other than the successful subsidiary integration of elements drawn from a particular environment; in other words, what the body is can be signified by this act of successful subsidiary integration or, perhaps better, incorporation.

21. We recall here the distinction Polanyi made between the functional, the phenomenological, the semantic, and the ontological dimensions of apprehension, all of which operate simultaneously in coordinating the molar achievement signified by our recognition and understanding of a complex entity or event.

22. See Polanyi, *Personal Knowledge*, 58-59.

23. Polanyi, *Personal Knowledge*, 60; cf. idem, *Tacit Dimension*, 16.

24. Cf. Polanyi, *Personal Knowledge*, 327.

25. Polanyi, *Personal Knowledge*, 323.

26. Cf. Polanyi, *Personal Knowledge*, 403.

27. Bruno V. Manno, *The Person and Meaning: a Study in the Post-Critical Thought of Michael Polanyi* (Ph.D. dissertation: Boston College, 1975).

28. Manno, *Person and Meaning*, 11-32.

29. Manno, *Person and Meaning*, 16-18.

30. Manno, *Person and Meaning*, 27-32.

31. Manno, *Person and Meaning*, 33-90.

32. Manno, *Person and Meaning*, 91-118.

33. Manno, *Person and Meaning*, 136-160.

34. Cf. "Understood in this comprehensive sense, religious education becomes a passionate life-long process of inquiry that opens the person to those ultimate concerns and values which give meaning, motivation, and direction to the deepest dimensions of a person's being," in Manno, *Person and Meaning*, 159.

35. E.g. "The use of the word 'person' in this thesis is restricted to the human being as one who knows or, in Polanyi's words, understands and comprehends," in Manno, *Person and Meaning*, 7.

36. See Manno, *Person and Meaning*, 56-60.

37. See Manno, *Person and Meaning*, 85-90.

38. Cf. "How a person assimilates the structures of language forms a paradigm for all processes through which the person grows and develops," in Manno, *Person and Meaning*, 139.

39. Cf. "As there is an increasing differentiation on the level of liabilities [i.e. the vulnerabilities to which one is opened by commitment] and capabilities there is an increasing consolidation of the center to which they are attributable," in Manno, *Person and Meaning*, 152.

40. David Rutledge criticizes Manno's project as failing to address the question of personhood in Polanyi's thought; see Rutledge, *Recovery of the Person*, 67 (note 3). This is, however, perhaps a bit stringent, for, as has been demonstrated above, Manno does offer some useful, if preliminary, suggestions towards the elucidation of a Polanyian view of personhood.

41. See Rutledge, *Recovery of the Person*, 9-20, wherein Rutledge also acknowledges several of the criticisms that have been leveled against Polanyi, including his reading of history, his notion of moral inversion, and the relative lack of structure that attends his thought.

42. Rutledge, *Recovery of the Person*, 4.

43. Rutledge, *Recovery of the Person*, 22-66.

44. Rutledge, *Recovery of the Person*, 83-86.

45. Rutledge, *Recovery of the Person*, 86-124.

46. Rutledge, *Recovery of the Person*, 135-143.

47. Rutledge, *Recovery of the Person*, 143-160.

48. Rutledge, *Recovery of the Person*, 160.

49. Rutledge, *Recovery of the Person*, 160-169.

50. Rutledge, *Recovery of the Person*, 170-189.

51. Rutledge, *Recovery of the Person*, 200-228.

52. Rutledge, *Recovery of the Person*, 228-250.

53. Rutledge, *Recovery of the Person*, 259-287.

54. Rutledge, *Recovery of the Person*, 287-303.

55. See, e.g., Raymond Martin, *The Rise and Fall of Soul and Self: an Intellectual History of Personal Identity* (New York: Columbia University Press, 2006); Robert C. Solomon, *Continental Philosophy Since 1750: the Rise and Fall of the Self*, History of Western Philosophy 7 (Oxford and New York: Oxford University Press, 1988); Calvin Schrag, *The Self after Post-Modernity* (New Haven: Yale University Press, 1997); etc.

56. E.g., "Moses said to God, 'If I come to the Israelites and say to them, "The God of your ancestors has sent me to you," and they ask me, "What is his name?" what shall I say to them?' God said to Moses, 'I AM WHO I AM.' He said further, 'Thus you shall say to the Israelites, "I AM has sent me to you",'" Ex 2.13-14 (NRSV).

57. Anthony Hoekema, *Created in God's Image* (Grand Rapids: Wm. B. Eerdman's, 1986), 213. Cf. Glenn F. Whitlock, "The Structure of Personality in Hebrew Psychology," in *Interpretation* 14 (1960), 3-13.

58. See, e.g., Ellis R. Brotzman, "Man and the Meaning of *Nephesh*," in *Bibliotheca Sacra* 145 (1988), 400-409; Robert Brachter, "Biblical Words Describing Man: Breath, Life, and Spirit," in *Bible Translator* 34 (1983), 201-209; Daniel Lys, "The Israelite Soul According to the LXX," in *Vestus Testamentum* 16 (1966), 181-228; et al.

59. Cf. "one of the most striking differences between the pagan and the Christian ethos seems to be in the latter's dynamic approach to the person–a dynamism grounded in the idea, inherited from Judaism but utterly unfamiliar in the Greco-Roman world, that ethics is the kernel of religious life," in Gedaliahu Stroumsa, "Caro Salutis Cardo: Shaping the Person in Early Christian Thought," in *History of Religions* 30 (1990), 29; cf. 44.

60. Stroumsa, "Caro Salutis Cardo," 30.

61. Cf. "just as it was being enlarged and unified through the integration of the body, the subject was at once broken again, this time in a new fashion. This time, the great divide was no longer between soul and body as representing lofty spirit and base matter, but cut right through the subject itself. The conception of original sin and, hence, of the radical asceticism appearing on a grand scale in the fourth century was again rooted in Jewish soil, more precisely in those marginal splinter groups of Encratites familiar to us from the

Dead Sea Scrolls and who seem to have left a deep imprint on early Jewish Christianity," in Stroumsa, "Caro Salutis Cardo," 30.

62. Belief in the possibility of a bodily resurrection, foreign to the Greek mindset, was slow to emerge in Jewish thought, "but already well established in the first Christian century," in Stroumsa, "Caro Salutis Cardo," 37.

63. Cf. "Greek philosophy does indeed provide the starting point for the development of the Western discovery of the self (in a subjective way) and of the person (in an objective way). Yet, the status of the individual had to remain unclear in Greece as long as marks of individuality were primarily perceived as signs of imperfection," in Stroumsa, "Caro Salutis Cardo," 32.

64. This entailed considerations of the relationship between simplicity and complexity, universality and specificity, unity and diversity, incorruptibility and corruptibility, etc. See Stephen A. Hipp, *"Person" in Christian Tradition and the Conception of Saint Albert the Great: a Systematic Study of its Concept as Illuminated by the Mysteries of the Trinity and the Incarnation*, Beiträge zur Geschichte der Philosophie und Theologie des Mittelalters 57 (Münster: Druckhaus Aschendorff, 2001), 38.

65. See W. Norris Clarke, "Substance and Accident," in *The New Dictionary of Theology*, ed. J.A. Komonchak, M. Collins, and D.A. Lane (Wilmington: Michael Glazier, Inc., 1987), 986-987.

66. Cf. F. LeRon Shults, *Reforming Theological Anthropology: After the Philosophical Turn to Relationality* (Grand Rapids and Cambridge: Wm. B. Eerdman's, 2003), 12-15.

67. See John of Damascus, *The Fount of Knowledge*, Fathers of the Church 37, ed. J. Deferrari, et al, trans. F.H. Chase (New York: Fathers of the Church, 1958), esp. XXIX, XXX, XLII-XLV, etc.

68. E.g. David Coffey (following Pannenberg) suggests that "'person' is a specifically Christian concept," one "acquired in the course of the formulation of christological and trinitarian theology and doctrine in the first five centuries of the Christian era as the functional categories of the New Testament needed to be translated into ontological one borrowed from Hellenism and then to be developed within this new context," in David Coffey, *Deus Trinitas: the Doctrine of the Triune God* (New York: Oxford University, 1999), 67.

69. C.J. de Vogel has argued forcefully against the thesis that the concept of personhood is a uniquely Christian contribution to Western thought. In his arguments he examines several different Greek literary and philosophical traditions, wherein he finds more or less fully developed notions of personality that predate Christian reflection on personhood. In particular, he examines the lyric and epic poetry of Homer, Herodotus, and Semonides, the political and philosophical musings of Cicero, Plato, Pythagoras, and the Stoics, and especially the transcendental philosophy of Plotinus (in whom he finds a "full-grown metaphysics of personality"). In each instance, he finds evidence of extended and sophisticated reflection on the question of personhood. It is thus in part against this background that he suggests early Christian reflection on personhood should be read (although he does not elaborate specific connections between these earlier Greek traditions and later Christian developments). See de Vogel's "Personality in Greek and Chris-

tian Thought," in *Studies in Philosophy and the History of Philosophy*, ed. J.K. Ryan (Washington, D.C.: Catholic University of America, 1963), 20-60. Cf. also the work of Adolf Trendelenburg, whose posthumously published essay, "A Contribution to the History of the Word Person" (in *The Monist* 20 [1910], 336-363), though not as focused as de Vogel's study and now dated in some of its scholarship, nonetheless provides a helpful review of some of the antecedents to the elaboration of the Christian view of persons.

70. Cf. Stroumsa's observation that the "maturing corpus of Christian thought, from the second to the fourth centuries, culminated with the notion of a radical reflexivity of the self" unparalleled by previous philosophical and theological speculation; see Stroumsa, "Caro Salutis Cardo," 27. Cf. also Stroumsa's observations regarding the importance of the notion of reflexive selfhood in the Western tradition: "This chapter is that of the transformation of a structure of thought, characterized by objectivation, into another one, focusing upon the recognition of the individual's irreducibility," in op. cit., 31.

71. Cf. C.S. Lewis's description of the "synthesis" of philosophy, science, and theology that provided the patristic and medieval periods with a "single, complex, harmonious mental Model of the Universe," in Lewis's *The Discarded Image: an Introduction to Medieval and Renaissance Literature* (Cambridge: Cambridge University, 1994), 11; relative to the ambitions of the current study, cf. esp. 92-121, 139-197.

72. See Shults, *Reforming Theological Anthropology*, 16-17.

73. Although precisely identifying the beginning and the end of the modernity can be a hazardous enterprise, we will content ourselves with a historical perspective that sees the modern period as including the years between 1543 (when Copernicus published his *De revolutionibus orbium coelestium*) and 1905 (when Albert Einstein introduced the theory of special relativity in his "Zür Elektrodynamik bewegter Körper," in *Annalen der Physik* 17 [1905], 891-921).

74. Ockham modified the prevailing view of his time regarding the notion of a first cause in the created order. Whereas postulating a necessary first cause for the continued existence of the world would put God at the end of an infinite and eternal regress of causes, Ockham suggested rather that it was by God's providence that the created order was sustained, thereby allowing him to affirm that an eternal first cause was not necessary and thus avoid an infinite and eternal regress of natural causes. This also had the happy consequence of making God's existence necessary for the existence of the world; cf. Wolfhart Pannenberg, *Toward a Theology of Nature: Essays on Science and Faith*, T. Peters, ed. (Louisville: Westminster John Knox, 1993), 19. However, Ockham's empiricist "theologism" also opened the door to the possibility of particular variations of skepticism and reductionistic determinism; see Etienne Gilson, *The Unity of Philosophical Experience* (San Francisco: Ignatius, 1964), 49-72.

75. Copernicus introduced a heliocentric cosmology, displacing the existing Ptolemaic terracentric view. Galileo's elaboration of causality and mechanics helped displace Aristotelian cosmology, and his astronomical discoveries confirmed many of the finding of Copernicus. Kepler's "laws of planetary motion" further ensconced both the theories of Copernicus as well as his methodology. Newton managed (among other things) to demonstrate the continuity between the insights of Coperniucs, Galileo, and Kepler, thereby presenting something of a "grand unified theory" of the universe.

76. Cf. Wolfhart Pannenberg's explication of the development of the doctrine of inertia, which had the effect of replacing "the dependence of physical reality on God's activity of continuous creation with the idea of self-preservation," thus making God unnecessary to explain the continued existence of the world, in Pannenberg's *Toward a Theology of Nature*, 19-20. Even though early developments of the principle of inertia left some room for God's activity (e.g. Descartes, who ultimately grounded his understanding of inertia in God's immutability), later developments would either make no explicit reference to God (e.g. Newton) or would identify the essence of spatio-temporal objects with their "perseverance in being," thus eliminating altogether the need for divine action in the conservation of nature (e.g. Spinoza); op. cit., 30-31.

77. Wolfhart Pannenberg has traced the development of modern approaches to the question of God and demonstrated the connection between the emergence of modern atheism and contemporaneous efforts to confront the question of God from a perspective informed primarily by the reality of the reflexive subject. He points out that Feuerbach's treatment of the question of God followed quite naturally from the work of Kant and (more closely) Fichte. Feuerbach pointed out that, inasmuch as we can say that God can be thought of as an object of human awareness and reflection, human subjectivity is relative to this question involved in the process of "positing the idea of its own source," in Wolfhart Pannenberg, *Metaphysics and the Idea of God*, trans. P. Clayton (Grand Rapids: Wm. B. Eerdman's, 1990), 46; cf. 43-44. Feuerbach's contention was subsequently developed (in different ways) by Marx, Nietzsche, Durkheim, and Freud.

78. Interestingly, Karl Barth judged modern atheism as philosophically marginal, a "phenomena not to be taken seriously," in Barth's *Protestant Theology in the Nineteenth Century: Its Background & History* (Valley Forge: Judson Press, 1973), 83. Barth argues that the modern period was as sensitive to theological questions as was any other; it simply attempted to reformulate the problem of theology according to its own standards. For a more complete account of the emergence and development of modern atheism, see Henri de Lubac, *The Drama of Atheist Humanism* (San Francisco: Ignatius, 1995); Michael Buckley, *At the Origins of Modern Atheism* (New Haven: Yale University, 1987).

79. Cf. Warren Bourgeois, *Persons: What Philosophers Say About You* (Waterloo: Wilfrid Laurier University, 1995), 77-79.

80. Keith Ward, "The Decline and Fall of Reason," in *Faith and Praxis in a Postmodern Age*, ed. U. King (London: Cassell, 1998), 23. The question of whether or not Descartes intended to develop a philosophical system based on "first principles" has recently received significant attention; see esp. Philip Clayton, *The Problem of God in Modern Thought* (Grand Rapids: Wm. B. Eerdman's, 2000), 51-114. Cf. Graham Ward's analysis of the early work of Jean-Luc Marion on Descartes, which Ward believes suggests a more complex image of Descartes than may typically be acknowledged: "Marion's Descartes is haunted by questions of God and eternal truths. Marion's work points out that the gaze of the *cogito* in Descartes exists both in harmony and in conflict with a second gaze–the gaze of God. ... An irreducible ambivalence emerges in Descartes's analysis of the *cogito*, for Descartes refuses to reduce the operation of consciousness upon the world either to anthropology or theology. Descartes, then, opens up *the question* of epistemological and ontological foundations," from Ward's "Postmodern Theology," in *The Modern Theologians: an Introduction to Christian Theology in the Twentieth Century*, D. Ford, ed. (Oxford: Blackwell, 1997), 593.

81. Cf. Bourgeois, *Persons*, 81-86.

82. See Shults, *Reforming Theological Anthropology*, 18-20.

83. Cf. Bourgeois, *Persons*, 103.

84. Cf. Nancey Murphy, *Beyond Liberalism and Fundamentalism: How Modern and Post-modern Philosophy Set the Theological Agenda* (Valley Forge: Trinity Press, 1996), 56-58; cf. 92. For a reconsideration of Hume's philosophical skepticism, see John Earman, *Hume's Abject Failure: the Argument Against Miracles* (New York: Oxford University, 2000).

85. Shults, *Reforming Theological Anthropology*, 20.

86. Cf. Bourgeois, *Persons*, 104-107; cf. 143.

87. *The Oxford Companion to Philosophy*, ed. T. Honderich (New York: Oxford University, 1995), 277-278.

88. Cf. the essay by David Bell on Kant in *The Blackwell Companion to Philosophy*, ed. N. Bunnin and E.P. Tsui-James (Oxford: Blackwell, 1996), esp. 590-598.

89. Cf. the essay by Michael Ironwood on Hegel in *The Blackwell Companion to Philosophy*, ed. N. Bunnin and E.P. Tsui-James (Oxford: Blackwell, 1996), 607-614; cf. also Bourgeois, *Persons*, 107-110.

90. There were, however, different ways of accounting for or describing "mind." While some held that mind could be said to exist fully only in some supernatural state (absolute idealism), others held that mind is more or less coterminous with the natural order (cosmic idealism). Similarly, while some held that mind signifies the collective consciousness of all rational beings (social or "panpsychistic" idealism), still others held that mind signifies only the consciousness of individual rational beings (individual idealism). Cf. *Cambridge Dictionary of Philosophy*, 2nd ed., ed. R. Audi (Cambridge: Cambridge University, 1999), 412. The *Cambridge Dictionary* describes what we have here termed "individual idealism" as "personal idealism." *The Encyclopedia of Philosophy*, v. 6, ed. P. Edwards (New York/London: Macmillan & The Free Press/Collier Macmillan, 1967), 108, describes social idealism as "panpsychistic."

91. One might well argue that the renewal of eschatological ontology, prevalent in the work of Jürgen Moltmann, Wolfhart Pannenberg, Robert Jenson, and others, serves as a signal indicator of Hegel's abiding influence; see F. LeRon Shults, *Reforming the Doctrine of God* (Grand Rapids: Wm. B. Eerdman's, 2005), 166-201.

92. Cf. the essay by David E. Cooper on modern European philosophy in *The Blackwell Companion to Philosophy*, ed. N. Bunnin and E.P. Tsui-James (Oxford: Blackwell, 1996), 702-717.

93. To say, however, that what we might call existential concerns are not manifest in the patristic and medieval theological traditions would be inaccurate; cf. John McIntyre, *The Shape of Christology: Studies in the Doctrine of the Person of Christ*, 2nd ed. (Edinburgh: T & T Clark, 1998), 130-132.

94. It helps to recall here Polanyi's notion of indwelling and his insistence that we can never both indwell a perspective and, through that indwelling, "observe" that same perspective.

95. Polanyi, *Personal Knowledge*, 347.

96. See Polanyi, *Personal Knowledge*, 371-373, 263-264.

97. Polanyi, *Personal Knowledge*, 327-328.

98. See David Kettle, "Michael Polanyi and Human Identity," in *Tradition and Discovery* 21, no. 3 (1994-1995), 5-18

99. See esp. Kettle, "Polanyi and Human Identity," 11-12.

100. See esp. Kettle, "Polanyi and Human Identity," 9-11.

101. Kettle, "Polanyi and Human Identity," 16 (emphasis in original). Kettle's work here parallels the earlier efforts of Bruno Manno. Manno's reading of Polanyi's notion of calling as the impetus that motivates the organization of a center of consciousness is comparable to Kettle's indeterminate pole of interiorty. Manno's reading of Polanyi's account of the acquisition of language (and thereby a worldview) is comparable to Kettle's description of the various indeterminate poles of exteriority. Thus, for both Kettle and Manno, personhood is understood to involve a process of increasing simultaneous individuation and socialization.

102. Jean Galot provides a more theologically grounded description of the emergence of relational personal being in terms that are very much in keeping with Kettle's suggestions; see Galot's *The Person of Christ: a Theological Insight*, trans. M.A. Bouchard (Chicago: Franciscan Herald Press, 1984), esp. 45-59.

103. See, e.g., Polanyi, *Personal Knowledge*, 318, 344; idem, *Science, Faith, and Society*, 37-41, 72-73; idem, *The Contempt of Freedom* (London: Watts & Co., 1940), 57.

104. These observations parallel somewhat the conclusions of David Rutledge, whose analysis of Polanyi's understanding of the "person as speaker" also notes that language gives a decisively social or relational tenor to the notion of personhood; see Rutledge's *Recovery of the Person*, 228-250.

105. Wolfhart Pannenberg makes a helpful connection regarding the idea of indwelling and its potential correspondence to field theory; see Pannenberg's *Toward a Theology of Nature: Essays on Science and Faith*, ed. Ted Peters (Louisville: Westminster/John Knox1993), 22-24, 37-41, etc.

106. Cf. Kettle's characterization, noted earlier, of the "interanimation" of interior and exterior poles or "indeterminacies."

107. Cf. the personal "is neither subjective nor objective. In so far as the personal submits to requirements acknowledged by itself as independent of itself, it is not subjective; but in so far as it is an action guided by individual passions, it is not objective either. It transcends the disjunction between subjective and objective," in Polanyi, *Personal Knowledge*, 300. Cf. too Marjorie Grene's description of the distinction Polanyi made between

the personal and the subjective, in her "The Personal and the Subjective," in *Tradition and Discovery* 22, no. 3 (1995-1996), 6-16, esp. 8-13.

108. Polanyi, *Personal Knowledge*, 327.

109. Cf. Drusilla Scott's brief explication of a Polanyian sense of personhood, in which she includes the notion of persons as individuals, persons as known by convivial indwelling, persons as both determined and free (the correlation of which signifies calling), persons as representative of a cosmic mystery, and persons as the foundation for all free societies; see Scott's *Everyman Revived: the Common Sense Philosophy of Michael Polanyi* (Grand Rapids: Wm. B. Eerdman's, 1995), 155-159. Cf. also Michael Hill's comparative analysis of Polanyi's incipient anthropology with one more beholden to biblical categories; see Michael Hill, "Reflections on Cloning and the Soul," in *The Reformed Theological Review* 56 (1997), 138-148.

110. Cf. Michael Polanyi, "The Body-Mind Relation," in *Man and the Science of Man*, W.R. Coulson and C.R. Rogers, eds. (Columbus: Charles E. Merrill, 1968), 96-102.

111. See esp. W. Norris Clarke, *Person and Being* (Milwaukee: Marquette University, 1993); idem, "To Be Is To Be Substance-In-Relation," in *Metaphysics as Foundation: Essays in Honor of Ivor Leclerc*, ed. P.A. Bogaard and G. Treash (Albany: State University of New York, 1993); idem, "Person, Being, and St. Thomas," in *Communio* 19 (1992), 601-618. Clarke's earlier work on the extent to which it is through an analysis of action that our awareness of persons in made possible is also relevant here; see his "Action as the Self-Revelation of Being: a Central Theme in the Thought of St. Thomas," in *History of Philosophy in the Making: a Symposium of Essays to Honor Professor James D. Collins on his 65th Birthday by his Colleagues and Friends*, ed. L.J. Thro (Washington, D.C.: University Press of America, 1982). Cf. Joseph Bracken, *Society and Spirit: a Trinitarian Cosmology* (London and Toronto: Associated University Press, 1991); idem, "*Ipsum Esse Subsistens*: Subsistent Being or Subsistent Activity? A Search for URAM in Systematic Theology," in *Ultimate Reality and Meaning* 14 (1991), 279-292; idem, "Subsistent Relation: Mediating Concept for a New Synthesis?" in *The Journal of Religion* 64, no. 2 (1984), 188-204.

112. Cf. Richard Allen, *Transcendence and Immanence in the Philosophy of Michael Polanyi and Christian Theism*, Rutherford Studies in Contemporary Theology 5 (Lewiston: Edwin Mellen Press, 1992), 16-29.

113. Recall Polanyi's demonstration, noted above (page 173, note 24), that a comprehensive knowledge of humanity is impossible because whenever we acquire knowledge we enlarge our understanding of the world, and thus we enlarge the world, and the process by which we come to new knowledge must always remain prior to our awareness of this process as an object of knowledge itself; see Polanyi, *Study of Man*, 11-12.

4. From Philosophy to Theology

1. See Richard Gelwick, *Michael Polanyi: Credere Aude–His Theory of Knowledge and Its Implications for Christian Theology* (Ph.D. dissertation: Pacific School of Religion, 1965). See also Richard C. Prust, *The Knowledge and Reality of God: the Theological Implications of Michael Polanyi's Epistemology and Ontology* (Ph.D. dissertation: Duke

University, 1970). Cf. other earlier essays dedicated to exploring the theological implications of Polanyi's thought, such as Robert T. Osborn, "Christian Faith as Personal Knowledge," in *Scottish Journal of Theology* 28 (1975), 101-126; John Apczynski, *Doers of the Word: Toward a Foundational Theology Based on the Thought of Michael Polanyi* (Missoula: Scholar's Press, 1977), and "Integrative Theology: a Polanyian Proposal for Theological Foundations," in *Theological Studies* 40 (1979), 23-43; Donald Thorsen, "Michael Polanyi: a Post-Critical Understanding of Religious Belief," in *Asbury Theological Journal* 41 (1986), 79-90; Colin Grant, "Dynamic Orthodoxy: a Polanyian Direction for Theology," in *Studies in Religion* 17 (1988), 407-419; etc.

2.   See, e.g., Torrance's review of Polanyi's assessment of the insufficiency of modern science and the emergence of postmodern physics, in Thomas F. Torrance, *Theological Science* (London: Oxford University, 1969), 92-93, 250, 261; cf. idem, *God and Rationality* (London: Oxford University, 1971), 3-25, 99-103; idem, *Christian Theology and Scientific Culture* (New York: Oxford University, 1981), 15-25. Torrance saw the advent of postmodern physics as a "profound recovery of ontology and objectivity," and understood Polanyi's thought to have better absorbed the implications of special and general relativity than any other philosophical program of the time; see idem, *Transformation and Convergence in the Frame of Knowledge: Explorations in the Interrelations of Scientific and Theological Enterprise* (Grand Rapids: Wm. B. Eerdman's, 1984), 107-189. See also Torrance's review of Polanyi's critique of objectivism, in idem, *Theological Science*, 114-115, as well as his review of Polanyi's critique of skepticism, op. cit., 122-123.

3.   See Alister E. McGrath, *Thomas F. Torrance: an Intellectual Biography* (Edinburgh: T & T Clark, 1999), esp. 228-234. See also John Douglas Morrison, *Knowledge of the Self-Revealing God in the Thought of Thomas Forsyth Torrance*, Issues in Systematic Theology 2 (New York: Peter Lang, 1997), esp. 90-97.

4.   Colin Weightman, *Theology in a Polanyian Universe: the Theology of Thomas Torrance*, American University Studies Series VII: Theology and Religion 174 (New York: Peter Lang, 1994), esp. 131-132, 203-206, 235-280. Note that McGrath has criticized Weightman for overstating Torrance's indebtedness to Polanyi; see McGrath, *Thomas F. Torrance*, 229 (note 100).

5.   Robert K. Martin, *The Incarnate Ground of Christian Education: the Integration of Epistemology and Ontology in the Thought of Michael Polanyi and Thomas F. Torrance* (Ph.D. dissertation: Princeton University, 1994).

6.   Colyer does not examine Torrance's reading of Polanyi in the light of Polanyi's work itself, but relies on Torrance's reading of Polanyi for his own description of personal knowledge; see his *How to Read T.F. Torrance: Understanding His Trinitarian and Scientific Theology* (Downer's Grove: IVP, 2001), esp. 334-344. Spjuth, in his *Creation, Contingency and Divine Presence in the Theologies of Thomas F. Torrance and Eberhard Jüngel* (Lund: Lund University, 1995), mentions Polanyi at several points but does not describe in any great detail the elements of his philosophy. Interestingly, though, Spjuth does at one point characterize Polanyi as a "personalistic thinker" in the tradition of John Macmurray and Martin Buber; see op. cit., 36.

7.   Thomas F. Torrance, *The Christian Frame of Mind: Reason, Order, and Openness in Theology and Natural Science* (Colorado Springs: Helmers & Howard, 1989); idem,

Transformation and Convergence; idem, "The Framework of Belief," in *Belief in Science and Christian Life: the Relevance of Michael Polanyi's Thought for Christian Faith and Life*, ed. T.F. Torrance (Edinburgh: Handsel, 1980).

8.   Torrance's essay, "The Place of Michael Polanyi in the Modern Philosophy of Science," in *Transformation and Convergence*, 108-173, is one of the very few places where he examines at length Polanyi's thought within its own intellectual milieu.

9.   See Torrance, "The Framework of Belief"; idem, *Christian Frame of Mind*, 114-116; idem, *Transformation and Convergence*, 195-204; idem, *Christian Theology and Scientific Culture*, 41-72.

10. Torrance, *Transformation and Convergence*, 76-87.

11. Thomas F. Torrance, *The Christian Doctrine of God, One Being Three Persons* (Edinburgh: T & T Clark, 1996), 27.

12. Torrance, *Reality and Scientific Theology* (Edinburgh: Scottish Academic Press, 1985), 33-34.

13. See Torrance, *Christian Frame of Mind*, 79-80, 96; cf. idem, *Transformation and Convergence*, 269.

14. Thomas F. Torrance, *Space, Time, and Resurrection* (Grand Rapids: Wm. B. Eerdman's, 1976), 15.

15. Torrance, *Reality and Scientific Theology*, 55.

16. Cf. the "rationality of nature objectively transcends our experience of it and so commands our respect for it that we are ready to *let it speak for itself*, so to say, and to subject our formulations and apprehensions to its criticism and guidance," in Torrance, *Theological Science*, 30; cf. 129-130 (emphasis in original).

17. Torrance, *Theological Science*, 30; cf. "verification of our knowledge of God must come to us from without from God Himself," op. cit., 197.

18. Torrance, *Theological Science*, 267. Note that Torrance's use of the phrase "from without" is somewhat awkward and may need modification. It is meant to signify that our knowledge of God must come from God and not from ourselves, and this is certainly true, but the spatial imagery suggested by the term "without" may be problematic inasmuch as it may equally be said that our knowledge of God may come from "within," from reflection on our experience of being persons, that is, our reflection on our experience of presence and being in the narrative interface between subjectivity and objectivity.

19. Torrance, *Space, Time, and Resurrection*, 188-193; cf. idem, *Christian Frame of Mind*, 60-61; idem, *Reality and Scientific Theology*, 49-50, 111; idem, *Christian Doctrine of God*, 84; idem, *Reality and Evangelical Theology: the Realism of Christian Revelation* (Philadelphia: Westminster, 1982), 35-36; idem, *The Ground and Grammar of Theology* (Charlottesville: University Press of Virginia, 1980), 141-143. See also Torrance's appropriation of Polanyi relative to the question of the distinction between natural and su-

pernatural explanation and the relative difficulty involved in bringing the two together, in idem, *God and Rationality* (London: Oxford, 1971), 72, 203-205.

20. Torrance, *Reality and Scientific Theology*, 131-159.

21. Torrance, *Theological Science*, 230; cf. 241-242. Torrance relies here on Polanyi's explication of the play of intellectual passions in the process of discovery; cf. idem, *Christian Frame of Mind*, 142-146; idem, *God and Rationality*, 45, 96; idem, *Ground and Grammar*, 58-60; idem, *Reality and Scientific Theology*, 76-80. See also Torrance's account of the way in which Polanyi's notion of dual control functions relative to the coordination of meaning in our awareness, in idem, *Divine and Contingent Order: Nihil constat de contingentia nisi ex revelatione* (Oxford: Oxford University, 1981), 102-103.

22. Cf. Torrance, *Divine and Contingent Order*, 16-25.

23. Torrance, *Space, Time, and Resurrection*, 11. Torrance, in an explication of the meaning of Jn 14.22-23, compares the knowledge and understanding of the resurrection granted to the disciples with Polanyi's notion of indwelling, a knowledge and understanding made possible only by standing "within its reality," op. cit., 37-38; cf. idem, *Transformation and Convergence*, 93-94; idem, *Reality and Scientific Theology*, 84-85; idem, *Christian Doctrine of God*, 37-38.

24. Torrance uses Polanyi's description of what happens when we don spectacles that invert our visual field as an example of what happens when reflection on general revelation is pursued outside of the horizon of reflection on special revelation; thus, still following Polanyi, Torrance recommends that "natural theology" be understood as necessarily existing within the context of "revealed theology," that is, that faith (commitment) takes precedence over understanding. See Torrance, *Reality and Scientific Theology*, 42-43; cf. idem, *Christian Frame of Mind*, 73-75.

25. Cf. Torrance, *Divine and Contingent Order*, 53-61.

26. Cf. "only a person can engage in genuinely objective knowledge, for only he or she can distinguish objective realities from subjective fantasies; only a person can discern a coherent pattern in nature and let his insight into it steer his researches to a successful result; and of course only a person can weigh evidence or judge the validity of an argument in response to the compelling claim of reality, and therefore engage in rigorous, critical scientific activity," in Torrance, *Christian Frame of Mind*, 45.

27. Torrance, *Theological Science*, 163.

28. Torrance, *Reality and Evangelical Theology*, 45; cf. "it is in commitment to the transcendent realty of truth over which we have no control, in acknowledgement of transcendent obligations, and in dedication to transcendent ideals which we affirm with universal intent that we have our freedom as rational beings," op. cit., 150. See also idem, *Ground and Grammar*, 113-114; idem, *Theological Science*, 305-312.

29. See Martin Moleski, *Personal Catholicism: the Theological Epistemologies of John Henry Newman and Michael Polanyi* (Washington, D.C.: Catholic University, 2000). Moleski is not the only one to have noticed the similarity between Newman and Polanyi; Torrance acknowledged it in his *Reality and Scientific Theology*, 99. See also W. Stephen

Gunter, *Resurrection Knowledge: Recovering the Gospel for a Postmodern Church* (Nashville: Abingdon, 1999); Jerry Gill, *On Knowing God: New Directions for the Future of Theology* (Philadelphia: Westminster, 1981); Avery Dulles, *Models of Revelation* (Maryknoll: Orbis, 1992); idem, *The Craft of Theology: from Symbol to System* (New York: Crossroad, 1992); Lesslie Newbigin, *Foolishness to the Greeks: the Gospel and Western Culture* (Grand Rapids: Wm. B. Eerdman's, 1986); idem, *The Gospel in a Pluralist Society* (Grand Rapids: Wm. B. Eerdman's, 1989); idem, *Proper Confidence: Faith, Doubt and Christian Discipleship* (Grand Rapids: Wm. B. Eerdman's. 1994); etc.

30. Barbara Dee Bennett Baumgarten, *Visual Art as Theology*, New Studies in Aesthetics 21 (New York: Peter Lang, 1994).

31. E.g. "The intention of art, to reveal ever deeper coherences of meaning which lie beyond the realm of articulation, emulates the intention of religion which seeks coherence of the whole of our world," in Baumgarten, *Visual Art*, 125.

32. A significant portion of Baumgarten's *Visual Art* (153-243) is devoted to exploring the aesthetic sensibilities of Paul Tillich, whom Baumgarten then uses as a foil in her development of a post-critical theological aesthetic. Our concern has more to do with her interpretation and appropriation of Polanyi's work, and thus we will not treat her examination of Tillich's aesthetics or her comparative analysis of Tillich and Polanyi.

33. E.g. "Polanyi's triadic structure of knowing may be employed to summarize the interworkings of beauty, imagination, and intellectual passions: beauty is the unspecifiable attracting aspect of a focally known reality; imagination is the seeker which aims for a meaningful relation of the subsidiaries to a focal whole; intellectual passions are the imagination's guide to discovery based on skills held subsidiarily," in Baumgarten, *Visual Art*, 75.

34. Like scientific discovery, creative discovery is spurred by the recognition of a problem; this is in part what makes the presence of a teacher or a mentor necessary, for it is only through modeling the successful, masterful behavior of a teacher that one is enabled to learn the skills necessary to overcome the problem. The same is true for the role of tradition: the "unspecifiable elements of knowledge possessed by one generation are received by its successors through mindbodily imitation and attention." See Baumgarten, *Visual Art*, 49-50.

35. E.g. Baumgarten's description of indwelling as "the act of extending our person into elements that are essential to the achievement of an aim and the appreciation of a comprehensive whole," Baumgarten, *Visual Art*, 55.

36. Baumgarten, *Visual Art*, 105.

37. Baumgarten, *Visual Art*, 65.

38. Baumgarten, *Visual Art*, 37.

39. Baumgarten, *Visual Art*, 38-39.

40. Baumgarten, *Visual Art*, 39. Cf. Drusilla Scott's understanding of the perception of "supra-natural" realities: she suggests that the "supra-natural" carries the meaning of a

"natural world revealing a meaning," a meaning which "belongs to a higher level ... and may be glimpsed on in a few clues on the natural level, but if it can be grasped it illuminates and can change the whole of every level," in Scott's *Everyman Revived: the Common Sense Philosophy of Michael Polanyi* (Grand Rapids: Wm. B. Eerdman's, 1995), 186-187. Cf. also Baumgarten's own later statement that "our understanding of art does require a much richer measure of imaginative integration" comparable to that required for both artistic and scientific discovery than does "possessing scientific knowledge," that is, abstracted maxims, in Baumgarten, *Visual Art*, 63.

41. Baumgarten, *Visual Art*, 48.

42. Baumgarten, *Visual Art*, 37.

43. Baumgarten goes far enough in her reliance on visual categories of apprehension as to suggest at one point that the exercise of aesthetic sensitivity can be traced to the anatomical and neurophysiological activity of the eye; see Baumgarten, *Visual Art*, 56.

44. E.g., "Visual perception is a purposive action and *requires some thrust of our imagination*. Perception, like all action in progress, aims at the future, and *we can only attend to the future in our imagination*," Baumgarten, *Visual Art*, 58 (emphasis added).

45. Baumgarten, *Visual Art*, 55.

46. Baumgarten, *Visual Art*, 127.

47. Joan Crewdson, *Christian Doctrine in Light of Michael Polanyi's Theory of Personal Knowledge: a Personalist Theology*, Toronto Studies in Theology 66 (Lewiston: Edwin Mellen, 1994).

48. Crewdson, *Christian Doctrine*, x.

49. Crewdson, *Christian Doctrine*, 1-65.

50. Crewdson, *Christian Doctrine*, 70-106.

51. Crewdson draws on John Macquarrie as a primary source in her development of a dialectical theology; see John Macquarrie, *In Search of Deity: an Essay in Dialectical Theism* (London: SCM, 1984).

52. Crewdson, *Christian Doctrine*, 110-176. It is unfortunate that Crewdson was not able to include in her analysis of late modern theology recent developments in the study of non-linear dynamics and the emergence of the contemporary panentheist school of thought, as it seems that such a comparative analysis would have revealed a significant degree of common ground. Philip Clayton is one of the more recognized advocates of contemporary panentheism: see his *God and Contemporary Science* (Edinburgh: Edinburgh University, 1997) and his "The Case for Christian Panentheism," in *Dialog* 37:3 (1998), 201-208, as well as the dialogue this essay generated, in T. Peters, ed., "A Case for Christian Panentheism," in *Dialog* 38:4 (1999), 281-293. See also Thomas Finger, "Trinity, Ecology, and Panentheism," in *Christian Scholar's Review* 27:1 (1997), 74-98; William French, "The World as God's Body: Biological Ethics and Panentheism," in *Broken and Whole*, ed. M.A. Tilley and S.A. Ross. (Lanham: University Press of America, 1995); Jo-

seph Bracken, "Panentheism from a Trinitarian Perspective," in *Horizons* 22:1 (1995), 7-28; William M. Thompson, "A Suffering World, a Loving God," in *Suffering and Healing in Our Day*, ed. F.A. Eigo (Villanova: Villanova University, 1990); S.A. Mousalimas, "The Divine in Nature: Animism or Panentheism?", in *Greek Orthodox Theological Review* 35:4 (1990), 367-375; etc.

53. Crewdson, *Christian Doctrine*, 183-220.

54. Crewdson, *Christian Doctrine*, 228-270. For a slightly more extensive consideration of Crewdson's arguments regarding the nature of freedom, see note 62, below, which explores the question of freedom relative to the relationship between God and the world.

55. Crewdson, *Christian Doctrine*, 302 (emphasis in the original).

56. Crewdson, *Christian Doctrine*, 275-312.

57. Crewdson, *Christian Doctrine*, 316-345.

58. Crewdson, *Christian Doctrine*, 348-398.

59. Crewdson, *Christian Doctrine*, 216-217.

60. Crewdson does at certain times point out the need to affirm the "great ontological gulf that separates God from the created order," but even in those instances in which she emphasizes God's transcendence, she affirms that God and the world exist as "part of one reality." God is seen within this context as "the ultimate, in the sense that he is the ultimate form of the personal in whom opposites coincide. But this kind of difference cannot prevent the Eternal from entering time or hinder finite personhood from participating in the life of God," in Crewdson, *Christian Doctrine*, 229; cf. 320-321, 349-350. Further, she is uncomfortable with the idea of an impassible God and insists that the God's "capacity for love and joy must be matched by a capacity for suffering and pain," in op. cit., 339-340.

61. Crewdson, *Christian Doctrine*, 84; cf. 229-230.

62. It is conceivable that Crewdson might respond to this critique by suggesting that the creation's "transcendence" over God is manifest in the real freedom the creation has, a freedom that is granted by God. Crewdson does, after all, go to some lengths to demonstrate that a Polanyian perspective on the doctrine of creation affirms the reality of the freedom of the creation; cf. Crewdson, *Christian Doctrine*, 90-97, 153-154, 237-243, etc. However, this rebuttal implies that the creaturely exercise of freedom away from the will or the being of God in no way compromises either the freedom or the being of the creatures who so choose to exercise their freedom; creatures in relative rebellion against God would thus be seen as the source of their own being (and freedom), and would have to create their own being (and freedom) *ex nihilo*. This idea, however, clashes with the Christian notion that it is God alone who is the source of all being (and freedom). Augustine of Hippo's characterization of non-being or privation as the result of rebellion against God immediately comes to mind; see, e.g., his *Confessions*, trans. H. Chadwick (New York: Oxford University, 1991), III.vii. Even Crewdson recognizes this: "Apart from God, the created order would only have such meaning as it gives itself–a precarious

meaning, as easy to dissolve as morning mist," in Crewdson, *Christian Doctrine*, 213; cf. "The truly free person does not act otherwise than his nature determines," op. cit., 238.

63. Richard Allen, in a work that predates Crewdson's *Christian Doctrine* by just a few years, acknowledges that Polanyi's work might in some ways lend itself to either a monistic, pantheistic or a panentheistic interpretation (such as Crewdson's interpretation suggests). Allen also convincingly demonstrates that such an interpretation of Polanyi's thought is not only problematic from a traditional Christian perspective, but also represents something of a misunderstanding of Polanyi's thought. See Richard T. Allen, *Transcendence and Immanence in the Philosophy of Michael Polanyi and Christian Theism*, Rutherford Studies in Contemporary Theology 5 (Lewiston: Edwin Mellen, 1992), 99-105, 111-143.

64. E.g., Crewdson contends that the "makers of Christian doctrine found it necessary to invent the doctrine of the Trinity in attempting to understand the nature of the God-world relation. The problem of relating incompatibles arose first in connection with the incarnation, which the Church fathers represented as a union of divine and human natures. The next problem, as the Church fathers saw it, was how to view Jesus as part of the Godhead, without violating the basic principle of God's oneness. The first necessity was to see God, not as an individual deity, but as a communion of love. It was then found necessary to give the Holy Spirit ontological weight and see this mediating factor as fully personal," in Crewdson, *Christian Doctrine*, 230-231. This passage represents very nearly the sum total of Crewdson's efforts to wrestle with her reception of early Christian reflection on the person and work of Christ and the nature of God.

65. E.g., "Throughout its history, Christianity has been a growing and changing movement under pressure to adapt its doctrines to harmonise with enlargements of human knowledge. In the nineteenth century, human beings had to be accepted as part of the evolutionary process. Similar pressures made it necessary to recognise that the books of the Bible were written by many hands in varying circumstances and cannot be accorded verbal divine authority. In the twentieth century, new insights have developed concerning the nature of the physical universe, persons and consciousness, giving rise to the idea that it may be time for another major theological adjustment," in Crewdson, *Christian Doctrine*, 275; cf. 315-318.

66. E.g., "Not until this century can it be said that human persons on any scale have begun to think in a mature way about the nature and form of personal being and to show themselves able to think about the supernatural as a spiritual reality, but not as miraculous in a magical sense," in Crewdson, *Christian Doctrine*, 287.

67. E.g., "Creation as a whole can only enjoy the redeemed state when human beings are fully reconciled to God and to one another—that is, when persons have learnt to relate to God as father in the unity of sonship and when the nations have learned the lessons of good stewardship. At one time, Christians thought this must mean the conversion of the entire world to Christianity. It seems more likely to mean that the major world faiths will eventually share the same cosmic perspective that is provided by the Christ of God and that mankind will move together towards that 'Omega point', when a united human family will share fully in the life of God, which the Bible symbolises in the phrase, 'a new heaven and a new earth'," in Crewdson, *Christian Doctrine*, 358.

68. Polanyi's remarks regarding Merleau-Ponty's work as "an abundance of brilliant flashes without a constructive system" come to mind here; see Michael Polanyi and Harry Prosch, *Meaning* (Chicago: University of Chicago, 1975), 47.

69. The work of Richard T. Allen, particularly his *Transcendence and Immanence*, deserves mention at this point for its influence on the shape of the current project. However, the structure of Allen's work in *Transcendence and Immanence* is not as amenable to brief review as was the work of Manno, Rutledge, Torrance, Baumgarten, and Crewdson, and will therefore be brought to bear as our argument continues to unfold.

70. There is a considerable literature dedicated to exploring this issue. For a more complete treatment, see, e.g., Michel Henry, *I Am the Truth: Toward a Philosophy of Christianity*, trans. S. Emmanuel (Stanford: Stanford University, 2003); James P. Mackey, *The Critique of Theological Reason* (Cambridge and New York: Cambridge University, 2000); Leo Sweeney, *Christian Philosophy: Greek, Medieval, Contemporary Reflections* (New York: Peter Lang, 1997); Nancey Murphy, *Beyond Liberalism and Fundamentalism: How Modern and Postmodern Philosophy Set the Theological Agenda* (Valley Forge: Trinity Press, 1996); Francis J. Ambrosio, ed., *The Question of Christian Philosophy Today* (New York: Fordham University, 1999); etc.

71. See Alister McGrath, *Thomas F. Torrance: an Intellectual Biography* (Edinburgh: T & T Clark, 1999), 228-232.

72. Allen, *Transcendence and Immanence*, 56-58; cf. Michael Polanyi, *Personal Knowledge: Towards a Post-Critical Philosophy*, rev. ed. (Chicago: University of Chicago, 1962), 282-286.

73. Allen, *Transcendence and Immanence*, 56; cf. "The framework provided by worship must first have a prior and non-religious appeal to the child or unbeliever by way of its dogma, narratives, morality and ritual exercises before he can religiously comprehend them. ... The Faith is not, after all, a closed circle but needs to commend itself historically, morally, metaphysically, scientifically, and aesthetically," in op. cit., 40.

74. Allen, *Transcendence and Immanence*, 56; cf. "religion and above all Christianity have roots in secular experience, especially history in the case of Christianity, so that such experience and religion do bear upon each other in certain respects. ... Secular experience is a lower level which does not determine but leaves open the higher level of its religious significance, although its breakdown will destroy it," in op. cit., 42.

75. Allen, *Transcendence and Immanence*, 58.

76. Allen, *Transcendence and Immanence*, 58; Allen sees in Polanyi's notion of a stratified universe a kind of implicit cosmological argument, especially when considered from the perspective of his explication of the tacit dimension.

77. Alister McGrath, *Nature*, A Scientific Theology 1 (Grand Rapids: Wm. B. Eerdman's, 2001); idem, *Reality*, A Scientific Theology 2 (Grand Rapids: Wm. B. Eerdman's, 2002): idem, *Theory*, A Scientific Theology 3 (Grand Rapids: Wm. B. Eerdman's, 2003).

78. McGrath, *Reality*, 56.

79. See McGrath, *Nature*, 75-76. For McGrath's exposition of critical realism, see esp. idem, *Reality*, 146-160, 195-226.

80. See, e.g., McGrath, *Reality*, 64-72; idem, *Theory*, 66-76; etc.

81. See McGrath, *Theory*, 245-313.

82. See McGrath, *Nature*, 59, 142-143, 155-159, 184-186; idem, *Reality*, 285-294; idem, *Theory*, 234-236; etc.

83. See McGrath, *Reality*, 297-313.

84. McGrath makes passing reference to Polanyi's work several times; see, e.g., McGrath, *Reality*, 185, 205-206, and idem, *Theory*, 138, etc. That he does not engage Polanyi's thought more extensively is something of a mystery, but may perhaps be chalked up to his determination to engage the "mainline debate over critical realism" as a way of reinserting theological studies into the contemporary intellective enterprise; see idem, *Reality*, 208. In other words, McGrath's relative marginalization of Polanyi's thought may follow from the neglect Polanyi's work has received from "mainline" philosophy.

85. See Polanyi, *Personal Knowledge*, 252-255, 311; idem, *Science, Faith, and Society*, 2nd Ed. (Chicago: University of Chicago, 1963), 81-82.

86. See Polanyi, *Personal Knowledge*, 281.

87. See Michael Polanyi, *Scientific Thought and Social Reality*, F. Schwarz, ed. (New York: International Universities, 1974), 129-130.

88. Cf. Polanyi, *Personal Knowledge*, 405.

89. Polanyi, *Personal Knowledge*, 285.

90. Polanyi, *Personal Knowledge*, 198.

91. Polanyi, *Personal Knowledge*, 285; cf. op. cit., 199.

92. Polanyi, *Personal Knowledge*, 199.

93. See Allen, *Transcendence and Immanence*, 34-36.

94. Torrance, *Space, Time, and Resurrection*, 15-17.

95. Torrance, *Space, Time, and Resurrection*, 11; cf. 12-14.

96. Torrance, *Space, Time, and Resurrection*, 17-18, 42-43.

97. Torrance, *Space, Time, and Resurrection*, 15.

98. See Bruce D. Marshall, *Trinity and Truth*, Cambridge Studies in Christian Doctrine 3 (Cambridge and New York: Cambridge University, 2000).

99. Marshall's understanding of realist epistemology is informed almost entirely by correspondence theories of truth, while his understanding of anti-realist epistemologies is informed almost entirely by pragmatic or utilitarian theories of truth. Marshall's rejection
of both of these alternatives follows from his engagement with late modern analytic philosophy, especially the work of Donald Davidson and, less so, Willard Quine and Gottlob
Frege. Marshall's engagement with analytic thought leans at times towards the abstruse
and the technical, and does not bear on our efforts herein; see Marshall, *Trinity and
Truth*, 72-107, 217-241.

100. Marshall, *Trinity and Truth*, 242.

101. Cf. "We recognize the ultimate epistemic right which belongs to Jesus Christ by organizing our total system of belief around the narratives which identify him, crucified and
risen. If we ascribe this epistemic significance to Jesus, we shall be unwilling to hold true
any belief which we recognize to be inconsistent with these narratives, and, conversely,
unwilling to regard these narratives as false for the sake of holding true any other belief,
should that belief conflict with them," in Marshall, *Trinity and Truth*, 180.

102. See Marshall, *Trinity and Truth*, 17-49, 108-140.

103. Marshall, *Trinity and Truth*, 246.

104. See Marshall, *Trinity and Truth*, 246-250, 260-261.

105. Cf. "The Father raises Jesus by his own free and sovereign action, which is to bestow his
Spirit upon the slain Jesus. This gift to the crucified Jesus fully enacts the Spirit's mission, *begun at Jesus' baptism*, to abide in and on the Son. The Spirit gives the dead Jesus
the divine freedom to rise from the dead, by including Jesus once again in an ordered but
mutual bond of being, knowledge, and love with the Father," in Marshall, *Trinity and
Truth*, 246 (emphasis added). Marshall would have done better to posit the beginning of
the Spirit's mission, not at the baptism of Jesus, but at his conception, itself an event attested to as a work of the Spirit (cf. Mt 1.18-19; Lk 1.35). Cf. John McIntyre, *The Shape
of Pneumatology: Studies in the Doctrine of the Holy Spirit* (Edinburgh: T & T Clark,
1997), 45-49.

106. Marshall suggests that while the Son's specific role in our apprehension of his resurrection is to act on our minds (i.e., by presenting himself as the risen one), the Spirit's specific role is to act on our wills such that we are enabled to believe the truthfulness of the
testimony of the risen Son; see Marshall, *Trinity and Truth*, 251.

107. See Marshall, *Trinity and Truth*, 266.

108. See Marshall, *Trinity and Truth*, 278-281.

109. Marshall, *Trinity and Truth*, 202-203.

110. Cf. "If Jesus Christ is 'the truth,' then we should expect the truth-bestowing action of the
triune God to unify all true beliefs, and not simply those about the Trinity. We are looking for a single, theologically adequate concept of the truth for all true beliefs," in Marshall, *Trinity and Truth*, 272. Cf. also "Believing the gospel ... necessarily commits
believers to a comprehensive view of the world centered epistemically on the gospel nar-

rative itself. On such a view there will be no regions of belief and practice which can isolate themselves from the epistemic reach of the gospel. But conversely having such a comprehensive view also means that Christians will not be able to isolate the gospel from the rest of their beliefs, to be held true for whatever restricted purposes, pious or otherwise, Christians may want to use it. On the contrary, believing the gospel at all means that Christians must always venture forth, prepared to engage as best they can all life and reality–to interpret and assess whatever alien or novel beliefs they may encounter–in light of the narratives which identify Jesus," in op. cit., 118.

111. See Marshall, *Trinity and Truth*, 108-115.

112. See Marshall, *Trinity and Truth*, 273-274.

113. Note that Marshall suggests (following Thomas) that it is the Spirit's identity as love that enables the Spirit to make manifest the truth, "for it belongs to love to disclose hidden things" (Marshall quotes here from Thomas's *Commentary on John*, XIV.4). Further, the particular character of the Spirit's action as love rules out the possibility of generating faith through coercive argument, but rather requires the cultivation of a spirit of charity and adoration; see Marshall, *Trinity and Truth*, 180-181, 204-212.

114. E.g., Marshall suggests that in light of the reality of finitude and contingence in the creation, and especially that of evil, "there will be some actual states of affairs which correspond to nothing in God, arrangements of the world for which there is nothing in God of which they are the likeness, even remotely," in Marshall, *Trinity and Truth*, 274.

115. Cf. "We may be able to take the creative, redeeming, and consummating actions of the Trinity as a basis for grasping the identities of the divine persons, but we cannot take our grasp of their identities to consist in the knowledge of these actions," in Marshall, *Trinity and Truth*, 263.

116. See Marshall, *Trinity and Truth*, 122-123, 270-271.

117. Marshall, *Trinity and Truth*, 212-213; cf. 268-269.

118. Marshall observes that the Trinity "cannot be thought of as waiting, the way we must, for things to exist in order to know them. [God's] very knowledge of them must be productive of their existence and attributes," Marshall, *Trinity and Truth*, 123.

119. Marshall, *Trinity and Truth*, 146.

120. Polanyi, *Personal Knowledge*, 267.

121. Cf. "Beliefs succeed in terminating justificatory arguments just in case we do not have to give reasons for them. Without a terminus to the regress of reasons we will lack a way to decide whether the reasons we have given are good ones that is, whether they actually support the belief which prompted our search for reason in the first place. This sort of decision has to rely, it appears, on a nexus of belief which can serve as a reason, but does not itself require the giving of reasons. ... So holding beliefs rationally requires not only the ability to give reasons, but the ability to distinguish between those occasions when we need to give reasons, and those when we do not," in Marshall, *Trinity and Truth*, 142; cf. 166-167.

122. Cf. "Being a bearer of Christ's image is therefore a cognitively dependent relation. Having affections, thoughts, and desires which succeed in making us like another person requires having a range of true beliefs–in this case not only the belief that Jesus is risen, but countless others about the way his action and passion embody the purpose of the tri-une God, about what counts as virtuous action and affection, about how we should treat our neighbors, and so forth. ... The act by which we come to have true beliefs concerning the divine persons is therefore apparently not an end in itself, but serves the Trinity's purpose of making us bearers of Christ's image," in Marshall, *Trinity and Truth*, 266-267.

123. See Marshall, *Trinity and Truth*, 204-212.

124. E.g. "the more persistently we try to uphold the truth of a belief, the wider the range of beliefs over which it has epistemic primacy, and thus the higher the epistemic status it has for us," in Marshall, *Trinity and Truth*, 127; cf. "since all [Christian] beliefs have to be consistent with the narratives which identify Jesus and the Trinity in order to be true, the scope of the Christian community's assimilative efforts has to match the scope of the community's epistemic priorities: both must be universal and unrestricted," in op. cit., 153; cf. 118.

125. See Marshall, *Trinity and Truth*, 147-158.

126. See Polanyi, *Personal Knowledge*, 160-171.

127. Marshall, *Trinity and Truth*, 218, note 3. Marshall finds both of these descriptions of correspondence at work in medieval theology, and suggests that the wholesale dismissal of the first in the modern period led to the concomitant rejection of the second.

128. Cf. "participationist versions of the pragmatic thesis end up in a paradox: the more excellently or successfully a person participates in the church's practice, the less need he has to treat those practices as evidence for the church's beliefs (or would have, were practice susceptible of being treated in this way in the first place)," in Marshall, *Trinity and Truth*, 191; cf. 182-194.

129. See Marshall, *Trinity and Truth*, 206-207.

130. E.g., "In the correspondence of person to person by which the Trinity makes us Christ's icons one may hear an echo of the ancient idea that truth is the correspondence of mind to reality, though here it is the whole self, and not just the intellect, which shares in the relevant conformity. In this sense created persons affected by the truth-bestowing action of the Trinity may themselves be seen as truth-bearers. As whole selves, they can become 'true' when the action by which the triune God enables them to have the relevant true beliefs brings about their conformity to the risen Christ," in Marshall, *Trinity and Truth*, 268.

131. Allen, *Transcendence and Immanence*, 99.

5. The Trinitarian Ground of Personal Being

1.   E.g., not only does the task of trinitarian theology involve analysis of questions related to God's redemptive self-revelation in Jesus Christ and the Holy Spirit, a more comprehensive treatment would also require that some attention be given to issues more often asso-

ciated with the doctrine of God philosophically conceived (e.g., divine attributes, divine knowledge and action, theodicy, etc.) and the place of trinitarian theology in ecumenical and interfaith dialogue. George Newlands's *God in Christian Perspective* (Edinburgh: T & T Clark, 1994) is one effort that attempts to acknowledge (if not fully accommodate) the respective demands of each of these areas of study.

2. E.g., in *The Conflict of the Faculties*, a collection of essays published in 1798, Immanuel Kant complained that "the doctrine of the Trinity, taken literally, has *no practical relevance at all*, even if we think we understand it; and it is even more clearly irrelevant if we realize that it transcends all our concepts" (emphasis in the original), in Immanuel Kant, *Religion and Rational Theology*, ed. and trans. A.W. Wood and G. Di Giovanni (Cambridge: Cambridge University, 2001), 264; cf. "But, if this very faith (in a divine Trinity) were to be regarded not just as the representation of a practical idea, but as a faith that ought to represent what God is in himself, it would be a mystery surpassing all human concepts, hence unsuited to a revelation humanly comprehensible, and could only be declared in this respect as mystery," from Kant's 1793 *Religion Within the Boundaries of Mere Reason*, in Kant, *Religion and Rational Theology*, 167.

3. Even a sampling of projects dedicated to exploring the trinitarian shape of various aspects of the Christian faith would be unwieldy (and unnecessary) at this point. A list of representative examples would include Samuel M. Powell, *Participating in God: Creation and Trinity* (Minneapolis: Fortress Press, 2003); David S. Cunningham, *These Three Are One: the Practice of Trinitarian Theology* (Malden: Blackwell, 1998); Colin E. Gunton, *The One, the Three, and the Many: God, Creation, and the Culture of Modernity* (Cambridge and New York: Cambridge University, 1993); etc.

4. E.g., "Images and ideas of God as abstract, undifferentiated ideas of omnipotence are not simply 'an extension of the world.' They are an extension of the world perceived in the absence of spirit and without bearing witness! Images and ideas of God as abstract, undifferentiated ideas of omnipotence are an extension of the world *not perceived as creation.* The abstract idea of omnipotence ignores the sensitivity of faith for relations of power, relations of powerlessness, and the manifold ways in which the two are interlaced. Busy with its speculation, it misses the creator and the creation," in Michael Welker, *Creation and Reality*, trans. J. Hoffmeyer (Minneapolis: Fortress, 1999), 74. See also Karl Rahner, *The Trinity*, trans. J. Donceel (New York: Herder and Herder, 1970), 22 (emphasis in the original).

5. For a concise description of major loci of reflection relative to late modern trinitarian theology, see F. LeRon Shults, "Sharing in the Divine Nature: Transformation, Koinonia, and the Doctrine of God," in *On Being Christian...and Human: Essays in Celebration of Ray S. Anderson*, ed. Todd H. Speidell (Eugene: Wipf & Stock, 2002), esp. 90-109.

6. See esp. Yves Congar, *The Word and the Spirit*, trans. D. Smith (London and San Francisco: G. Chapman and Harper & Row, 1986). Cf. also Gary Badcock's observation that the development of Spirit-christology in the patristic period was probably frustrated in part by the fact that pneumatologically rich accounts of the incarnation were developed by individuals whose views were later determined to be heretical because of their subordinationism (e.g., Paul of Samosota, Theodotus of Byzantium); see Gary D. Badcock, *Light of Truth and Fire of Love: a Theology of the Holy Spirit* (Grand Rapids: Wm. B. Eerdman's, 1997), 39-42.

7. Robert J. Palma, "Polanyi and Christological Dualisms," in *Scottish Journal of Theology* 48 (1995), 212.

8. Palma, "Polanyi and Christological Dualisms," 221. Palma suggests that Dietrich Bonhoeffer is representative of the "ontological" approach to christology, and that Oscar Cullmann is representative of the "functional." Palma here seems to miss Bonhoeffer's own insistence on the unity of the person of Christ and the extent to which this unity discounts any question of distinguishing decisively between the divine and human natures, or between the person and work of Jesus; cf. "The separation of the question of christology from that of soteriology is necessary only to establish a theological method. For the christological question, by its very nature, must be addressed to the one complete Christ. This complete Christ is the historical Jesus, who can never in any way be separated from his work," in Dietrich Bonhoeffer, *Christ the Center*, trans. E.H. Robertson (New York: Harper-Collins, 1978), 39; cf. 27-38.

9. Cf. John McIntyre's description of the biblical witness to the person of Christ, in which "the indicator to the presence of the human nature operates automatically as the marker for the divine nature, so completely are they regarded as elements in a single situation. The matter of one being present with the other is not even mentioned: it is taken for granted," in John McIntyre, *The Shape of Christology: Studies in the Doctrine of the Person of Christ* (Edinburgh: T & T Clark, 1997), 85.

10. Cf. Gerald O'Collins's observations regarding the "near functional identity" in the biblical record between the presence and activity of the risen Christ and that of the Holy Spirit, in Gerald O'Collins, *Christology: a Biblical, Historical, and Systematic Study of Jesus Christ* (Oxford and New York: Oxford University, 1995), 150.

11. R.L. Sturch, "The Metaphysics of the Incarnation," in *Vox Evangelica* 10 (1977), 71-72.

12. For a thorough review of the themes traditionally associated with this question, see Wolfhart Pannenberg, *Jesus: God and Man*, trans. L.L. Wilkins and D.A. Priebe (Philadelphia: Westminster Press, 1968), 115-187.

13. Cf. Pannenberg's suggestion that it was primarily in terms of the "concept of the Spirit" that the early church most often attempted "to express God's presence in Jesus," in Pannenberg, *Jesus: God and Man*, 116; cf. 169-179.

14. See Jaroslav Pelikan, *The Emergence of the Catholic Tradition (100-600)*, The Christian Tradition: a History of the Development of Doctrine 1 (Chicago: University of Chicago, 1971), 211-225; Basil Studer, *Trinity and Incarnation: the Faith of the Early Church*, ed. Andrew Louth, trans. Matthias Westerhoff (Edinburgh and Collegeville: T & T Clark and Liturgical Press, 1993), 139-153.

15. See McIntyre, *Shape of Christology*, 286-288. Cf. "Christ possesses all the attributes and qualities of human nature, but they are vitalized by the divine relational being of the Son of God. This takes nothing away from the perfection of Christ's human nature and guarantees that the incarnate Word is consubstantial with us in his humanity," in Jean Galot, *The Person of Christ: a Theologial Insight*, trans. M.A. Bouchard (Chicago: Franciscan Herald Press, 1984), 5.

16. Cf. Jean Galot's observation that the question of why the human nature of Christ cannot be thought to be a person is a "particularly delicate problem, since it requires us to determine the formal constituent of the person in such a way that when we affirm the absence of this constituent in Christ's human nature we take away none of its perfection. The absence of human personality cannot involve any incompleteness or imperfection in the human nature assumed by the Word," in Galot, *Person of Christ*, 12.

17. Cf. Karl Rahner, *Hominisation: The Evolutionary Origin of Man as a Theological Problem*, trans. W.T. O'Hara (New York, NY: Herder & Herder, 1965), esp. 62-93.

18. Leontius suggested that the human nature of Christ exists, not anhypostatically (i.e., without its own *hypostasis*), but enhypostatically (i.e., rightly possessing its own *hypostasis* in the divine *hypostasis* of the Son). Similarly, Ephraim employed the phrase "*synthetos he hypostasis*" to describe the manner in which the two *hypostases* signified by the two natures of Christ are blended in a way that the natures themselves are not. See McIntyre, *Shape of Christology*, 89-103. It was, however, John of Damascus that brought the doctrine of the enhypostasia to fruition; see his *Fount of Knowledge*, ed. J. Deferarri, et al, trans. F.H. Chase, Fathers of the Church 37 (New York: Fathers of the Church, 1958), esp. XLIV. The Damascene recognized three ways in which the idea of an "enhypostaton" might be understood, and saw in the incarnation the definitive example of that "which has been assumed by another hypostasis and in this has its existence." The other two ways in which John understood enhypostatic existence included, first, entities that do not subsist in themselves but are nonetheless regarded by way of their subsistence (e.g., particular instantiations of a universal), and second, "compound" entities consisting of two substances coming together in a single hypostasis (e.g., spirit and body).

19. Cf. "The harmony of similarity between the two natures, that makes possible the manifestation of one through the other, does not imply their unity. We even know that to insist on unity in this instance would open the way to Monophysitism. The constitution of Christ demands proper emphasis on the distinction of his natures, which are united without alteration or confusion," in Galot, *Person of Christ*, 12.

20. This suggests intriguing possibilities for revisioning the distinction offered by Maximus the Confessor between the natural and the gnomic will, i.e., we might conceive of the various boundary conditions established by the human nature of Christ in terms of the human energy or will of Christ and the marginal control exercised by the divine nature of Christ in terms of the divine energy or will of Christ. Since the human nature of Christ does not itself signify a form of distinct personal being, Christ could not be said to evince what Maximus refers to as the gnomic will, but rather subsists entirely in obedience to the divine will of the Son (i.e., under the power of the natural will). Cf. Andrew Louth, *Maximus the Confessor* (London and New York: Routledge, 1996), 51-59.

21. Cf. Lars Thunberg's suggestion that Maximus's notion of theandric christology highlights the "entirely unique and new relationship that is established in Jesus Christ as being both fully human and fully divine: God and man cooperating for the benefit of the whole creation, not separated and yet not mixed, not confused and yet in full harmony," in Lars Thunberg, *Man and the Cosmos: the Vision of St. Maximus the Confessor* (Crestwood: St. Vladimir's Seminary, 1985), 71.

22. Adrian Thatcher seems to make just this mistake in his *Truly a Person, Truly God: a Post-Mythical View of Jesus* (London: SPCK, 1990), esp. 80-92. Thatcher suggests that

we can affirm that the divine nature as well as the human nature of Jesus can be said to have had a form of personal being without having to say that there are two persons in Christ provided we recognize that we do not mean the same thing when speaking of the "person" of Jesus' human nature as we do when speaking of the "Person" of Jesus' divine nature, the former representing the modern understanding(s) of the term "person" and the latter representing the "ancient metaphysical concept" of the term "person." This, however, seems to resemble Nestorian christology, not to mention leaving us with an understanding of the concept of the person that invites confusion. The distinction between "person" and "hypostasis" proposed by Jean Galot, whereby "person" signifies "who" and "hypostasis" signifies "how," seems more in keeping with orthodox christology; see Galot, *Person of Christ*, 9-11.

23.   This last statement anticipates the further elaboration of a trinitarian theology of creation explicated along the lines of the contiguity of *logos* and *pneuma* in creation; cf. Gunton's exposition of the role of the Spirit in securing the integrity of creation, in Colin Gunton, *The Triune Creator: a Historical and Systematic Study*, Edinburgh Studies in Constructive Theology (Edinburgh: Wm B. Eerdman's and Edinburgh University, 1998), 10, 143-144, 160-161, 184.

24.   Cf. Galot's comments on the need to read the incarnation through a soteriological lens: the "determination of the formal constituent of the person [of Christ] must not be made in the abstract. It must provide a better understanding of Christ's mission," in Galot, *Person of Christ*, 13.

25.   In addition to the developments discussed in what follows, we might also profitably examine the emergence and development of contemporary panentheism as represented by, e.g., Joseph Bracken, Philip Clayton, and others. See Joseph Bracken, *Christianity and Process Thought: Spirituality for a Changing World* (Philadelphia and London: Templeton Press, 2006); idem, *The One in the Many: a Contemporary Reconstruction of the God-World Relationship* (Grand Rapids and Cambridge: Wm. B. Eerdman's, 2001); idem, *Society and Spirit: a Trinitarian Cosmology* (Cranbury: Associated University Press, 1991); Philip Clayton, *The Problem of God in Modern Thought* (Grand Rapids: Wm. B. Eerdman's, 2000): idem, *God and Contemporary Science*, Edinburgh Studies in Constructive Theology (Edinburgh: Edinburgh University, 1997); etc.

26.   Catherine Mowry LaCugna, *God for Us: the Trinity & Christian Life* (New York: Harper Collins, 1993). See also Dorothea Wendebourg, "From the Cappadocian Fathers to Gregory Palamas: the Defeat of Trinitarian Theology," in *Studia Patristica* XVII:1, ed. Elizabeth A. Livingstone (Oxford: Pergamon, 1982).

27.   LaCugna explores these themes and their interdependence as she develops her ontology of personhood; see esp. LaCugna, *God for Us*, 243-305.

28.   See LaCugna, *God for Us*, 377-411.

29.   See esp. LaCugna, *God for Us*, 283-288.

30.   I am indebted here to the summary of Rahner's thought provided in Stanley J. Grenz and Roger E. Olson, *20th Century Theology: God and the World in a Transitional Age* (Downer's Grove: InterVarsity Press, 1992), 238-254.

31. Grenz and Olson, *20th Century Theology*, 172-186.

32. Grenz and Olson, *20th Century Theology*, 186-199.

33. See Paul D. Molnar, *Divine Freedom and the Doctrine of the Immanent Trinity: in Dialogue with Karl Barth and Contemporary Theology* (London and New York: T & T Clark, 2002).

34. See, e.g., Molnar, *Divine Freedom*, 61-81.

35. See, e.g., Molnar, *Divine Freedom*, 197-233.

36. See, e.g., Molnar, *Divine Freedom*, 125-166.

37. See, e.g., Molnar, *Divine Freedom*, 235-271.

38. See esp. Molnar, *Divine Freedom*, 172-181.

39. See Richard Allen, *Transcendence and Immanence in the Philosophy of Michael Polanyi and Christian Theism*, Rutherford Studies in Contemporary Theology 5 (Lewiston: Edwin Mellen, 1992), esp. 154-156.

40. Cf. Allen, *Transcendence and Immanence*, 112-118.

41. Cf. "In terms of Polanyi's philosophy, the denial of Natural Theology entails that the theologian does not participate in his theology. For if man contributes nothing, from his own experience and reasoning, to his knowledge of God, then there results a theological Objectivism as equally at fault as the Objectivism in natural and human sciences which Polanyi opposed," in Allen, *Transcendence and Immanence*, 52.

42. Cf. Allen's account of the complementarity of apophatic and kataphatic theology, in Allen, *Transcendence and Immanence*, 81-83.

43. See Michael Polanyi, *Science, Faith, and Society* (Chicago: University of Chicago, 1964), 84.

44. See Michael Polanyi, *The Tacit Dimension* (Chicago: University of Chicago, 1966), 92.

45. Michael Polanyi, *Personal Knowledge: Towards a Post-Critical Philosophy*, Revised Edition (Chicago: University of Chicago, 1962), 311; cf. 104.

46. Polanyi, *Personal Knowledge*, 82-87.

47. Cf. "What emerges from contemporary theology is that a doctrine of the immanent Trinity is possible to the extent that it is itself explicitly constructed *sub specie temporis*, an idea that is clearly based on the presupposition that a doctrine of the Trinity *sub specie temporis* can and does yield a doctrine of the immanent Trinity," in Badcock, *Light of Truth and Fire of Love*, 177. Cf. also the reconsideration of Rahner's trinitarian axiom provided by Bruce D. Marshall in Marshall's *Trinity and Truth* (Cambridge and New York: Cambridge University, 2000), 259-265.

48. See, e.g., Thomas F. Torrance, *The Christian Doctrine of God: One Being, Three Persons* (Edinburgh: T & T Clark, 1996), 140-141. Torrance seeks to follow both Gregory of Nyssa and Gregory of Nazianzus in saying that it is God the Father who, as the "uncaused cause" of all things, grounds the relations of the divine persons.

49. See Polanyi, *Personal Knowledge*, 381-405. It is worth noting that Polanyi's concern was not the concept of the person *per se*, but rather the appearance of self-conscious life situated within a context of transcendent responsibility; cf. "While the first rise of living individuals overcame the meaninglessness of the universe by establishing in it centres of subjective interests, the rise of human thought in its turn overcame these subjective interests by its universal intent. The first revolution was incomplete, for a self-centred life ending in death has little meaning. The second revolution aspires to eternal meaning, but owing to the finitude of man's condition it too remains blatantly incomplete. Yet the precarious foothold gained by man in the realm of ideas lends sufficient meaning to his brief existence; the inherent stability of man seems to me adequately supported and certified by his submission to ideals which I believe to be universal," in ibid., 389.

50. Polanyi, *Personal Knowledge*, 383-384 (emphases in the original).

51. Cf. esp. Polanyi, *Personal Knowledge*, 195-200.

52. Polanyi, *Personal Knowledge*, 198. A study of the ramifications of Polanyi's notion of indwelling for understanding Christian worship is provided in Ronald E. Parker, *Religious Indwelling: a Post-Critical Understanding of Ritual Based on Michael Polanyi's Epistemology* (Ph.D. dissertation: Graduate Theological Union, 1974).

53. The simultaneity of what we are here referring to in terms of active and passive participation through indwelling recapitulates both the principle of "*adaequatio intellectus et rei*," that is, the conformity of the mind to the object(s) of its apprehension, as well as the congruence between the *ordo essendi* and the *ordo cognoscendi*. Cf. "truth is defined as conformity between intellect and thing. Hence to know that conformity is to know truth. ... Truth, then, can be present in sense, or in intellect knowing a meaning, as in a thing that is true; but not as the object known is in the knower, which is implied by the word 'truth'; for the perfection of the intellect is truth as known. Therefore properly speaking truth is in the intellect in its function of affirming and denying one reality of another; and not in sense, nor in intellect knowing the meaning," in Thomas Aquinas, *Summa theologiæ*, v. 2, ed. T. Gilby (New York and London: Blackfriars in conjunction with McGraw-Hill and Eyre & Spottiswoode, 1964), I.16.ii.

54. Cf. Torrance, *Christian Doctrine of God*, 140-141.

55. We might even say that the Father's generation of the Son evinces a certain passivity inasmuch as it signifies the Father's willingness to allow the Son to actualize his own personal being as the Son of the Father rather than imposing this on him.

56. The Son's active integration and interiorization of his relation with the Father does not so much signify that relation itself as much as it does the Son's self-actualization of his own identity as the Son.

57. To the question of whether or not the Father alone might generate the Spirit in a manner different from that of the Son, we can respond that the result would be a Spirit subordi-

nate in divinity to the Father and the Son. The Father, in other words, can bestow nothing other than the gift of personal being (through the translation of the transcendent personalizing dynamics of the Godhead), a gift that by virtue of the perfection and simplicity of the divine nature does not admit to multiple recipients, so to speak.

58. I.e., as the Son proceeds, not from the person of the Father but from the being of the Father (which is the being of God), so too can the Spirit be said to proceed, not from the persons of the Father and the Son, but from their being (which is of course the being of the Spirit as well, but only inasmuch as he receives it from the Father and the Son).

59. This last statement anticipates the elaboration of a trinitarian theology of creation explicated along the lines of the extension of personal being by way of indwelling, a subject to which we will briefly return later in this chapter.

60. See esp. Polanyi, *Personal Knowledge*, 299-324; idem, *Tacit Dimension*, 79-81, wherein Polanyi describes the extent to which the "personal boundary conditions" of one's "geography" evoke both particular opportunities and responsibilities.

61. For two recent (and disparate) explorations of the question of the absolute personhood of God , cf. Thomas Torrance, *Christian Doctrine of God*, 123-135, 140-141, 155-167, and David Coffey, *Deus Trinitas: the Doctrine of the Triune God* (New York: Oxford University Press, 1999), 66-76.

62. See Polanyi, *Personal Knowledge*, 86.

63. See Anselm of Canterbury, *Proslogion* II, in *A Scholastic Miscellany: Anselm to Ockham*, ed. and trans. E.R. Fairweather, The Library of Christian Classics 10 (Philadelphia: Westminster Press, 1956), 73-74. Anselm, in an effort to preserve the mystery of divine being, later asserts that not only is God "that than which a greater cannot be thought," but is even "something greater than can be thought," in op. cit., XV.

64. See Anselm of Canterbury, *Proslogion*, XXIII.

65. Examples of recent works dedicated to exploring the viability of a theology of perfect being include Joshua Hoffman and Gary S. Rosenkrantz, *The Divine Attributes* (Oxford and Malden: Blackwell, 2002); Katherin A. Rogers, *Perfect Being Theology* (Edinburgh: Edinburgh University, 2000); Ermanno Bencivenga, *Logic and Other Nonsense: the Case of Anselm and His God* (Princeton: Princeton University, 1996); Gerard J. Hughes, *The Nature of God* (London and New York: Routledge, 1995); Graham Oppy, *Ontological Arguments and Belief in God* (Cambridge and New York: Cambridge University, 1995); etc.

66. Should it seem that our direction here departs significantly from the course we have followed in this and the previous chapter, we can note (with slight modification) George Newlands's suggestion that the consideration of divine being and action "*remoto Christo*" can be useful "in order to stretch our theological imagination as far as possible precisely in order to do justice to the difference that the Christological [and pneumatological] dimension makes," in Newlands, *God in Christian Perspective*, 104.

67. Cf. Coffey, *Deus Trinitas*, 66, 81-83.

68. Cf. "The claim to transcend-yet-preserve [*Aufhebung*] religion or religious representations within the realm of the concept, paradigmatically expressed in Hegel's system, is thus only the symptom of a more general lack. This lack does not merely concern the relationship of philosophy to religion and theology; it is the symptom of disregarding the finitude of philosophical thought, or at least of neglecting the significance of this fact for the form taken by philosophical reflection. ... Any renewal of metaphysics that wishes to rise above such objections must give adequate place to human finitude, the finitude that results from the historicity of every starting point for metaphysical reflection," in Wolfhart Pannenberg, *Metaphysics and the Idea of God*, trans. Philip Clayton (Grand Rapids: Wm. B. Eerdman's, 1990), 92; cf. 61-62.

69. Cf. "Unlike the old idea of 'simple substance', which was held to be indissoluble and so immortal (and thus really in conflict with Theism), a comprehensive entity is manifestly contingent. It is contingent as not being self-explanatory and also in being liable to dissolution. For it bears within itself the possibility that the lower level can escape the control of the higher. There is always the logical possibility of breakdown," in Allen, *Transcendence and Immanence*, 61-62.

70. Cf. Allen, *Transcendence and Immanence*, 146-148.

71. Thomas's analysis of the correlation of essence and existence in God relies on a formal distinction between them in order to prove that they are inseparable; see Aquinas, *Summa theologiæ*, Ia.3.iv. See also Wolfhart Pannenberg's brief but helpful description of the introduction of the distinction between "essence" and "existence" and the notion of God as "*actus essendi*" in Western thought, in Pannenberg's *Metaphysics and the Idea of God*, 69-70; cf. also Coffey, *Deus Trinitas*, 73-75.

72. Cf. "For God, we said, is not composed of extended parts, since he is not a body; nor of form and matter; nor does he differ from his own nature; nor his nature from his existence; nor can one distinguish in him genus and difference; nor substance and accidents. It is clear then that there is no way in which God is composite, and he must be altogether simple," in Aquinas, *Summa theologiæ*, Ia.3.vii.

73. E.g., "Every conception of the absolute One must today prove its worth by showing itself to be not only the source and completion of the world but also the constitutive ground and highest good of subjectivity," in Pannenberg, *Metaphysics*, 62.

74. E.g., recent reconsiderations of the notion of divine impassibility in Thomas G. Weinandy, *Does God Suffer?* (Edinburgh and Notre Dame: T & T Clark and University of Notre Dame, 2000); Kristiaan Depoortere, *A Different God: a Christian View of Suffering* (Louvain and Grand Rapids: Peeters Press and Wm. B. Eerdman's, 1995); I.A. Dorner, *Divine Immutability: a Critical Reconsideration* (Minneapolis: Fortress Press, 1994); Joseph M. Hallman, *The Descent of God: Divine Suffering in History and Theology* (Minneapolis: Fortress Press, 1991); Paul S. Fiddes, *The Creative Suffering of God* (Oxford: Clarendon Press, 1988).

75. A paradigmatic example is Thomas's analysis of the attributes he includes as part of his explication of the existence and nature of God; see Aquinas, *Summa theologiæ*, Ia.2-11.

76. Our earlier review of Torrance's suggestion that we understand divine being "not simply in terms of the self-grounded Being of God, but as the Being of God *for others*" is apropos here; see Torrance, *Christian Doctrine of God*, 132.

77. Relative to the different ways absolute divine personhood has been expounded in contemporary trinitarian theology, we seem to be moving closer here to Thomas Torrance than to David Coffey (see note 63, above); cf. "to say that God is intrinsically personal does not mean that we must think of the one God as *a* Person in the relational sense of the the three divine Persons in their objective relations to one another, in the same way that the Father, Son, and the Holy Spirit are each *a* Person in relation to the other two Persons, but rather that God is completely personal in himself," in Torrance, *Christian Doctrine of God*, 161.

78. Cf. Kathryn Tanner on the "non-competitive" character of God's relationship with the world, in Tanner's *Jesus, Humanity, and the Trinity: a Brief Systematic Theology* (Minneapolis: Fortress Press, 2001), 2-13, 41-46.

79. Joan Crewdson explores a similar possibility by way of an appropriation (via Moltmann) of the doctrine of *zimzum*, which suggests that the world comes into being in a "space" ceded by God, who withdraws himself so as to allow for the emergence and development of a free creation. Unlike Moltmann, however, Crewdson insists that the space ceded by God wherein the world comes into being must be understood, not as a negation (or "nihil"), but very much in personal terms. See Crewdson, *Christian Doctrine*, 186-194, 234-237, 319-320.

80. Cf. Basarab Nicolescu, "Levels of Representation and Levels of Reality: Towards an Ontology of Science," in *The Concept of Nature in Science and Theology–Part Two*, ed. N.H. Gregersen, M.W.S. Parsons, and C. Wassermann (Geneva: Labor et Fides, 1998), esp. 97-99.

81. See Stratford Caldecott, "A Science of the Real: the Renewal of Christian Cosmology," in *Communio* 25, no. 3 (1998), 462-479. Caldecott's project in many ways resembles Colin Gunton's *Enlightenment and Alienation: an Essay Towards a Trinitarian Theology* (Grand Rapids: Wm. B. Eerdman's, 1985).

82. Caldecott, "Science of the Real," 476. Caldecott quotes here from C.S. Lewis's *The Abolition of Man*. Lewis continues, "The analogy between the *Tao* of Man and the instincts of an animal species would mean for it new light cast on the unknown thing, Instinct, by the inly known reality of conscience and not a reduction of conscience to the category of Instinct. Its followers would not be free with the words *only* and *merely*. In a word, it would conquer Nature without being at the same time conquered by her and buy knowledge at a lower cost than that of life," in C.S. Lewis, *The Abolition of Man* (New York: Macmillan, 1955), 89-90.

83. See Caldecott, "Science of the Real," 472.

84. Caldecott (following Balthasar) observes that in the doctrine of the Trinity, we recognize that "the distinction of one person from another deepens in direct proportion to their unity in love," a principle we can also apply to the relationship between God and the world; see Caldecott, "Science of the Real," 473-474; cf. "the triune God is the one who, as creator and sustainer of a real world of which we are a part, makes it possible for us to

know our world," in Gunton, *Enlightenment and Alienation*, 52. Note, too, that this provides yet another perspective on the insufficiency of Joan Crewdson's efforts at the construction of a Polanyian theology, and provides a further rationale as to why her understanding of the relationship between God and the creation lapses into pantheism.

85. Caldecott's analysis recapitulates in many ways Polanyi's description of the development of moral inversion; see Caldecott, "Science of the Real," 463-472. Cf. Gunton, *Enlightenment and Alienation*, 1-25, 57-70; Philip Sherrard, "The Desanctification of Nature," in *Sanctity and Secularity: Papers Read at the Eleventh Annual Meeting and the Twelfth Annual Meeting of the Ecclesiastical Historical Society*, ed. D. Baker (Oxford: Basil Blackwell, 1973).

86. Caldecott describes human knowing such that the act of apprehension is seen as a creative one, something that actualizes "what was merely potential into a single definite outcome," thus mirroring (in a contingent, not to mention a fallen or sinful, manner) both the creative and sovereign work of God; see Caldecott, "Science of the Real," 469-470.

87. Caldecott, "Science of the Real," 470-471; cf. Gunton, *Enlightenment and Alienation*, 71-89.

88. Caldecott, "Science of the Real," 478. Cf. "If love is the deepest meaning of the objective universe, the scientist and the mathematician are fully vindicated in their intuition that beauty (or 'elegance') must somehow be the signature of truth. Central to Balthasar's thought is the *Gestalt* that enables a recovery of the notion of substantial form, and it is this which makes beauty possible," in op. cit., 477.

89. Cf. "The whole point of the perspective described here is that the connection between subjective and objective is no longer arbitrary (as for Cartesian science) but intrinsic: knower and known, while eternally distinct, belong to one single reality, and the meaning at the center of that reality is the Person of the Logos. The unity-in-distinction of the Trinity is the basis for an analogy that runs right through creation as a kind of watermark: the analogy of 'spousal' union between subject and object, self and other. The life of love revealed in Christ promises to each of us no mere absorption into the Beloved, but our own integrity and fulfillment in the very measure we give ourselves away," in Caldecott, "Science of the Real," 477.

90. Avery Dulles, "Faith, Church, and God: Insights from Michael Polanyi," in *Theological Studies* 45, no. 3 (1984), 550.

Bibliography

Books by Michael Polanyi

Polanyi, Michael. *The Contempt of Freedom*. London: Watts & Co., 1940.

———. *Full Employment and Free Trade*. Cambridge: Cambridge University, 1945.

———. *The Planning of Science*. Oxford: Society for Freedom in Science, 1946.

———. *The Foundations of Academic Freedom*. Oxford: Society for Freedom in Science, 1947.

———. *The Logic of Liberty: Reflections and Rejoinders*. Chicago: University of Chicago, 1951.

———. *Pure and Applied Science and Their Appropriate Forms of Organization*. Oxford: Society for Freedom in Science, 1953.

———. *The Magic of Marxism and the Next Stage of History*. Manchester: Committee on Science and Freedom, 1956.

———. *The Study of Man*. Chicago: University of Chicago, 1959.

———. *Beyond Nihilism*. Cambridge: Cambridge University, 1960.

———. *Personal Knowledge: Towards a Post-Critical Philosophy*, Revised Edition. Chicago: University of Chicago, 1962.

———. *Science, Faith, and Society*. 2nd Ed. Chicago: University of Chicago, 1963.

———. *The Tacit Dimension*. Chicago: University of Chicago, 1966.

———. *Knowing and Being: Essays by Michael Polanyi*. Ed. M. Grene. London and Chicago: Routledge & Kegan Paul and University of Chicago, 1969.

———. *Scientific Thought and Social Reality*. Ed. F. Schwarz. New York: International Universities, 1974.

———. *Society, Economics, and Philosophy: Selected Papers*. Ed. R.T. Allen. New Brunswick: Transaction, 1997.

Polanyi, Michael, and Harry Prosch. *Meaning*. Chicago: University of Chicago, 1975.

Essays and Articles by Michael Polanyi

Polanyi, Michael. "Science: its Reality and Freedom." *The Nineteenth Century* 135 (1944): 78-83.

———. "The Foundations of Freedom in Science." *Physical Science and Human Values*. Ed. E.P. Wigner. Princeton: Princeton University, 1947.

———. "From Copernicus to Einstein." *Encounter* 5 (1955): 54-63.

———. "Faith and Reason." *Journal of Religion* 41 (1961): 237-247.

———. "Tacit Knowing: Its Bearing on Some Problems of Philosophy." *Review of Modern Physics* 34 (1962): 601-616.

————. "The Unaccountable Element in Science." *Philosophy* 37 (1962):1-14.

————. "Science and Religion: Separate Dimensions or Common Ground?" *Philosophy Today* 7 (1963): 4-14.

————. "Science and Man's Place in the Universe." *Science as a Cultural Force.* Ed. H. Woolf. Baltimore: Johns Hopkins, 1964.

————. "The Structure of Consciousness." *Brain* 88 (1965): 799-810.

————. "The Creative Imagination." *Chemical and Engineering News* 44 (1966): 85-93.

————. "The Logic of Tacit Inference." *Philosophy* 41 (1966): 1-18.

————. "The Message of the Hungarian Revolution." *American Scholar* 35 (1966): 261-276.

————. "Life Transcending Physics and Chemistry." *Chemical and Engineering News* 45 (1967): 54-66.

————. "The Growth of Science in Society." *Minerva* 5 (1967): 533-545.

————. "Do Life Processes Transcend Physics and Chemistry?" *Zygon* 3 (1968): 442-472.

————. "The Body-Mind Relation." *Man and the Science of Man.* Ed. W.R. Coulson and C.R. Rogers. Columbus: Charles E. Merrill, 1968.

————. "The Growth of Science in Society." *Man and the Science of Man.* Ed. W.R. Coulson and C.R. Rogers. Columbus: Charles E. Merrill, 1968.

————. "Life's Irreducible Structure." *Science* 160 (1968): 1308-1312.

————. "Logic and Psychology." *American Psychologist* 23 (1968): 27-43.

————. "The Determinants of Social Action." *Roads to Freedom.* Ed. E. Streissler. New York: A.M. Kelley, 1969.

————. "On Body and Mind." *The New Scholasticism* 43 (1969): 195-204.

————. "Life's Irreducible Structure." *Journal of the American Scientific Affiliation* 22 (1970): 123-131.

————. "Transcendence and Self-Transcendence." *Soundings* 53 (1970): 88-94.

————. "What is a Painting?" *American Scholar* 39 (1970): 655-669.

————. "Why Did We Destroy Europe?" *Studium Generale* 23 (1970): 909-916.

————. "Discoveries of Science." *Science, Philosophie, Foi.* Ed. S. Dockx, et al. Paris: Beauchesne, 1974.

————. "The Creative Imagination." *The Concept of Creativity in Science and Art.* Ed. D. Dutton and M. Krauz. The Hague: Martinus Nijhoff, 1981.

————. "Forms of Atheism." *Convivium* 13 (1981): 5-13.

Audio Recordings of Lectures Presented by Michael Polanyi

Polanyi, Michael. *The Destruction of Reality.* History and Hope 1. Los Angeles: Pacifica Tape Library, 1962.

————.*The Realm of the Unspoken.* History and Hope 2. Los Angeles: Pacifica Tape Library, 1962.

————.*The Vindication of Realities.* History and Hope 3. Los Angeles: Pacifica Tape Library, 1962.

————.*A Society of Explorers.* History and Hope 4. Los Angeles: Pacifica Tape Library, 1962.

Secondary Books and Monographs

Allen, Richard T. *Polanyi*. London: Routledge, 1990.

———. *Transcendence and Immanence in the Philosophy of Michael Polanyi and Christian Theism*. Rutherford Studies in Contemporary Theology 5. Lewiston: Edwin Mellen, 1992.

Anselm of Canterbury. *Proslogion. A Scholastic Miscellany: Anselm to Ockham*. Ed. and Trans. E.R. Fairweather. The Library of Christian Classics 10. Philadelphia: Westminster Press, 1956.

Apczynski, John. *Doers of the Word: Toward a Foundational Theology Based on the Thought of Michael Polanyi*. Missoula: Scholar's Press, 1977.

Aquinas, Thomas. *Summa Theologiæ* 1-60. Ed. T. Gilby. New York and London: Blackfriars in conjunction with McGraw-Hill and Eyre & Spottiswoode, 1964.

Badcock, Gary D. *Light of Truth and Fire of Love: a Theology of the Holy Spirit*. Grand Rapids: Wm. B. Eerdman's, 1997.

Bagood, Albert. *The Role of Belief in Scientific Discovery: Michael Polanyi and Karl Popper*. Ph.D. dissertation: University of Fribourg, 1998.

Barth, Karl. *Protestant Theology in the Nineteenth Century: Its Background and History*. Valley Forge: Judson Press, 1973.

Baumgarten, Barbara Dee Bennett. *Visual Art as Theology*. New Studies in Aesthetics 21. New York: Peter Lang, 1994.

Beckermann, A., H. Flohr, and J. Kim, eds. *Emergence or Reduction? Essays on the Prospects of Nonreductive Physicalism*. Berlin: Walter de Gruyter, 1992.

Bonhoeffer, Dietrich. *Christ the Center*. Trans. E.H. Robertson. New York: Harper-Collins, 1978.

Bourgeois, Warren. *Persons: What Philosophers Say About You*. Waterloo: Wilfrid Laurier University, 1995.

Brown, Colin. *From the Ancient World to the Age of Enlightenment*. Christianity and Western Thought: a History of Philosophers, Ideas, and Movements 1. Downer's Grove: IVP, 1990.

Clarke, W. Norris. *Person and Being*. Milwaukee: Marquette University, 1993.

Clayton, Philip. *God and Contemporary Science*. Edinburgh Studies in Constructive Theology. Edinburgh: Edinburgh University, 1997.

———. *Explanation from Physics to Theology: an Essay in Rationality and Religion*. New Haven: Yale, 1989.

———. *The Problem of God in Modern Thought*. Grand Rapids: Wm. B. Eerdman's, 2000.

Coats, J.B. *The Crisis of the Human Person: Some Personalist Interpretations*. London: Longman, Green & Co., 1949.

Coffey, David. *Deus Trinitas: the Doctrine of the Triune God*. New York: Oxford University, 1999.

Crewdson, Joan. *Christian Doctrine in Light of Michael Polanyi's Theory of Personal Knowledge: a Personalist Theology*. Toronto Studies in Theology 66. Lewiston: Edwin Mellen, 1994.

Del Colle, Ralph. *Christ and the Spirit: Spirit-Christology in Trinitarian Perspective*. Oxford and New York: Oxford University, 1994.

de Margerie, Bertrand. *The Christian Trinity in History.* Trans. E.J. Fortman. Studies in Historical Theology 1. Petersham: St. Bede's Publications, 1982.

den Bok, Nico. *Communicating the Most High: a Systematic Study of Person and Trinity in the Theology of Richard of St. Victor (†1173).* Bibliotheca Victorina 7. Paris: Brepols, 1996.

Dulles, Avery. *Models of Revelation.* Maryknoll: Orbis, 1992.

———. *The Craft of Theology: from Symbol to System.* New York: Crossroad, 1992.

Forte, Bruno. *The Trinity as History: Saga of the Christian God.* 3rd Ed. Trans. P. Rotondi. Staten Island: Alba House, 1989.

Galot, Jean. *The Person of Christ: a Theological Insight.* Trans. M.A. Bouchard. Chicago: Franciscan Herald Press, 1984.

Gelwick, Richard. *The Way of Discovery.* New York: Oxford University, 1977.

Gill, Jerry. *On Knowing God: New Directions for the Future of Theology.* Philadelphia: Westminster, 1981.

———. *The Tacit Mode: Michael Polanyi's Postmodern Philosophy.* Albany: State University of New York, 2000.

Gilson, Etienne. *The Unity of Philosophical Experience.* San Francisco: Ignatius, 1964.

Gregersen, N.H., W.B. Drees, and U. Görman, eds. *The Human Person in Science and Theology.* Grand Rapids: Wm. B. Eerdman's, 2000.

Gregersen, N.H., U. Görman, and C. Wassermann, eds. *The Interplay Between Scientific and Theological Worldviews, Parts 1-2.* Geneva: Labor et Fides, 1999.

Gregersen, N.H., M.W.S. Parsons, and C. Wasserman, eds. *The Concept of Nature in Science and Theology, Parts 1-2.* Geneva: Labor et Fides, 1997.

Gregersen, N.H., and J.W. van Huyssteen, eds. *Rethinking Theology and Science: Six Models for the Current Dialogue.* Grand Rapids: Wm. B. Eerdman's, 1998.

Gunton, Colin E. *Enlightenment and Alienation: an Essay Towards a Trinitarian Theology.* Grand Rapids: Wm. B. Eerdman's, 1985.

———. *The Triune Creator: a Historical and Systematic Study.* Edinburgh Studies in Constructive Theology. Grand Rapids and Edinburgh: Wm. B. Eerdman's and Edinburgh University, 1998.

Hipp, Stephen A. *"Person" in Christian Tradition and the Conception of Saint Albert the Great: a Systematic Study of its Concept as Illuminated by the Mysteries of the Trinity and the Incarnation.* Beiträge zur Geschichte der Philosophie und Theologie des Mittelalters 57. Münster: Druckhaus Aschendorff, 2001.

Hoekema, Anthony. *Created in God's Image.* Grand Rapids: Wm. B. Eerdman's, 1986.

Hoy, Terry. *Praxis, Truth, and Liberation: Essays on Gadamer, Taylor, Polanyi, Habermas, Gutierrez, and Ricoeur.* Lanham: University Press, 1988.

Ignotus, Paul, ed. *The Logic of Personal Knowledge: Essays Presented to Michael Polanyi on His Seventieth Birthday 11th March 1961.* Glencoe: Free Press, 1961.

Kane, Jeffrey. *Beyond Empiricism: Michael Polanyi Reconsidered.* American University Studies Series XIV: Education 6. New York: Peter Lang, 1984.

Kelly, John N.D. *Early Christian Creeds.* 3rd Ed. New York: David McKay Co., 1972.

———. *Early Christian Doctrines.* 5th Ed. New York: Harper Collins, 1978.

Kennedy, Terrence. *The Morality of Knowledge: Transcendence and the Intellectual Life in the Thought of Michael Polanyi*. Ph.D. dissertation: Pontificia Universitas Lateranensis, 1979.

LaCugna, Catherine Mowry. *God For Us: the Trinity and Christian Life*. New York: Harper Collins, 1993.

Langford, Thomas A., and William H. Poteat, eds. *Intellect and Hope: Essays in the Thought of Michael Polanyi*. Durham: Duke University, 1968.

Long, Eugene T. *Twentieth-Century Western Philosophy of Religion, 1900-2000*. Dordrecht: Kluwer Academic, 2000.

Louth, Andrew. *Maximus the Confessor*. London and New York: Routledge, 1996.

Mackintosh, H.R. *The Doctrine of the Person of Jesus Christ*. New York: Charles Scribner's Sons, 1912.

Manno, Bruno V. *The Person and Meaning: a Study in the Post-Critical Thought of Michael Polanyi*. Ph.D. dissertation: Boston College, 1975.

Marshall, Bruce D. *Trinity and Truth*. Cambridge Studies in Christian Doctrine 3. Cambridge and New York: Cambridge University, 2000.

Martin, Robert K. *The Incarnate Ground of Christian Education: the Integration of Epistemology and Ontology in the Thought of Michael Polanyi and Thomas F. Torrance*. Ph.D. dissertation: Princeton University, 1994.

McGrath, Alister E. *Thomas F. Torrance: an Intellectual Biography*. Edinburgh: T & T Clark, 1999.

———. *Nature*. A Scientific Theology 1. Grand Rapids: Wm. B. Eerdman's, 2001.

———. *Reality*. A Scientific Theology 2. Grand Rapids: Wm. B. Eerdman's, 2002.

———. *Theory*. A Scientific Theology 3. Grand Rapids: Wm. B. Eerdman's, 2003.

McIntyre, John. *The Shape of Pneumatology: Studies in the Doctrine of the Holy Spirit*. Edinburgh: T & T Clark, 1997.

———. *The Shape of Christology: Studies in the Doctrine of the Person of Christ*. 2nd Ed. Edinburgh: T & T Clark, 1998.

Meyendorff, John. *Byzantine Theology: Historical Trends and Doctrinal Themes*. 2nd Ed. New York: Fordham University, 1979.

Moleski, Martin X. *Personal Catholicism: the Theological Epistemologies of John Henry Newman and Michael Polanyi*. Washington, D.C.: Catholic University Press, 2000.

Molnar, Paul D. *Divine Freedom and the Doctrine of the Immanent Trinity: in Dialogue with Karl Barth and Contemporary Theology*. Edinburgh and New York: T & T Clark, 2002.

Morrison, John D. *Knowledge of the Self-Revealing God in the Thought of Thomas Forsyth Torrance*. Issues in Systematic Theology 2. New York: Peter Lang, 1997.

Murphy, Nancey. *Beyond Liberalism and Fundamentalism: How Modern and Postmodern Philosophy Set the Theological Agenda*. Valley Forge: Trinity Press, 1996.

Musser, Donald W. *Theological Language and the Epistemology of Michael Polanyi*. Ph.D. dissertation: University of Chicago, 1981.

Need, Stephen W. *Human Language and Knowledge in the Light of Chalcedon*. American University Studies Series VII: Theology and Religion 187. New York: Peter Lang, 1996.

Nellas, Panayiotis. *Deification in Christ: the Nature of the Human Person*. Trans. N. Russell. Contemporary Greek Theologians 5. Crestwood: St. Vladimir's Seminary, 1987.

Newbigin, Lesslie. *Foolishness to the Greeks: the Gospel and Western Culture*. Grand Rapids: Wm. B. Eerdman's, 1986.

———. *The Gospel in a Pluralist Society*. Grand Rapids: Wm. B. Eerdman's, 1989.

———. *Proper Confidence: Faith, Doubt and Christian Discipleship*. Grand Rapids: Wm. B. Eerdman's. 1994.

Newlands, George. *God in Christian Perspective*. Edinburgh: T & T Clark, 1994.

Newman, Paul W. *A Spirit Christology: Recovering the Biblical Paradigm of Christian Faith*. Lanham: University Press of America, 1987.

O'Collins, Gerald. *Christology: a Biblical, Historical, and Systematic Study of Jesus Christ*. Oxford and New York: Oxford University, 1995.

O'Donnell, John J. *The Mystery of the Triune God*. Mahwah: Paulist Press, 1990.

Pannenberg, Wolfhart. *Jesus: God and Man*. Trans. L.L. Wilkins and D.A. Priebe. Philadelphia: Westminster Press, 1968.

———. *Metaphysics and the Idea of God*. Trans. P. Clayton. Grand Rapids: Wm. B. Eerdman's, 1990.

———. *Toward a Theology of Nature: Essays on Science and Faith*. Louisville: Westminster/John Knox, 1993.

Patterson, Sue. *Realist Christian Theology in a Postmodern Age*. Cambridge and New York: Cambridge University, 1999.

Paul, Ian. *Knowledge of God: Calvin, Einstein, and Polanyi*. Edinburgh: Scottish Academic, 1987.

Pelikan, Jaroslav. *The Emergence of the Catholic Tradition (100-600)*. The Christian Tradition: a History of the Development of Doctrine 1. Chicago: University of Chicago, 1971.

———. *The Spirit of Eastern Christendom (600-1700)*. The Christian Tradition: a History of the Development of Doctrine 2. Chicago: University of Chicago, 1974.

Prestige, G.L. *God in Patristic Thought*. London: S.P.C.K., 1956.

Prosch, Harry. *Michael Polanyi: a Critical Exposition*. Albany: State University of New York, 1986.

Prust, Richard C. *The Knowledge and Reality of God: the Theological Implications of Michael Polanyi's Epistemology and Ontology*. Ph.D. dissertation: Duke University, 1970.

Rahner, Karl. *The Trinity*. Trans. J. Donceel. London: Burns and Oates, 1970.

Rutledge, David W. *The Recovery of the Person in the Post-Critical Thought of Michael Polanyi*. Ph.D. dissertation: Rice University, 1979.

Sanders, Andy. *Michael Polanyi's Post-Critical Epistemology: A Reconstruction of Some Aspects of 'Tacit Knowing.'* Amsterdam: Rodopi, 1988.

Scott, Drusilla. *Everyman Revived: the Common Sense Philosophy of Michael Polanyi*. Grand Rapids: Wm. B. Eerdman's, 1995.

Shults, F. LeRon. *Reforming Theological Anthropology: After the Philosophical Turn to Relationality*. Grand Rapids and Cambridge: Wm. B. Eerdman's, 2003.

———. *Reforming the Doctrine of God*. Grand Rapids and Cambridge: Wm. B. Eerdman's, 2005.

Sputh, Roland. *Creation, Contingency and Divine Presence in the Theologies of Thomas F. Torrance and Eberhard Jüngel*. Lund: Lund University, 1995

Stevenson, J., ed. *Creeds, Councils, and Controversies: Documents Illustrating the History of the Church A.D. 337-461*. Rev. ed. with additional documents by W.H.C. Frend. London: SPCK, 1989.

Studer, Basil. *Trinity and Incarnation: the Faith of the Early Church*. Ed. A. Louth. Trans. M. Westerhoff. Collegeville: Michael Glazier, 1993.

Templeton, J.M., and R.L. Herrmann. *The God Who Would be Known: Revelations of the Divine in Contemporary Science*. Radnor: Templeton Foundation Press, 1998.

Thatcher, Adrian. *Truly a Person, Truly God: a Post-Mythical View of Jesus*. London: SPCK, 1990.

Thunberg, Lars. *Man and the Cosmos: the Vision of St. Maximus the Confessor*. Crestwood: St. Vladimir's Seminary, 1985.

Torrance, Thomas F. *Theological Science*. London: Oxford University, 1969.

———. *God and Rationality*. London: Oxford University, 1971.

———. *Space, Time and Resurrection*. Grand Rapids: Wm. B. Eerdman's, 1976.

———. *Theology in Reconciliation: Essays Towards Evangelical and Catholic Unity in East and West*. Grand Rapids: Wm. B. Eerdman's, 1976.

———. *The Ground and Grammar of Theology*. Charlottesville: University Press of Virginia, 1980.

———, ed. *Belief in Science and in Christian Life: the Relevance of Michael Polanyi's Thought for Christian Faith and Life*. Edinburgh: Handsel, 1980.

———. *Christian Theology and Scientific Culture*. New York: Oxford University, 1981.

———. *Divine and Contingent Order: Nihil constat de contingentia nisi ex revelatione*. London: Oxford University, 1981.

———. *Reality and Evangelical Theology: the Realism of Christian Revelation*. Philadelphia: Westminster, 1982.

———. *Transformation and Convergence in the Frame of Knowledge: Explorations in the Interrelations of Scientific and Theological Enterprise*. Grand Rapids: Wm. B. Eerdman's, 1984.

———. *Reality and Scientific Theology*. Edinburgh: Scottish Academic Press, 1985.

———. *The Christian Frame of Mind: Reason, Order, and Openness in Theology and Natural Science*. Colorado Springs: Helmers & Howard, 1989.

———. *Trinitarian Perspectives: Toward Doctrinal Agreement*. Edinburgh: T & T Clark, 1994.

———. *The Christian Doctrine of God: One Being, Three Persons*. Edinburgh: T & T Clark, 1996.

Ward, Graham. *Theology and Contemporary Critical Theory*. 2nd Ed. London and New York: Macmillan and St. Martin's, 2000.

Webb, Eugene. *Philosophers of Consciousness: Polanyi, Lonergan, Voegelin, Ricoeur, Girard, Kierkegaard*. Seattle: University of Washington, 1988.

Weightman, Colin. *Theology in a Polanyian Universe: the Theology of Thomas Torrance*. American University Studies Series VII: Theology and Religion 174. New York: Peter Lang, 1994.

Welker, Michael. *Creation and Reality*. Minneapolis: Fortress Press, 1999.

Wilczak, Paul. *Faith, Motive, and Community: an Interpretation of the Philosophy of Michael Polanyi*. Ph.D. dissertation: University of Chicago, 1973.

Zizioulas, John. *Being as Communion: Studies in Personhood and the Church*. Contemporary Greek Theologians 4. Crestwood: St. Vladimir's Seminary, 1997.

Secondary Essays and Articles

Aghiorgoussis, Maximos. "Christian Existentialism of the Greek Fathers: Persons, Essence, and Energies of God." *Greek Orthodox Theological Review* 23 (1978): 15-41.

Anastos, Thomas L. "Gregory Palamas' Radicalization of the Essence, Energies, and Hypostasis Model of God." *Greek Orthodox Theological Review* 38 (1993): 335-349.

Apczynski, John. "Integrative Theology: a Polanyian Proposal for Theological Foundations." *Theological Studies* 40 (1979): 23-43.

―――. "Are Religion and Science Distinct or Dichotomous Realms?" *Tradition and Discovery* 15, no. 1 (1987-1988): 4-14.

―――. "Torrance on Polanyi and Polanyi on God: Comments on Weightman's Criticisms." *Tradition and Discovery* 24, no. 1 (1997-1998): 32-34.

Baker, Lynne. "Need a Christian be Mind-Body Dualist?" *Faith and Philosophy* 12 (1997): 489-504.

Bielfeldt, Dennis. "God, Physicalism, and Supervenience." *Center for Theology and Natural Science Bulletin* 15 (1995): 1-12.

―――. "Nancey Murphy's Nonreductive Physicalism." *Zygon* 34 (1999): 619-628.

―――. "Can Western Monotheism Avoid Substance Dualism?" *Zygon* 36 (2001): 153-177.

Bracken, Joseph. "Panentheism from a Trinitarian Perspective." *Horizons* 22 (1995):7-28.

―――. "Supervenience and Basic Christian Belief." *Zygon* 36 (2001): 137-152.

Caldecott, Stratford. "A Science of the Real: the Renewal of Christian Cosmology." *Communio* 25, no. 3 (1998): 462-479.

Campbell, Donald. "'Downward Causation' in Hierarchically Organized Systems." *Studies in the Philosophy of Biology: Reduction and Related Problems*. Ed. F.J. Ayala and T. Dobzhansky. London: Macmillan, 1974.

Cannon, Dale. "Sanders' Analytic Rebuttal to Polanyi's Critics With Some Musings on Polanyi's Idea of Truth." *Tradition and Discovery* 23, no. 3 (1996-1997):17-23.

―――. "Some Aspects of Polanyi's Version of Realism." *Tradition and Discovery* 26, no. 3 (1999-2000): 51-61.

Charlesworth, James H. "The Jewish Roots of Christology: the Discovery of the Hypostatic Voice." *Scottish Journal of Theology* 39 (1986): 19-41.

Clark, Mary T. "The Trinity in Latin Christianity." *Christian Spirituality: Origins to the Twelfth Century*. Ed. B. McGinn, J. Meyendorff, and J. Leclerq. New York: Crossroad, 1996.

Clarke, W. Norris. "Action as the Self-Revelation of Being: a Central Theme in the Thought of St. Thomas." *History of Philosophy in the Making: a Symposium of Essays to Honor Professor James D. Collins on his 65th Birthday by his Colleagues and Friends*. Ed. L.J. Thro. Washington, D.C.: University Press of America, 1982.

————. "Substance and Accident." *The New Dictionary of Theology*. Ed. J.A. Komonchak, M. Collins, and D.A. Lane. Wilmington: Michael Glazier, Inc., 1987.

————. "To Be Is To Be Substance-In-Relation." *Metaphysics as Foundation: Essays in Honor of Ivor Leclerc*. Ed. P.A. Bogaard and G. Treash. Albany: State University of New York, 1993.

Clayton, Philip. "The Case for Christian Panentheism." *Dialog* 37 (1998): 201-208.

Coakley, Sarah. "Why Three? Some Further Reflections on the Origins of the Doctrine of the Trinity." *The Making and Remaking of Christian Doctrine: Essays in Honour of Maurice Wiles*. Ed. S. Coakley and D. Pailin. Oxford: Clarendon, 1993.

Cousins, Ewert. "A Theology of Interpersonal Realtions." *Thought* 45 (1970): 56-82.

Crawford, R.G. "The Relation of the Divinity and the Humanity in Christ." *Evangelical Quarterly* 53 (1981): 237-240.

Crewdson, Joan. "Nature and the Noosphere: Two Realities or One?" *Tradition and Discovery* 15, no. 1 (1987-1988): 18-24.

Cullen, Lindsay. "Nancey Murphy, Supervenience, and Causality." *Science and Christian Belief* 13 (2001): 39-50.

de Vogel, C.J. "Personality in Greek and Christian Thought." *Studies in Philosophy and the History of Philosophy*. Ed. J.K. Ryan. Washington, D.C.: Catholic University of America, 1963.

Dulles, Avery. "Revelation and Discovery." *Theology and Discovery: Essays in Honor of Karl Rahner, S.J.* Ed. W.J. Kelly. Milwaukee: Marquette University, 1980.

————. "Faith, Church, and God: Insights from Michael Polanyi." *Theological Studies* 45 (1984): 537-550.

Farrugia, Edward. "*Tropos Tes Hyparxeos Ton Theion Prosopon*: the Fate of a Greek Patristic Formula in Modern Western Theology." *Melita Theologica* 49, no. 2 (1998): 31-37.

Finger, Thomas. "Trinity, Ecology, and Panentheism." *Christian Scholar's Review* 27 (1997): 74-98.

Fox, Robert W. "The Athanasian Meaning of 'Being of One Substance with the Father'." *Lutheran Quarterly* 12 (1960): 205-216.

French, William. "The World as God's Body: Biological Ethics and Panentheism." *Broken and Whole*. Ed. M.A. Tilley and S.A. Ross. Lanham: University Press of America, 1995.

Friedman, Russell L. "Divergent Traditions in Later-Medieval Trinitarian Theology: Relations, Emanations, and the Use of Philosophical Psychology, 1250-1325." *Studia Theologica* 53 (1999), 13-25.

Gelwick, Richard. "Discovery and Theology." *Scottish Journal of Theology* 28 (1975): 301-322.

————. "Post-Critical Belief." *The Sources of Hope*. Ed. R. Fitzgerald. Elmsford: Pergamon, 1979.

————. "Science, Reality, and Religion: a Reply to Harry Prosch." *Zygon* 17 (1982): 25-40.

————. "The Polanyi-Tillich Dialogue of 1963: Polanyi's Search for a Post-Critical Logic in Science and in Theology." *Tradition and Discovery* 22, no. 1 (1995-1996): 11-19.

Gill, Jerry. "Tacit Knowing and Religious Belief." *International Journal for the Philosophy of Religion* 6 (1975): 73-88.

————. "Reasons of the Heart." *Religious Studies* 14 (1978): 143-157.

Gockel, Matthias. "A Dubious Christological Formula? Leontius of Byzantium and the 'Anhypostasis-Enhypostasis' Theory." *Journal of Theological Studies* 51 (2000): 515-532.

Grabowski, John S. "Person: Substance and Relation." *Communio* 22 (1995): 139-163.

Grant, Colin. "Polanyi: the Augustinian Component." *The New Scholasticism* 48 (1974): 438-463.

———. "Identifying the Theological Enemy: Polanyi's Near Miss." *Modern Theology* 3 (1987): 255-268.

———. "Dynamic Orthodoxy: a Polanyian Direction for Theology." *Studies in Religion/ Studies Religieuses* 17, no. 4 (1988): 407-419.

Gregersen, Niels Henrik. "Freedom and Evolution: Systems Theoretical and Theological Perspectives." *Free Will and Determinism.* Ed. V. Mortensen and R.C. Sorensen. Aarhus: Aarhus University, 1987.

———. "Theology in a Neo-Darwinian World." *Studia Theologica* 48 (1994):125-149.

———. "The Idea of Creation and the Theory of Autopoietic Processes." *Zygon* 33 (1998): 333-367.

———. "Autopoiesis: Less Than Self-Constitution, More Than Self-Organization." *Zygon* 34 (1999), 117-138.

Grene, Marjorie. "The Personal and the Subjective." *Tradition and Discovery* 22, no. 3 (1995-1996): 6-16.

Gulick, Walter. "An Unlikely Synthesis: What Kant Can Contribute to a Polanyian Theory of Selfhood." *The Personalist Forum* 9 (1993): 81-107.

Hefner, Philip. "Freedom in Evolutionary Perspective." *Free Will and Determinism: Papers from an Interdisciplinary Research Conference, 1986.* Ed. V. Mortensen and R.C. Sorensen. Aarhus: Aarhus University, 1987.

Hill, Michael. "Reflections on Cloning and the Soul." *The Reformed Theological Review* 56 (1997): 138-148.

Hopko, Thomas. "The Trinity in the Cappadocians." *Christian Spirituality: Origins to the Twelfth Century.* Ed. B. McGinn, J. Meyendorff, and J. Leclerq. New York: Crossroad, 1996.

Hussey, M. Edmund. "The Persons-Energy Structure in the Theology of St. Gregory Palamas." *St. Vladimir's Theological Quarterly* 18 (1973): 22-43.

Jacobs, Struan. "Michael Polanyi and Spontaneous Order, 1941-1951." *Tradition and Discovery* 24, no. 2 (1997-1998): 14-27.

Kettle, David. "Michael Polanyi and Human Identity." *Tradition and Discovery* 21, no. 3 (1994-1995): 5-18.

Kroger, Joseph. "Theology and Notions of Reason and Science: a Note on the Point of Comparison Between Lonergan and Polanyi." *Journal of Religion* 56 (1976): 157-161.

———. "Some Reflections on Michael Polanyi and Catholic Thought." *Tradition and Discovery* 18, no. 2 (1992): 10-14.

Lang, U.M. "Anhypostatos-Enhypostatos: Church Fathers, Protestant Orthodoxy, and Karl Barth." *Journal of Theological Studies* 49 (1998): 630-657.

Langford, Thomas A. "Michael Polanyi and the Task of Theology." *Journal of Religion* 46, no. 1 (1966): 45-55.

Lienhard, Joseph T. "The 'Arian' Controversy: Some Categories Reconsidered." *Theological Studies* 48 (1987): 415-437.

Lonergan, Bernard. "Theology in Its New Context." *Conversion: Perspectives on Personal and Social Transformation.* Ed. W.E. Conn. Staten Island: Alba House, 1978.

Lynch, John J. "Prosopon in Gregory of Nyssa: a Theological Word in Transition." *Theological Studies* 40 (1979): 728-738.

Manno, Bruno V. "Michael Polanyi and Erik Erikson: Toward a Post-Critical Identity of Human Identity." *Religious Education* 75 (1980): 205-214.

———. "Ways of Viewing Reality: a Proposed Convergence of Polanyi, Lonergan, and Tracy." *Journal of Christian Education* 81 (1984): 5-10.

Maritain, Jacques. "On the Notion of Subsistence." *Progress in Philosophy: Philosophical Studies in Honor of Rev. Doctor Charles A. Hart.* Ed. J.A. McWilliams, et al. Milwaukee: Bruce, 1955.

Martland, T.R. "A Study of Cappadocian and Augustinian Trinitarian Methodology." *Anglican Theological Review* 47 (1965): 252-263.

McCoy, Charles T. "The Postcritical and Fiduciary Dimension in Polanyi and Tillich." *Tradition and Discovery* 22, no. 1 (1995-1996): 5-10.

Mousalimas, S.A. "The Divine in Nature: Animism or Panentheism?" *Greek Orthodox Theological Review* 35 (1990): 367-375.

Mullins, Phil. "Nascent Ritual and the Real." *The Polanyi Society* 11, no. 2 (1983-1984): 4-9.

Murphy, Nancey. "Downward Causation and Why the Mental Matters." *Center for Theology and Natural Science Bulletin* 19 (1999): 13-21.

———. "Physicalism Without Reductionism: Toward a Scientifically, Philosophically, and Theologically Sound Portrait of Human Nature." *Zygon* 34 (1999): 551-572.

Musser, Donald W. "Polanyi and Tillich on History." *Tradition and Discovery* 22, no. 1 (1995-1996): 20-30.

Olding, A. "Polanyi's Notion of Hierarchy." *Religious Studies* 16 (1980): 97-102.

Osborn, Robert T. "Christian Faith as Personal Knowledge." *Scottish Journal of Theology* 28, no. 2 (1975): 101-126.

Palma, Robert J. "Polanyi and Christological Dualisms." *Scottish Journal of Theology* 48(1995): 211-224.

Poirier, Maben W. "Harry Prosch's Modernism." *Tradition and Discovery* 16, no. 2 (1988-1989): 32-39.

Prosch, Harry. "Polanyi's View of Religion in *Personal Knowledge*: a Response to Richard Gelwick." *Zygon* 17 (1982): 41-48.

———. "Those Missing 'Objects'." *Tradition and Discovery* 17, no. 1-2 (1990-1991): 17-21.

Ratzinger, Joseph. "Concerning the Notion of Person in Theology." Trans. M. Waldstein. *Communio* 17 (1990): 439-454.

Sanders, Andy. "Criticism, Contact with Reality, and Truth." *Tradition and Discovery* 23, no. 3 (1996-1997): 24-37.

Scott, Drusilla. "Quality but Bristling with Difficulties: on Polanyi's View of Reality." *Tradition and Discovery* 15, no. 1 (1987-1988): 14-17.

Scott, William. "The Question of a Religious Reality: Commentary on the Polanyi Papers." *Zygon* 17 (1982): 83-87.

Shults, F. LeRon. "A Dubious Christological Formula: from Leontius of Byzantium to Karl Barth." *Theological Studies* 57 (1996): 431-446.

Slusser, Michael. "The Exegetical Roots of Trinitarian Theology." *Theological Studies* 49 (1988): 461-476.

Stead, G. Christopher. "The Concept of Divine Substance." *Vigiliae Christianae* 29 (1975): 1-14.

Stroumsa, Gedaliahu G. "Caro Salutis Cardo: Shaping the Person in Early Christian Thought." *History of Religions* 30 (1990): 25-50.

Sturch, R.L. "The Metaphysics of the Incarnation." *Vox Evangelica* 10 (1977): 65-76.

Thorsen, Donald. "Michael Polanyi: a Post-Critical Understanding of Religious Belief." *Asbury Theological Journal* 41 (1986): 79-90.

Turcescu, Lucian. "Prosopon and Hypostasis in Basil of Caesarea's *Against Eunomius* and the Epistles." *Vigiliae Christianae* 51 (1997): 374-395.

———. "The Concept of Divine Persons in Gregory of Nyssa's *To His Brother Peter, on the Difference Between Ousia and Hypostasis*." *Greek Orthodox Theological Review* 42 (1997): 63-82.

Turner, Harold. "The Theological Significance of Michael Polanyi." *Stimulus* 5 (1997): 12-19.

Van Inwagen, Peter. "Dualism and Materialism: Athens and Jerusalem?" *Faith and Philosophy* 12 (1998): 475-488.

von Balthasar, Hans Urs. "On the Concept of Person." Trans. P. Verhalen. *Communio* 13 (1986): 18-26.

Whitlock, Glenn F. "The Structure of Personality in Hebrew Psychology." *Interpretation* 14 (1960): 3-13.

Williams, Rowan. "'Person' and 'Personality' in Christology." *Downside Review* 94 (1976): 253-260.

Zizioulas, John. "Human Capacity and Human Incapacity: a Theological Exploration of Personhood." *Scottish Journal of Theology* 28 (1975): 401-447.

———. "The Church as Communion." *St. Vladimir's Theological Quarterly* 38 (1994): 3-16.

———. "Communion and Otherness." *St. Vladimir's Theological Quarterly* 38 (1994): 347-361.